Mary Jones and Matthew Parkin

Cambridge International AS and A Level

Biology

Workbook

CAMBRIDGE
UNIVERSITY PRESS

University Printing House, Cambridge CB2 8BS, United Kingdom

One Liberty Plaza, 20th Floor, New York, NY 10006, USA

477 Williamstown Road, Port Melbourne, VIC 3207, Australia

4843/24, 2nd Floor, Ansari Road, Daryaganj, Delhi – 110002, India

79 Anson Road, #06–04/06, Singapore 079906

José Abascal, 56–1°, 28003 Madrid, Spain

Cambridge University Press is part of the University of Cambridge.

It furthers the University's mission by disseminating knowledge in the pursuit of education, learning and research at the highest international levels of excellence.

Information on this title: education.cambridge.org

First published 2016

20 19 18 17 16 15 14 13 12 11 10 9 8 7 6 5 4 3 2

Printed in Spain by GraphyCems

A catalogue record for this publication is available from the British Library

ISBN 978-1-107-58947-6 Paperback with CD-ROM for Windows® and Mac®

How to use this book

A **Chapter outline** appears at the start of every chapter to set the scene and to help with navigation through the book.

Chapter outline

The questions in this chapter cover the following topics:

- the structure of animal, plant and bacterial cells, and of viruses
- the use of light microscopes and electron microscopes to study cells
- drawing and measuring cell structures
- the variety of cell structures and their functions
- the organisation of cells into tissues and organs

Each **Exercise** in every chapter helps students to practise the necessary skills for studying Biology at AS and A Level.

Exercise 8.3 Interpreting graphs of heart rate and blood pressure

Understanding how graphs relate to the topic under investigation and using them to extract numerical data are important skills. The topic of mammalian transport uses numerous graphical representations.

1 Figure 8.6 shows a typical electrocardiogram (ECG) from a healthy human. We can use ECG traces to calculate the heart rate.

   a First, calculate the time that one **small** square represents.

   b Now determine how many small squares one heart cycle takes (good places to use are the tops of the R waves).

1 large square = 0.2 s

TIP

Be careful converting from seconds to minutes. Remember that 0.5 of a minute is 30 s.

Detailed **Learning support** is provided throughout to help students to tackle the different exercises and build confidence to answer questions independently.

Exam-style questions allow students to thoroughly prepare for examinations and check answers which are provided on the CD-ROM at the back of the book.

Exam-style questions

1   Figure 9.5 shows two magnifications of a section through part of an airway.

Figure 9.5 Tissue maps showing the wall of a region of the airways.

a   The part of airway that the section was taken from was the:

   A   bronchus

   B   terminal bronchiole

   C   respiratory bronchiole

   D   alveolar duct.   [1]

Contents

v

Chapter outline

The questions in this chapter cover the following topics:

- the structure of animal, plant and bacterial cells, and of viruses
- the use of light microscopes and electron microscopes to study cells
- drawing and measuring cell structures
- the variety of cell structures and their functions
- the organisation of cells into tissues and organs

Exercise 1.1 Units for measuring small objects

Cells are small, and the organelles that they contain are sometimes very, very small. In this exercise, you will practise converting between the different units that we use for measuring very small objects. You will also make sure that you are able to write numbers in standard form.

1   The units that we use when measuring cells are millimetres (mm), micrometres (µm) and nanometres (nm).

   Copy and complete:

   a $1\,µm = 1000\,nm = 10^{\cdots}\,nm$

   b $1\,nm = \ldots\ldots\ldots\,µm = 10^{\cdots}\,µm$

   c $1\,nm = \ldots\ldots\ldots\,mm = 10^{\cdots}\,mm$

> **TIP**
> $1\,mm = 1000\,µm$
> $= 10^3\,µm$
> So $1\,µm = 1/1000\,mm$
> $= 10^{-3}\,mm$

Standard form is a way of writing down large or small numbers simply. The rules are:

- Write down the digits as a number between 1 and 10.
- Then write $\times\,10^{\text{power of the number}}$.

To work out the correct power, imagine moving the decimal point to the right or left, until you get a number between 1 and 10. Count how many moves you have to make, and that is the power of ten you should write.

For example, if your number is 4297, you would move the decimal point like this:

4.297

So we write this number as 4.297×10^3.

Here are some examples of writing large numbers in standard form:
$6000 = 6 \times 10^3$
$6248 = 6.248 \times 10^3$
$82\,910 = 8.291 \times 10^4$
$547.5 = 5.475 \times 10^2$

2 Write these numbers in standard form:
    a 5000

    b 63

    c 63 000

    d 63 497

    e 8521.89

Here are some examples of writing small numbers in standard form:
$$0.678 = 6.78 \times 10^{-1}$$
$$0.012 = 1.2 \times 10^{-2}$$
$$0.0057 = 5.7 \times 10^{-3}$$

3 Write these numbers in standard form:
    a 0.1257

    b 0.0006

    c 0.0104

4 A cell measures 0.094 mm in diameter.
    a Convert this to micrometres.

    b Express this value in standard form.

5 A cell organelle is 12 nm long.
   Express this value in µm, in standard form.

6 A mitochondrion is 1.28×10^2 µm long.
   Express this value in nm.

7 A chloroplast is 2.7×10^3 nm in diameter.
   Express this value in µm.

Exercise 1.2 Magnification calculations

This exercise will help you to gain confidence in doing magnification calculations, as well as providing further practice in using different units and converting numbers to standard form. You will also need to think about selecting a suitable number of significant figures to give in your answers. In general, you should use the same number of significant figures as there are in the value with the smallest number of significant figures that you used in your calculations.

$$\text{magnification} = \frac{\text{image size}}{\text{actual size}}$$

TIP

Remember – magnification has no units.

1 A light micrograph of a plant cell shows the cell to be 5.63 cm long. The real size of the cell is 73 µm. Follow the steps to find the magnification of the micrograph.

    Step 1   Convert 5.63 cm to µm.

    Step 2   Substitute into the magnification equation:

$$\text{magnification} = \underline{\qquad\qquad}$$

    Step 3   Calculate the magnification. Write the answer as ×................

2 An electron micrograph of a nucleus shows it to be 44 mm in diameter. The actual diameter of the nucleus is 6 µm. Calculate the magnification of the electron micrograph.

3   An electron micrograph of a **mitochondrion** shows its diameter as 28 mm. The magnification of the image is given as ×22 700. Follow the steps to find the actual diameter of the mitochondrion.

Step 1   Convert 28 mm to μm.

Step 2   Rearrange the magnification equation, and then substitute into it:

$$\text{actual size} = \frac{\text{image size}}{\text{magnification}}$$

$$= \underline{\hspace{3cm}}$$

Step 3   Calculate the actual diameter of the mitochondrion. Remember to give your answer to the same number of significant figures as the value with the smallest number of significant figures that you used in your calculation.

4   An image of a **chloroplast** in an electron micrograph is 36 mm long. The magnification of the micrograph is ×1285. Calculate the actual length of the chloroplast.

5   The micrograph shows a group of *Legionella* bacteria. The image has been magnified ×980.

   a   Measure the maximum length of bacterium **A**.

   b   Calculate the actual length of this bacterium. Show all the steps in your working.

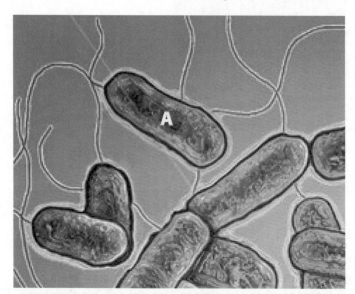

Figure 1.1 Micrograph of *Legionella* bacteria.

6   The micrograph shows some plant cells containing starch grains. There is a scale bar beneath the image.

   a   Measure the length of the scale bar in mm.

   b   Convert this measurement to μm.

   c   Use this image size of the scale bar, and the actual size that we are told it represents, to calculate the magnification of the image.

   d   Measure the maximum diameter of the central cell in the micrograph.

   e   Use the value of the magnification you have calculated to find the actual diameter of this cell.

20 μm

Figure 1.2 Micrograph of plant cells with starch grains.

3

7   The micrograph shows a cell from the **pancreas** of a mammal. Several mitochondria are visible.

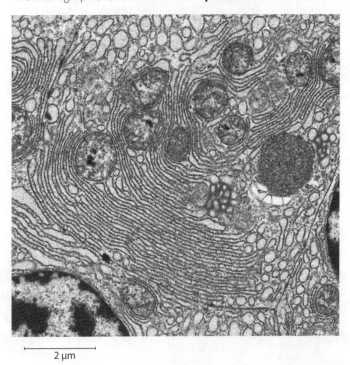

2 μm

Figure 1.3 Micrograph of a cell from the pancreas.

Use the scale bar to calculate the actual diameter of the largest mitochondrion.

Exercise 1.3 Drawing from light micrographs

Being able to draw good diagrams from micrographs, or from what you can see when using a microscope, is nothing to do with being good at art. Your task as a biologist is to make a clear, simple representation of what you can see. Use a sharp, medium hard (e.g. HB) pencil and have a good eraser to hand. Each line should be clean and not have breaks in it – unless there really are breaks that you want to represent.

1   This drawing was made by a student from the electron micrograph of the plant cells shown in the micrograph Figure 1.2 in Exercise 1.2.6.

Figure 1.4 Student's drawing of plant cells.

a Use these criteria to assess the quality of the student's drawing. Copy the table, and put a tick in one box in each row. You could also add a brief comment explaining why you made each decision.

Feature	Done very well	Done fairly well	Poorly done
suitably large diagram – makes good use of space available but does not extend over any text			
clean, clear, continuous lines			
overall shape and proportions look approximately correct			
correct number of starch grains shown, each carefully drawn the right shape and size			
relative sizes of starch grains and cell size correctly shown			
no shading has been used			
good and correct detail of cell walls shown			

b Now make your own drawing of the cells shown in the same electron micrograph, Figure 1.2, taking care to meet all of the criteria fully.

2 The micrograph in Figure 1.5 shows a **lymphocyte**, a type of white blood cell found in mammals.

Figure 1.5 Micrograph of lymphocyte.

a Make a drawing of the lymphocyte.

b Construct a list of criteria for your drawing, using the criteria from 1.3.1a as a guide.

c Assess the standard of your drawing against your criteria. Alternatively, or as well, you could exchange your drawing with a partner, and assess each other's drawings.

d The magnification of the micrograph of the lymphocyte is ×4750.

Calculate the actual diameter of the lymphocyte. Give your answer in μm, using standard form.

e Use your answer to **d** to calculate the magnification of your drawing.

Exercise 1.4 Electron microscopes and optical (light) microscopes

The micrographs in this chapter have been made using different kinds of microscopes. In this exercise, you will practise identifying features that distinguish images taken with different types of microscope, and then summarise the differences between what we can see using optical (light) microscopes and electron microscopes.

1 Copy and complete this table. In the 'type of microscope' column, choose from optical microscope, transmission electron microscope or scanning electron microscope.

Micrograph	Type of microscope used to produce the micrograph	Reason for your decision
Figure 1.2		
Figure 1.3		
Figure 1.5		

2 Copy and complete this table, to compare what can be seen in typical animal cells and plant cells using optical microscopes and electron microscopes. Put a tick or a cross in each box.

Organelle	Visible in plant cells		Visible in animal cells	
	Visible using optical microscope	Visible using electron microscope	Visible using optical microscope	Visible using electron microscope
nucleus				
mitochondrion				
membranes within mitochondrion				
Golgi body				
ribosomes				
endoplasmic reticulum				
chloroplast				
internal structure of chloroplast				
centriole				

Exercise 1.5 Using an eyepiece graticule and stage micrometer

An eyepiece graticule, calibrated using a stage micrometer, enables you to work out the actual size of objects you can see using a microscope. This exercise provides practice in this technique, and also involves decisions about how many significant figures to give in your answers.

An eyepiece graticule is a tiny piece of glass or plastic that you can put into the eyepiece of a microscope.

Figure 1.6 shows a group of palisade cells, as they look through a light microscope with an eyepiece graticule. The highest power objective lens of the microscope is being used.

The small divisions on the graticule scale can be referred to as 'graticule units'. Measure the total width of the four palisade cells **A**, **B**, **C** and **D** in graticule units.

> **TIP**
> When you are doing this using your own microscope, you will need to swivel the eyepiece and/or move the slide, so that your eyepiece graticule scale lies neatly over the thing you want to measure.

Figure 1.6 Micrograph of palisade cells seen using an eyepiece graticule.

In order to find out the true size represented by one eyepiece graticule unit we now need to calibrate the eyepiece graticule using a stage micrometer. This is a slide that is accurately marked off in small divisions of 0.01 mm.

Figure 1.7 shows what is seen when the slide with the palisade cells is replaced on the microscope stage by a stage micrometer.

> **TIP**
> It's essential to use the same objective lens – the one that you used when you measured the palisade cells in eyepiece graticule units. Again, you may need to swivel the eyepiece, and move the slide on the stage, to get them lined up against one another.

Figure 1.7 Stage micrometer seen using an eyepiece graticule.

1 **a** Look for a good alignment of marks on the two scales, as far apart as possible. The 0s of both scales match up, and there is another good match at 80 small divisions on the eyepiece graticule.

How many small divisions on the micrometer equal 80 small divisions on the eyepiece graticule?

b Remember that one small division on the micrometer is 0.01 mm. Use your answer to **a** to calculate how many micrometres (μm) are represented by one small division on the eyepiece graticule.

c Use your answer to **b** to find the total width of the four palisade cells in the micrograph.

d Now calculate the mean width of a palisade cell.

7

2 Explain why it is not possible to see both the palisade cells and the stage micrometer scale at the same time.

3 Figure 1.8 shows a light micrograph of some villi in the small intestine, seen using an eyepiece graticule.

Figure 1.9 shows the same eyepiece graticule, using the same objective lens, but this time with a stage micrometer on the microscope stage.

Use the two images to calculate the length of the villus that can be seen beneath the eyepiece graticule. Show each step in your working.

Figure 1.8 Light micrograph of villi seen using an eyepiece graticule.

Figure 1.9 Stage micrometer seen using the eyepiece graticule.

Exercise 1.6 Membranes in different types of cells

Most cells in multicellular organisms become specialised for a particular set of functions. In this exercise, you will consider data relating to the membranes in two different types of cell, and use your biological knowledge to suggest explanations for patterns that you can pick out in these data.

All cells are surrounded by a **cell surface membrane**, and also contain many other membranes within them. Researchers estimated the total quantity of membranes in 20 liver cells and 20 exocrine pancreas cells, and then calculated the percentage of these membranes in all the different membrane-containing structures in the cells. Their results are shown in the table.

Source of membrane	Mean percentage of all membranes	
	Liver cells	Exocrine pancreas cells
cell surface membrane	1.8	4.7
mitochondrial membranes	39.4	22.3
nuclear membrane	0.5	0.7
rough endoplasmic reticulum	33.4	61.9
smooth endoplasmic reticulum	16.3	0.1
Golgi apparatus	7.9	10.3
lysosomes	0.4	0
other small vesicles	0.3	0

1 Explain why we *cannot* use these results to draw the conclusion that the mean quantity of cell surface membrane in liver cells is less than that in exocrine pancreas cells.

2 Which of the sources of membranes listed in the table are made up of two membranes (an envelope)?

3 Using the data in the table, state the organelle that contains the greatest mean percentage of membrane in:

   a liver cells

   b pancreas cells.

4 Liver cells have a wide variety of functions in metabolism, including synthesising proteins, breaking down toxins, synthesising cholesterol and producing bile. Exocrine pancreas cells have a single main role, which is the production and secretion of digestive enzymes.

   Use this information to suggest explanations for the differences between the percentages for mitochondria and rough endoplasmic reticulum in the liver cells and the pancreas cells.

Exercise 1.7 Command words

In examinations, you will only rarely see a question that ends with a question mark. Almost all questions start with a word that tells you what to do. These are called command words. It is extremely important that you identify the command word in each question part, and understand what it means. If you don't do what the command word asks, you are likely to get few, or perhaps no, marks for your answer.

1 Some of the command words used in examination questions are listed below:

describe	**explain**	**discuss**	**list**	**suggest**
outline	**name**	**state**	**deduce**	**define**

Match each description with the correct command word:

   a Give a concise answer, with no supporting argument.

   b Give a formal statement, possibly one that you have learnt by heart.

   c Write an account to help someone else to 'see' something you are looking at, e.g. a graph; or give a step-by-step account of a structure or process.

   d Work out an answer from information you have been given.

   e Give the technical term, e.g. for a structure or a process.

   f Give a brief account, picking out the most important points and omitting detail.

   g Give reasons; use your knowledge of biology to say why or how something happens.

   h State points on both sides of an argument, e.g. reasons for and against a particular viewpoint, or how a set of results could be interpreted to support or reject a hypothesis.

   i Use information provided, and your biological knowledge, to put forward possible answers; there is often more than one possible correct answer.

   j State, very briefly, a number of answers to the question; if a particular number is asked for, you should give exactly that number of answers.

Exam-style questions

1 The table below lists some features of prokaryotic and eukaryotic cells.

Feature	Prokaryotic cell	Eukaryotic cell
cell surface membrane		
nucleus		
ribosomes		
mitochondria		
chloroplasts		

a Copy and complete the table. If a feature can be present in the cell, write a tick in the box. If it cannot be present, write a cross. You should write either a tick or a cross in each box. [5]

b Viruses are not usually considered to be living organisms and are not made of cells. Outline the key features of the structure of a virus. [2]

[Total: 7 marks]

2 The diagram is a drawing of a cell from the body of a mammal.

Figure 1.10 Diagram of a micrograph of a mammalian body cell.

a State the type of microscope that would be used to allow this amount of detail to be seen in the cell. [1]

b List the letters of the structures in the drawing which are made up of, or are surrounded by, phospholipid membranes. [3]

c Describe the functions of :

i structure **B** [2]

ii structure **E** [2]

iii structure **G**. [2]

[Total: 10 marks]

3 The diagram shows a method for separating the different components of cells. This technique is called ultracentrifugation.

Step 1:
Break up cells and then suspend in ice-cold buffer solution, with a water potential equal to that of the cells.

centrifuge tube

cell fragments suspended in buffer

Step 2:
Centrifuge at 1300 g for 5 min at 4 °C.

P, pellet containing nuclei

Step 3:
Centrifuge at 17 000 g for 15 min at 4 °C.

Q, pellet containing mitochondria

Step 4:
Centrifuge at 80 000 g for 60 min at 4 °C.

R, pellet containing cell surface membranes

Step 5:
Centrifuge at 150 000 g for 3 hours at 4 °C.

supernatant containing cytosol

S, pellet containing ribosomes

Figure 1.11 Ultracentrifugation.

a Suggest why the solution in which the broken-up cells were suspended:

  i was ice-cold [1]

  ii contained a buffer [2]

  iii had the same water potential as the cells. [2]

b Suggest why ribosomes do not collect in the pellet until the final stage of the ultracentrifugation. [1]

c Give the letter of the component or components in which you would expect to find:

  i DNA [1]

  ii phospholipids. [1]

d If this process were carried out using plant cells, which other cell organelles might you expect to find in the pellet containing mitochondria? Explain your answer. [2]

[Total: 10 marks]

Examination questions often contain something new, such as an unfamiliar micrograph. But a combination of your own knowledge and the information in the question should help you work out suitable answers. Look carefully at the mark allocations, which guide you in how detailed an answer you need to give.

4   The photograph shows a micrograph of parts of two cells from the small intestine of a mammal. The structures along the surfaces of the two cells are microvilli.

Figure 1.12 Micrograph of cells from the small intestine.

a   State the type of microscope that was used to obtain this micrograph. Give a reason for your answer.   [2]

b   Identify organelle **A**.   [1]

c   i   The magnification of the micrograph is × 12 500. Calculate the length of the microvillus between points **X** and **Y**. Show your working.   [3]

  ii   Microvilli greatly increase the surface areas of the cells. Suggest why the cells lining the small intestine have microvilli.   [2]

[Total: 8 marks]

Chapter 2
Biological molecules

Chapter outline

The questions in this chapter cover the following topics:

- how large biological molecules are made from smaller molecules
- the structure and function of carbohydrates, lipids and proteins
- biochemical tests to identify carbohydrates, lipids and proteins
- some key properties of water that make life possible

Exercise 2.1 Taking notes

Note taking is an important skill, and your own notes should be able to extract the relevant information from complex writing. There is little value in writing down the whole passage of information.

1   Read the passage below about carbohydrates carefully and then copy and complete the table below to make a summary of the structures and functions of the different **polysaccharides**.

Polysaccharides are **polymers** of **monosaccharides** and are made by joining the monosaccharides with **glycosidic bonds**. Glucose is the **monomer** for many polysaccharides. It is a highly soluble and reactive molecule and would affect the osmotic potential of cells and interfere with biochemical reactions. In plants, glucose is stored as starch, which is a mixture of two substances – amylose and amylopectin. In animals, glucose is stored as glycogen. **Amylose** is made of α-glucose molecules joined by α (1 → 4) glycosidic bonds, resulting in a very compact, helical molecule. **Amylopectin**, also made of α-glucose molecules, has many α (1 → 4) glycosidic bonds and has side branches joined by α (1 → 6) glycosidic bonds. **Glycogen** is made of α-glucose joined with both α (1 → 4) glycosidic and α (1 → 6) glycosidic bonds to make an even more branched molecule. Large numbers of branches enable rapid hydrolysis into glucose molecules. **Cellulose** is a polymer of β-glucose. In β-glucose, the –OH group on carbon number 1 points upwards, so that in cellulose molecules every other glucose molecule is inverted 180°. Cellulose molecules do not have branches and are long straight chains. About 60–70 cellulose molecules bind to each other using **hydrogen bonds** to form microfibrils. Several microfibrils bind together to form fibres, and these fibres make up the cell wall. Cellulose fibres have very high tensile strength, preventing cells from bursting, but allow free passage of water and water-soluble molecules.

Polysaccharide	Name of monomer	Bonds joining monomers	Description	Function
amylose	α-glucose	α (1 → 4)	long helical compact	cellular storage of glucose (energy) does not affect osmotic potential found in plants
amylopectin				
glycogen				
cellulose				

Exercise 2.2 Calculating the concentration of solutions and making dilutions

It is essential to be able to accurately produce different concentrations of solutions. You can be asked to make up concentrations as either percentages (%) or as the number of moles per unit volume (mol dm^{-3}).

GETTING THE UNITS RIGHT

It is important to understand the units of volume and mass when making up solutions of different concentrations, and you may have to do some conversions.

The SI unit of mass is the kilogram (kg). In biology, you will often come across mass measured in kilograms (kg), grams (g), milligrams (mg), micrograms (μg) and sometimes even nanograms (ng).

- 1 kg is equivalent to 1000 g.
- 1 g is equivalent to 1000 mg.
- 1 mg is equivalent to 1000 μg.
- 1 μg is equivalent to 1000 ng.

In order to convert your value to smaller units you need to multiply by 1000, and to convert to larger units you need to divide by 1000.

For example, 0.005 kg is equivalent to:

$$0.005 \times 1000 = 5 \text{ g}$$

and is also equivalent to:

$$0.005 \times 10^6 = 5000 \text{ mg.}$$

The SI unit of volume is the cubic metre (m^3). In biology, you will usually come across volumes as cubic decimetres (dm^3), cubic centimetres (cm^3) and cubic millimetres (mm^3).

- 1 cubic decimetre (dm^3) is equivalent to 1000 cubic centimetres (cm^3).
- 1 cubic centimetre (cm^3) is equivalent to 1000 cubic millimetres (mm^3).

In order to convert values given in cubic decimetres to cubic centimetres, you need to multiply by 1000 and to convert cubic centimetres into cubic decimetres you need to divide by 1000.

1 Carry out the following unit conversions:
   a 150 mg into g
   b 225 mg into kg
   c 0.005 kg into mg
   d 100 ng into g
   e 100 cm^3 into dm^3
   f 0.005 cm^3 into mm^3
   g 150 mm^3 into dm^3
   h 0.000005 dm^3 into mm^3.

CALCULATING CONCENTRATIONS AS PERCENTAGES OF TOTAL VOLUME

When the concentration of a solution is given as a percentage, e.g. 1.0% sucrose solution, it means that 1 g of sucrose was dissolved in distilled water and made up to a total volume of 100 cm³.

Percentage concentration may be calculated using the formula:

$$\text{percentage concentration} = \frac{\text{mass of solute in grams}}{\text{volume of solution in cm}^3} \times 100\%$$

2 Place the following statements about making up 100 cm³ of a 5% sucrose solution in the correct order:

   A Make up to 100 cm³ by adding distilled water.

   B Dissolve in a small amount of distilled water.

   C Place dissolved sucrose into a 100 cm³ volumetric flask.

   D Use a top pan balance to measure out 5 g of sucrose.

3 Calculate the sucrose concentrations in percentages of the following solutions:

   a 5 g of sucrose made up to a volume of 100 cm³

   b 10 g of sucrose made up to a volume of 500 cm³

   c 0.5 g sucrose made up to a volume of 500 cm³

   d 37.5 g sucrose made up to a volume of 150 cm³

   e 450 g sucrose made up to a volume of 1 dm³

   f 0.005 g sucrose made up to a volume of 100 mm³.

4 Calculate the mass of sucrose required to make the following solutions:

   a 100 cm³ of 0.5% sucrose solution

   b 250 cm³ of 12% sucrose solution

   c 500 cm³ of 25% sucrose solution

   d 750 cm³ of 50% sucrose solution

   e 500 mm³ of 10% sucrose solution

   f 1 dm³ of 45% sucrose solution.

CALCULATING CONCENTRATIONS AS MOLARITIES

Concentrations of solutions are often given as molarities. This tells you how many moles of solute are dissolved in one cubic decimetre of water. A **mole** is the relative molecular mass of a substance in grams.

The molarity of a solution can be calculated using the following equation:

$$\text{molarity (mol dm}^{-3}) = \frac{\text{number of moles of solute}}{\text{total volume of solution in dm}^3}$$

To make a 1 mol dm⁻³ solution of a substance, you need to weigh out **1 mole** of the substance, place it into a 1 dm³ volumetric flask and add distilled water up to a total volume of 1 dm³.

For example, if you wish to make a 1 mol dm⁻³ glucose solution:

Step 1 Find out the molecular formula of glucose ($C_6H_{12}O_6$).

Step 2 Determine the relative molecular mass of glucose.

The relative atomic masses of the elements are: carbon 12, hydrogen 1, and oxygen 16, so the relative mass of glucose is:

$(12 \times 6) + (1 \times 12) + (16 \times 6) = 72 + 12 + 96 = 180.$

Step 3 Weigh out 180 g of glucose.

Step 4 Dissolve the glucose in a small amount of distilled water.

Step 5 Place the glucose solution into a 1 dm³ volumetric flask and add distilled water to make a final volume of 1 dm³.

5 Calculate the masses of solutes required to make up the following solutions:

   a 1 dm³ of 1 mol dm⁻³ glucose solution
   b 1 dm³ of 1 mol dm⁻³ maltose solution
   c 1 dm³ of 1 mol dm⁻³ glycine ($C_2H_5O_2N$) solution
   d 100 cm³ of 2 mol dm⁻³ glucose solution
   e 100 cm³ of 2 mol dm⁻³ sucrose solution.

You should also be able work out what molarity of solution is made when you are given a mass of solution and the volume that it is made up to with distilled water.

$$\text{molarity (mol dm}^{-3}) = \frac{\text{number of moles of solute}}{\text{total volume of solution in dm}^3}$$

For example, 171 g of sucrose was dissolved by addition of distilled water and made up to 0.5 dm³. To calculate the molarity of the solution, you must follow the steps below:

Step 1 Calculate the mass of 1 mole of sucrose ($C_{12}H_{22}O_{11}$):

$(12 \times 12) + (22 \times 1) + (11 \times 16) = 144 + 22 + 176 = 342$ g

Step 2 Calculate how many moles are present in 171 g of sucrose:

$(171 \div 342) = 0.5$ moles

Step 3 Calculate the molarity by dividing the number of moles by the volume of water in dm³:

$(0.5 \div 0.5) = $ **1 mol dm⁻³**

6 Now try to work out the molar concentrations of the following solutions:

   a 171 g sucrose dissolved in 1 dm³ distilled water
   b 150 g glycine ($C_2H_5O_2N$) dissolved in 1 dm³ distilled water
   c 4.5 g glucose dissolved in 100 cm³ distilled water
   d 1.8 g glucose dissolved in 1 dm³ distilled water
   e 342 mg sucrose dissolved in 1 cm³ distilled water.

TIP

Be careful to make sure that you convert units! Often dilute solutions are given as mmol dm⁻³ where 1000 mmoles is equivalent to 1 mole.

Exercise 2.3 Graph plotting and using calibration curves

Benedict's test is a test for reducing sugars. Benedict's reagent is initially blue due to the presence of copper (II) sulphate. When heated in the presence of a reducing sugar, the copper (II) sulphate is reduced into insoluble red copper (I) oxide. Higher concentrations of reducing sugar will cause the solution to have less blue colour. The degree of blue colour can be quantified by using a colorimeter.

MAKING DILUTIONS

To decide what concentration of reducing sugar is in a particular solution, we must produce a calibration curve graph using a range of known concentrations. These are created by diluting stocks of reducing sugar solutions of known concentrations.

1   Copy and complete the table below to show how to make a range of concentrations when given a 1% standard solution of sucrose. The first two are done for you.

Concentration of sucrose / %	Volume of 1% glucose solution / cm³	Volume of added water / cm³
0.9	9	1
0.8	8	2
0.7		
0.6		
0.5		
0.4		
0.3		
0.2		
0.1		

To make wider ranges of dilutions you will need to be able to perform serial dilutions. An example of this is shown in the lower diagram below.

Figure 2.1 Producing a range of concentrations from standard solutions.

2 Describe how you could make up the following glucose concentrations when given a 1% standard solution (there may be several different ways for each!):

   a 0.02%

   b 0.003%

   c 0.0005%.

PLOTTING A CALIBRATION CURVE

A calibration curve is a graph with the known concentrations plotted against their percentage absorbance.

The table below shows the percentage of red light absorbed using a colorimeter from Benedict's tests performed on a variety of glucose concentrations.

Concentration of glucose / %	Absorption of light / %
1.0	5
0.8	35
0.6	45
0.4	64
0.2	85
0.1	92
0	96

3 Plot a calibration curve of concentration of glucose against absorption of light. Follow the steps below to plot your graph:

   Step 1 Label the x-axis with the independent variable, in this case, concentration of glucose / %.

   Step 2 Label the y-axis with the dependent variable, in this case, absorption of light / %.

   Step 3 Select appropriate linear scales on both axes. Make sure that you can fit all the plots along each axis, but try to use at least half of each axis. You do not need to start the axes at 0 if it is not appropriate.

   Step 4 Plot the points carefully with a sharp pencil.

   Step 5 Draw a smooth line or curve of best fit through the points. It is appropriate to use a line or curve of best fit when we can safely assume the intermediate points would lie along the line. If we cannot be sure of this we should join the points with straight lines.

4 A mystery sample of glucose was analysed using a Benedict's test. The colorimeter gave an absorption reading of 74%.

   a Using a ruler, draw a straight line across from 74% to meet the curve then drop the line down to the x-axis. Record the concentration of glucose that would give an absorption of 74%.

   b Repeat this for an absorption of 53%.

5 When comparing different solutions of glucose using this method, it is important to control many factors in order to make a valid comparison.

   List **three** factors that need to be kept constant.

Exercise 2.4 Processing and analysing data

You will need to be able to apply your factual knowledge in order to interpret unfamiliar data. Do not be put off by the fact that you have not seen the information in that context before – look carefully at the information and use your knowledge.

1 Look carefully at the fatty acids in Figure 2.2 and answer the questions.

Figure 2.2 The structure of four different fatty acids.

a Copy out and complete the table below identifying which fatty acids are saturated, monounsaturated and polyunsaturated.

Fatty acid	Type of fatty acid	Melting point / °C
lauric acid		
oleic acid		
linoleic acid		
arachidonic acid		

b The melting points of these fatty acids are: 45 °C, 13 °C, −49 °C, −11 °C. The presence of C=C bonds causes the melting point of fatty acids to be lowered. Match each fatty each with its corresponding melting point and enter the data in the table.

c Suggest why the melting points of the different fatty acids are different.

Now look at the table below which shows the proportions of saturated, monounsaturated and polyunsaturated fatty acids found in lipids extracted from different organisms.

Organism	Total mass of lipid material tested / g	Saturated fatty acids / g	Monounsaturated fatty acids / g	Polyunsaturated fatty acids / g
sheep (animal)	100	40.8	43.8	9.6
cow (butter) (animal)	100	54.0	19.8	2.6
duck (animal)	50	16.7	24.5	6.8
mackerel (animal)	10	2.4	3.2	2.3
olive oil (plant)	200	28.0	139.4	22.4
corn oil (plant)	100	12.7	24.7	57.8
sunflower oil (plant)	100	11.9	20.2	63.0
hemp oil (plant)	75	7.5	10.0	50.0
coconut oil (plant)	150	127.8	9.9	2.5

When you compare data you need to make sure that it is a fair comparison. The masses of fatty acids for the different species in the table were taken from different starting masses of total lipid. You will need to make each class of fatty acid proportional to the total mass of lipid, in other words grams (g) per 100 g of total lipid.

To convert the mass of each type of fat into mass per 100 grams, carry out the following steps:

Step 1 Calculate the mass of each type of fat per gram of total lipid:

$$\text{mass per gram} = \frac{\text{mass of fat}}{\text{total lipid mass}}$$

Step 2 Calculate the amount of each type of fat per 100 g:

$$\text{mass per 100 g of lipid} = \text{mass per gram} \times 100\,\text{g}$$

For example, in duck fat there are 16.7 g of saturated fat in 50 g of total lipid.

- In 1 g of total lipid there will be $(16.7 \div 50) = 0.334$ g saturated fat per gram of total lipid.
- If there is 0.334 g of saturated fat in 1 g of fatty material, there will be $0.334\,\text{g} \times 100 = 33.4\,\text{g}$ of saturated fat in 100 g of total lipid.

2 a Copy out and complete the table below.

Organism	Saturated fatty acids / g per 100 g	Monounsaturated fatty acids / g per 100 g	Polyunsaturated fatty acids / g per 100g
sheep (animal)	40.8	43.8	9.6
cow (butter) (animal)	54.0	19.8	2.6
duck (animal)			
mackerel (animal)			
olive oil (plant)			
corn oil (plant)	12.7	24.7	57.8
sunflower oil (plant)	11.9	20.2	63.0
hemp oil (plant)			
coconut oil (plant)			

Now that you have all the masses in the form of grams per 100 g of total lipid, you can start to evaluate the data.

b   Identify any patterns that you can see in the data.

c   Are there any results that do not seem to fit in with the patterns you have identified?

d   Can you now suggest any explanations for any of the patterns? You will now need to use some of your knowledge about fatty acids here.

Exercise 2.5 Drawing molecular structures

Most biochemical reactions are best represented by drawing them out. Accuracy when drawing molecular structures is important, and it is easy to make mistakes that can cost marks in exams.

1   You need to be able to understand the formation of glycosidic bonds in **disaccharides** and **polysaccharides** and be able to draw chemical structures.

a   Copy the diagram of two glucose molecules shown in Figure 2.3.

Figure 2.3 Two α-glucose molecules.

Step 1	Draw a ring around the hydrogen in the –OH group on carbon number 1 of the α-glucose on the left.
Step 2	Now draw a ring around the –OH group on carbon number 4 of the α-glucose on the right.
Step 3	Draw the reversible arrows as shown in the diagram.
Step 4	Draw out the disaccharide maltose and label it underneath the arrows. Also label the glycosidic bond.
Step 5	Show on the arrows where water (H₂O) is added or taken away.
Step 6	Next to the arrows, write the names of the reactions that would have taken place in each direction (**hydrolysis** and **condensation**).

b   Now use your knowledge of dipeptide formation to repeat this procedure in order to show the formation of a **peptide bond** between the two amino acids shown in Figure 2.4.

Figure 2.4 Molecular structure of the amino acids glycine (left) and serine (right).

21

2 Below is an example of an exam question and the answer given by a student. Use the attached mark scheme to identify what is correct and what is incorrect. When you have marked the student's answer, write your own, corrected answer.

i Complete the diagram below showing the formation of a **triglyceride**. [2]

Figure 2.5 The formation of a triglyceride.

ii Name the type of reaction that would have taken place.

condensation / hydrolysis

[1]

Mark scheme

i	3 water molecules on right of arrow	1 mark
	correct bonds drawn on the triglyceride	1 mark
ii	condensation	1 mark

Exercise 2.6 Planning experiments that generate reliable results

You need to be able to plan experiments that will enable you to generate valid conclusions. This means that your experiment will need:

- repeats – to improve reliability and make it easier to spot anomalous values
- to have one variable changed at a time. All other variables must be controlled.

1 Read this experimental plan written by a student and then answer the questions.

An experiment to determine the temperature at which egg white protein (albumin) denatures.

Apparatus:

4 test tubes
test tube rack
measuring cylinder
4 eggs
thermometer
glass marker pen

Bunsen burner
stop clock.
thermometer
Method:

The test tubes will be placed into the test-tube rack. Into each test-tube I will pour the clear liquid egg white from one egg. I will place a thermometer into the egg white of each tube. I will heat the tubes to different temperatures using the Bunsen burner for 5 minutes and see in which ones the albumin goes white. I will carry out the experiment at 20 °C, 25 °C, 50 °C and 55 °C. The lowest temperature at which the albumin goes white is the temperature at which it denatures.

a State the **independent variable** the student was testing.

b State the **dependent variable** the student was measuring.

c Will this experiment generate valid data? Explain your answer.

d Write an improved method that would produce more reliable, valid data. In your method you should think about:

  i how you will change the independent variable, what range you will use and how you will monitor it

  ii how you will measure the dependent variable more accurately and reliably

  iii what variables you will control and how you will control each one

  iv how you will make the results more reliable.

Exercise 2.7 Extended writing skills

Any higher level study of biology requires you to be able to write well organised, factual essays. A good essay has factual detail in keeping with A level standard and is planned so that it flows and does not jump around from topic to topic. The number of words is a guide, although a shorter essay with more scientific detail and relevance to the question is better than a longer one with less relevance.

1 a Write an essay on the biological importance of water (maximum 500 words).

Start by planning it to include the following:

- water as a solvent
- water as a transport medium
- high specific heat capacity
- high latent heat of vaporisation
- density and freezing properties
- high surface tension and cohesion
- water as a reagent.

For each of these properties you need to:

- explain how water achieves it
- give biological examples.

Try to give examples of both plants and animals.

b When you have written it use the mark scheme in the Answers to decide how many marks you would gain – be critical of yourself!

Exam-style questions

1 a Chemical bonds are found in all biological molecules. Complete the table below to match up different bonds with some biological molecules.

	Hydrogen bond	Disulfide bond	Ionic bond	α (1 → 4) glycosidic bond
found in the tertiary structure of a protein				
found in amylose				
found in cellulose				
found in the secondary structure of a protein				

[4]

b Figure 2.6 shows two amino acids.

Figure 2.6 Diagram to show the joining of two amino acids.

i Complete the diagram to show the dipeptide formed by joining these two amino acids. [2]

ii Name the type of reaction that occurs to join the two amino acids. [1]

[Total: 7 marks]

2 Figure 2.7 shows a diagram of the enzyme RNase.

Figure 2.7 Diagram to represent the structure of RNase.

a State the level of protein structure shown in Figure 2.7. [1]

b Addition of a substance called b-mercaptoethanol causes the reduction of disulfide bonds.

Explain the effect this would have on RNase activity. [4]

[Total: 5 marks]

3 A student set up a series of reactions to test the activity of the enzymes amylase and sucrase. Biochemical tests were carried out on each of the reaction mixtures after incubating at 37 °C for three hours.

The table below shows the reactions and tests carried out.

Tube	Contents	Iodine test	Benedict's test	Biuret test
A	starch and amylase			
B	starch and sucrase			
C	sucrose and sucrase			
D	sucrose and amylase			

a Complete the table by indicating which tests would give positive (+) and negative (−) results. [3]

b Explain how you could carry out a biochemical test to show that a solution contained a mixture of both glucose and sucrose. [4]

[Total: 7 marks]

4 Figure 2.8 shows the structure of the disaccharide sucrose.

CH₂OH
H O H
OH H
OH
H OH
CH₂OH
H O H
H HO
CH₂OH
OH H

Figure 2.8 Diagram to show the structure of sucrose.

a i Name the two monosaccharides produced by the breakdown of sucrose. [1]

ii Draw the structure of the two monosaccharides produced by the breakdown of sucrose. [2]

iii Name the type of reaction that is shown by the breakdown of sucrose. [1]

b Figure 2.9 shows a light micrograph of potato tuber cells.

Figure 2.9 Light micrograph of potato tuber cells.

i Add labels on the diagram to show the locations of cellulose and starch. [2]

ii Explain how the structure of cellulose enables it to carry out its function. [4]

iii Explain the advantages of storing starch rather than glucose in plant cells [3]

[Total: 13 marks]

5 **a** Describe how you could test a sample of sesame seeds for the presence of lipids. [3]

b Figure 2.10 shows the general structure of a triglyceride.

Figure 2.10 Diagram of a triglyceride.

Complete the diagram to show the products of hydrolysis of this triglyceride. [2]

c The table below shows the molecular formulae and melting points of three fatty acids.

Fatty acid	Molecular formula	Melting point / °C
linoleic acid	$C_{18}H_{32}O_2$	−5
oleic acid	$C_{18}H_{34}O_2$	13
stearic acid	$C_{18}H_{36}O_2$	69

Using the information in the table, suggest reasons for the different melting points of the fatty acids. [4]

[Total: 9 marks]

6 **a** The p53 gene is a tumour suppressor gene. It codes for the p53 protein which binds to other cellular proteins to regulate cell division. Tumour cells often contain mutated p53 protein where an amino acid called arginine is replaced by a different amino acid called proline. Figure 2.11 shows the structures of arginine and proline.

Arginine   Proline

Figure 2.11 The structures of the amino acids arginine and proline.

Arginine is a hydrophilic amino acid that has a net positive charge.
Proline is a hydrophobic uncharged amino acid.

i Draw the R-group of arginine. [1]

ii Using the example above, explain how changing the primary sequence of a **polypeptide** could affect its function. [3]

b Collagen is a fibrous protein found in many animal tissues including bones and cartilage. Explain how the structure of fibrous proteins such as collagen gives them high tensile strength. [3]

[Total: 7 marks]

Chapter outline

The questions in this chapter cover the following topics:

- how enzymes work
- the factors that affect enzyme activity, including inhibitors
- finding and using V_{max} and K_m
- how to carry out experiments with enzymes
- the advantages of using immobilised enzymes

Exercise 3.1 Answering questions about graphs

Exam questions often provide a graph, and then ask various questions relating to it. In this exercise, you practise answering questions involving three different command words, all about the same graph. You then calculate a rate by drawing a **tangent** to one of the curves.

When you are asked to **describe** a graph, your task is to change the information shown by the line into words. You don't use your biological knowledge for this. Concentrate on the overall trend, then any obvious changes in gradient. Quote figures, referring to both the *x*- and *y*-axes, and remember to give units.

Explaining a graph, however, requires to you to say *why* the graph is the shape that it is.

When asked to **compare** two graphs, try to make statements that include words such as 'but', 'however', and comparative terms such as 'faster', 'higher', 'greater'. Quote comparative figures for particular values that look significant to you; you could subtract one from the other, or calculate how many times greater one is than the other.

A student extracted catalase from 100 g of carrot and 100 g of apple. He added the two extracts to two tubes of hydrogen peroxide solution and measured the oxygen given off over a period of 10 minutes.

The graph shows the results he obtained.

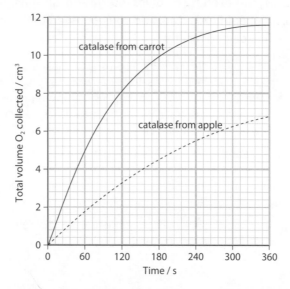

Figure 3.1 Graph showing the time course of the reaction for two sources of catalase.

1   **a**   Describe the curve for the catalase from carrot.

    b   Explain the shape of this curve.

2   Compare the curves for catalase from carrot and catalase from apple.

We can calculate the rate at which oxygen is given off at a particular time. Here's how to do this for the apple catalase curve:

1 Draw a vertical line from the *x*-axis time at which you want to calculate the rate.

2 Draw a tangent at the point where your vertical line meets the curve.

3 Make the next step easy for yourself by making your tangent end where it is easy to read off the values of *x* and *y*.

4 Draw two more lines to complete a right-angled triangle.

5 Calculate the length of the horizontal side of the triangle (this is the change in the value of *x*) and the vertical side (the change in the value of *y*).

6 Calculate the rate:
change in *y* ÷ change in *x* $= \dfrac{9.0}{300} = 0.03$ cm³ min⁻¹

Figure 3.2 Calculating a gradient by drawing a tangent.

3   Calculate the rate at which oxygen is given off at 30 s for the carrot catalase curve.

Exercise 3.2 Effects of temperature and pH on enzyme activity

Like Exercise 3.1, this exercise involves interpreting graphs. Here, however, some of the data are rather unexpected, and you are asked to think about what might be causing these unexpected results.

Spondias is a South American tree whose fruit is used for making juices and ice cream. Like the cells of many fruits, the cells of *Spondias* contain an enzyme called polyphenol oxidase. The substrate for this enzyme is a group of colourless compounds, which the enzyme converts to brown quinones. Normally, the enzyme and its substrate are kept in separate cellular compartments, but when the fruit is damaged they meet and the damaged tissue turns brown.

Producers of fruit juice and other products from *Spondias* need to understand how this enzyme works, so that they can prevent browning in their products. A team of researchers added an extract from *Spondias* fruits to a solution of pyrocatechol, which is a substrate for polyphenol oxidase. They measured the degree of browning using a colorimeter.

The graphs in Figures 3.3 and 3.4 show how temperature and pH affected the rate of activity of polyphenol oxidase from *Spondias* fruits.

Figure 3.3 The effect of temperature on the rate of activity of polyphenol oxidase.

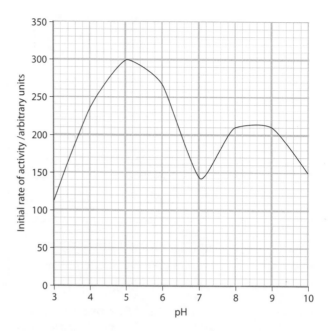

Figure 3.4 The effect of pH on the rate of activity of polyphenol oxidase.

1 **a** Describe the effect of temperature on the rate of activity of polyphenol oxidase from *Spondias* fruits.

  b Explain the effects you have described in your answer to **a**.

2 **a** Describe how the effect of pH on the rate of activity of polyphenol oxidase from *Spondias* fruits differs from the usual effect of pH on the activity of an enzyme.

  b The researchers concluded that the extract they had made from the *Spondias* fruits probably contained more than one type of polyphenol oxidase. What is the evidence for this conclusion?

3 The researchers recommended that the food manufacturers could reduce the browning of products made from *Spondias* fruits by adding lemon juice during their processing. Use the data in the graphs to explain how this might work.

Exercise 3.3 Finding V_{max} and K_m

In this exercise, you first plot a graph, and then use it to find V_{max} and the Michaelis–Menten constant, K_m.

Lipase is an enzyme that hydrolyses lipids to fatty acids and glycerol.

A researcher extracted lipase from *Burkholderia cepacia*, a species of bacterium. The lipase was added to an emulsion of olive oil. The rate of activity of the enzyme was measured by finding how much fatty acid was released from the olive oil in one minute.

The researcher investigated the effect of substrate concentration on the initial rate of reaction, V, of the lipase. The results are shown in the table.

Concentration of substrate / %	Initial rate of activity of lipase / µmol of fatty acid produced per minute
0	0
5	8
10	16
15	22
20	26
25	29
30	31
35	32
40	33
45	33
50	33

1   Which **two** of these variables would the researcher keep constant in the experiments:
   - the concentration of the lipase
   - the concentration of the olive oil
   - the temperature?

2   On a sheet of graph paper, construct a line graph to display these data. Draw a best fit line.

3   V_{max} is the initial rate of reaction at which substrate concentration is no longer limiting the reaction rate. Use your graph to find V_{max}.

4   The Michaelis–Menten constant for the enzyme, K_m, is the substrate concentration at which the rate of activity of the enzyme is ½ V_{max}.

   Step 1   On the y-axis of your graph, find the value that is exactly half the value of V_{max}.

   Step 2   Draw a horizontal line from this point on the y-axis, until it hits the curve.

   Step 3   Draw a vertical line from this point on the curve, down to the x-axis.

   Step 4   Read off the value of x at this point. This is K_m.

5   The researcher repeated this experiment using lipase extracted from a different species of bacterium. He found that K_m for this species was lower than that for B. cepacia.

   What can you conclude about the relative affinity for their substrates of the lipases from the two species of bacteria?

Exercise 3.4 Planning an investigation into the effect of inhibitor concentration on urease activity

Many experiments involve finding the effect of one variable (the independent variable) on another (the dependent variable). Any other variables that might affect your results should be kept the same – these are often known as controlled variables. It's often necessary to do some preliminary trials, to try to decide on the values of the independent and controlled variables that might work best. In this exercise, you will think about how you could do such an experiment.

Here is some information about urease, its substrate and an inhibitor that slows down its action.

- Urease is an enzyme that converts urea to ammonia:

$$CO(NH_2)_2 + H_2O \rightarrow 2NH_3 + CO_2$$

- Farmers often add fertilisers containing urea to the soil, which is a way of providing slow-release nitrogen compounds for their crops. These fertilisers sometimes also contain a urease inhibitor. This reduces the production of ammonia.
- You can obtain an extract containing urease by soaking soya beans in water overnight, then liquidising the mixture in a blender (or use a pestle and mortar). Filter the mixture, and keep the filtrate to use as your enzyme extract.
- Urea can be bought as a powder, which dissolves in water.
- The inhibitor can also be bought as a powder, which dissolves in water.
- Ammonia dissolves in water to form a solution with a pH above 7.

The rate of production of ammonia can be followed by measuring the pH of the enzyme–substrate mixture, using an indicator solution or a pH meter.

Answer the questions below, to explain how you would plan an experiment to investigate how the concentration of the inhibitor affects the rate of activity of the enzyme.

1   **a**   What is your independent variable?
     b   What is your dependent variable?
     c   List the important variables that you must keep the same.

2   What risks can you identify? What can you do to keep yourself and others safe?

3   You will need to do some preliminary work to find out a suitable concentration of substrate to use, so that you can obtain results in a reasonable length of time.

     a   Imagine that you have been provided with a bottle of urea powder. Describe how you could make up a 10% solution of urea in water.

     b   Imagine that you have made a solution containing urease from soya beans (as described above). You try adding 5 cm³ of this urease solution to 5 cm³ of the 10% urea solution, and measure the pH change. You find that the change in pH is very slow.

         Complete the sentence to suggest how you could make the reaction happen more quickly:

         You could use a .... concentrated solution of urease.

4   Imagine you have been provided with a 10% solution of the inhibitor.

     a   Describe how you could use this solution to make up a range of solutions with different concentrations.

     b   Suggest a suitable range and interval for the concentration of the inhibitor. Remember that the range is the spread between your lowest and highest value, and the interval is the difference between each value. You should have at least five values.

5   Describe how you will carry out your experiment.

6   Draw a results chart, with full headings, that you would be able to fill in as you collect your results.

Remember:

- The results chart should be drawn using a ruler. Each row and column should be separated from the next by a ruled line.
- The independent variable should be in the first column of your table.
- The repeat readings for the dependent variable should be in the next columns.
- The mean values of the dependent variable should be in the last column of the table.

7   Sketch the curve that you would expect to obtain if the inhibitor is a non-competitive inhibitor.

Exercise 3.5 Calculating actual and percentage error

We can never be absolutely certain that a value that we measure is a true value. It is possible to estimate the actual error in a reading quantitatively. We can then use this to estimate the percentage error in a reading.

Whenever you make a measurement with an instrument – such as a measuring cylinder, pipette, thermometer – you cannot be certain that the reading is exactly correct. There is an **uncertainty** or error in your measurement.

In general, we say that the size of the error is equivalent to half the size of the smallest division on the scale you are reading from.

For example, imagine you have a thermometer marked off in °C. When you read the thermometer, you can read the scale to the nearest 0.5 °C. However, we must accept that there is an uncertainty in this reading of 0.5 °C. So, if you read a temperature of 17.5 °C, you can show this by writing it as 17.5 ± 0.5 °C. This is the **error** in our measurement.

1   A 1000 cm³ measuring cylinder is marked off in intervals of 10 cm³. What is the actual error in each reading of volume that you make using this measuring cylinder?

If you are measuring a *change* in a quantity, then you must take into account that there are uncertainties in the readings for both the starting value and the final value. For example, if you measure a temperature at the start of an experiment as 22.0 °C, and at the end as 27.5 °C, then you must add together the 0.5 °C uncertainties for each reading. The change in temperature is therefore given as an increase of 5.5 ± 1 °C.

2   A 100 cm³ measuring cylinder is marked off in intervals of 2 cm³. What is the size of the actual error if you measure a change in volume using this measuring cylinder?

Once we have worked out the size of the error in the measurements, we can use this to calculate the **percentage error**:

$$\text{percentage error} = \frac{\text{size of the error in the reading}}{\text{the reading}} \times 100$$

So, if we measure a volume of 28 cm³ using a 50 cm³ measuring cylinder marked off in intervals of 1 cm³, the error in that measurement is ± 0.5 cm³, and the percentage error is:

$$\frac{0.5}{28} \times 100 = 1.8\%$$

3 A student measures out a volume of 10 cm³ of an enzyme solution, using a graduated pipette marked off in intervals of 0.1 cm³. Calculate the percentage error in her measurement of this volume.

4 A student measures a change in the length of a seedling over a period of 3 days. He measures the length with a ruler marked off in 1 mm intervals. The initial measurement is 2.15 cm, and the final measurement is 5.50 cm. What is the percentage error in his measurement of the change in length of the seedling?

5 A student measures a change in the mass of a potato strip after it has been immersed in a sucrose solution. He uses a top pan balance that gives readings to the nearest 0.01 g. He measures the initial mass of the strip as 1.63 g, and the final mass as 1.56 g. What is the percentage error in his measurement of the change in mass?

Exam-style questions

Take care in this question to focus on the command words for each part. Remember that 'suggest' means you are not expected to know the answer – you should use your biological knowledge and skills to work out a suitable answer.

1 Amylase digests starch to the reducing sugar maltose. The graphs show the activity of a sample of amylase produced by a fungus, at different pH values and at three different temperatures.

Figure 3.5 Effect of pH and temperature on the activity of amylase.

a Suggest how the researchers could measure the rate of activity of the amylase sample. [3]

b i With reference to the graph, describe the effect of pH on the activity of amylase at 60 °C. [2]

ii Explain the reasons for the effects that you have described in **i**. [3]

c i Describe the effect of temperature on the activity of this sample of amylase. [2]

ii Suggest how the optimum temperature of this sample of amylase could be determined. [3]

[Total: 13 marks]

Enzymes have a huge number of uses, and this question is about a medical application of knowledge that we have about an enzyme made by a bacterium.

2 Stomach ulcers are caused by a bacterium called *Helicobacter pylori*. This bacterium produces the enzyme urease, which converts urea to ammonia and carbon dioxide. To diagnose the presence of *H. pylori* in a person's stomach, the urea breath test is used. The person swallows a tablet of urea labelled with ^{13}C. The presence of ^{13}C in their breath indicates infection with *H. pylori*.

a Explain why the urea is labelled with ^{13}C. [1]

b Outline how carbon dioxide produced in the stomach is eventually exhaled in the breath. [3]

c The graph shows the results of urea breath tests carried out in two people, **A** and **B**.

Figure 3.6 Urea breath test results for two people.

Compare the results for person **A** and person **B**. [2]

d Suggest why the urea breath test is a good way of diagnosing the presence of *H. pylori* in a person's stomach. [1]

[Total: 7 marks]

Immobilised enzymes are very widely used in industry. Here you are asked to interpret data about the activity of free and immobilised enzymes, and then to use your own knowledge to answer the final part of the question.

3 Pectinase is an enzyme that breaks down pectin, a component of plant tissues that helps to hold adjacent cell walls together. Pectinase is used in the food industry to increase the quantity of juice that can be extracted from fruit, and also to clarify fruit juice.

Pectinase obtained from a fungus, *Aspergillus niger*, was immobilised onto an alginate support. This enzyme is known to be damaged by temperatures above 40 °C.

An experiment was carried out to compare the effect of exposure to a high temperature on the activity of free and immobilised pectinase.

- The enzymes were kept at a temperature of 50 °C for 30 minutes.
- The activity of the enzymes was then tested, and was recorded as a percentage of their activity before heating.

The results are shown in Figure 3.7.

Figure 3.7 Heat stability of free and immobilised pectinase.

a Compare the effect of exposure to a temperature of 50 °C on the free and immobilised samples of pectinase. [3]

b Suggest **two** variables that should have been kept the same when comparing the activity of the free and immobilised pectinase after exposure to 50 °C. [2]

c Explain how these results indicate that using immobilised pectinase could be advantageous for commercial manufacturers of fruit juice. [2]

d Use your knowledge of immobilised enzymes to list **two** other advantages of using immobilised pectinase rather than free pectinase. [2]

[Total: 9 marks]

Chapter 4
Cell membranes and transport

Chapter outline

The questions in this chapter cover the following topics:

- the structure of cell membranes
- how substances move through membranes
- finding the water potential of plant tissues through experiment

Exercise 4.1 Investigating the effect of surface area to volume ratio on the time taken for diffusion

A simple way of investigating how surface area to volume ratio affects the time taken for diffusion is to use blocks of agar with different surface areas and volumes. You need to be able to calculate surface areas, volumes and surface area : volume ratios. This exercise also gives you practice in constructing results charts and graphs, and identifying systematic and random errors.

1   A student made up a quantity of agar jelly by dissolving agar powder in slightly acidic water. She put a couple of drops of Universal Indicator solution into the water, and so made the jelly red.

The student used a ruler to measure the jelly, and cut cubes from it using a sharp scalpel. She cut cubes with sides of 4.0 cm, 3.0 cm, 2.0 cm, 1.0 cm and 0.5 cm.

   a   Calculate the surface area of each cube. Show your working.
   b   Calculate the volume of each cube. Show your working.
   c   Calculate the surface area : volume ratio of each cube. Show your working.
   d   Plot a graph of surface area : volume ratio (*y*-axis) against length of side of the cube (*x*-axis). Join the points with a smooth curve.

2   The student made three sets of cubes. She then placed one cube into a glass dish, and poured dilute sodium hydroxide solution around it. As the sodium hydroxide diffused into the agar cube, the colour changed to green and then blue. The student measured the time for the cube to turn completely blue. Although the timer measured to 0.01 s, the student decided to measure the time to the nearest quarter of a minute. She repeated this with each cube.

These are the results she wrote down.

4 cm cube: 12.25 minutes, 12.5 minutes, 12 minutes

3 cm cube: 8.5 minutes, 9.25 minutes, 8.5 minutes

2 cm cube: 6 minutes, 5.75 minutes, 6 minutes

1 cm cube: 3.25 minutes, 3.5 minutes, 3 minutes

0.5 cm cube: 1 minute, 0.75 minutes, 1.25 minutes

   a   Do you agree with the student's decision to measure the time to the nearest quarter of a minute? Explain your answer.
   b   Construct a results chart, and record the student's results. Remember:
       • Draw the chart with a ruler.
       • Head each column and/or row fully, including units.

- Make sure that each entry for a particular set of readings is given to the same number of decimal places, which is determined by the method of measuring the value.
- When calculating a mean value, the number of significant figures should be the same as (or one more than) the value with the least number of significant figures used in your calculation.

3 a Plot a graph of mean time taken for the colour to change (*y*-axis) against the surface area : volume ratio of the cube (*x*-axis).

b Use your graph to write a brief conclusion for the student's experiment. Your conclusion should summarise how the dependent variable is affected by the independent variable in the student's experiment.

c The student stated that the rate of diffusion, that is the distance travelled by the dye in a certain amount of time, was probably the same for all of the cubes. Do you agree with this statement?

4 The student was asked to identify significant sources of error in her experiment, and to state whether each one was random or systematic. She was told:

- **Systematic errors** are generally caused by lack of accuracy or precision in measuring instruments, and by the limitations of reading the scale. They tend to be always the same size, and act in the same direction, on all of the readings and results.
- **Random errors** are often caused by difficulties in keeping control variables (standardised variables) constant. They can also be caused by difficulties in measuring the dependent variable. They may be of different sizes, and act in different directions, at different times or stages of the experiment.

These are the sources of error that the student listed. For each one:

- State whether you think this was likely to be a significant source of error or not.
- If you think it was a significant source of error, state whether it was a random or systematic error.

a It was difficult to cut the agar blocks to the exact size.

b Temperature changes might have made diffusion happen faster or slower.

c One side of the block was resting on the base of the dish, so was not exposed to the sodium hydroxide solution.

d It was very difficult to decide exactly when the whole block had changed colour.

Exercise 4.2 Planning an experiment to determine how concentration affects diffusion rate

This exercise involves planning an experiment. You may need to look back at Chapter 2 to help you with some of the questions. You may be able to carry out your experiment after your teacher has checked your plan.

You are going to plan an investigation to find out how the concentration of a glucose solution affects the rate of diffusion.

The diagram shows the apparatus you can use. Visking tubing allows both water molecules and glucose molecules to move through it.

distilled water

Visking tubing, a partially
permeable membrane

glucose solution

Figure 4.1 Apparatus for diffusion experiment.

1 Suggest a testable hypothesis for this experiment.

2 Identify the independent and dependent variables.

3 You will be given a 10% solution of glucose.
   a Suggest the values of concentrations of glucose solution that you will use.
   b Describe how you will make up these concentrations of glucose solutions.

4 Which of the following variables should be controlled? For each variable that you decide should be controlled, explain how you would do this:
   a temperature of the solution and the water
   b light intensity
   c pH
   d time for which the apparatus is left.

5 You can measure your dependent variable by finding the concentration of glucose in the water outside the Visking tubing.
   a Explain how you can use the Benedict's test and a colorimeter to do this.
   b Suggest how you could estimate the concentration of glucose if you do not have access to a colorimeter.

6 Construct a results chart, with full headings, in which you could write your results. Remember to include spaces for repeats.

7 Draw and label the axes of the graph that you would plot. (You will not be able to draw a scale for the y-axis, because you cannot predict the values of the results.) Sketch the shape of the curve that you would expect to get if your hypothesis is correct.

Exercise 4.3 Determining the water potential of a plant tissue

In this exercise, you will practise constructing good results tables, and will also think back to earlier work on calculating magnification.

A student carried out an experiment, using flower petals, to estimate the water potential of the cells in the epidermis of the petals.

He made up a range of sucrose solutions of different concentrations between 0 and 1 mol dm^{-3}. He cut small pieces of flower petal epidermis and immersed three pieces in each solution, and also in distilled water. He left all of the pieces for 20 minutes.

He then mounted each piece of tissue on a slide. He recorded the number of cells he could see that were plasmolysed and non-plasmolysed. He moved the slide a little and continued to count until he had recorded results for 100 cells for each tissue sample.

Figure 4.2 shows a piece of the petal epidermis that was immersed in 1 mol dm^{-3} sucrose solution.

50 µm

Figure 4.2 Plant epidermis cells after immersion in 1 mol dm^{-3} sucrose solution.

1   Use the scale bar to calculate the mean length of cells **X**, **Y** and **Z**. Show all of your working.

2   **a**   Name the parts labelled **A**, **B** and **C** on the diagram.
    b   What is present in the part labelled **D**? Explain your answer.
    c   State the percentage of cells in this sample that are plasmolysed.
    d   Explain why these cells are plamolysed.

3   This is the results chart that the student completed.

Number of plasmolysed cells	Number of non-plasmolysed cells	Concentration of solution
0	100	0
0	100	0
0	100	0
14	86	0.2
19	81	0.2
12	88	0.2
29	71	0.4
63	37	0.4
31	69	0.4
45	55	0.6
43	57	0.6
46	54	0.6
82	18	0.8
89	11	0.8
87	13	0.8
100	0	1.0
100	0	1.0
100	0	1.0

a Which set of results could be omitted from the results chart, without losing any useful information?

b Identify the result that appears to be anomalous.

c Identify the mistakes that the student made in designing his results chart.

d Draw a fully correct results chart to show these results. (Remember that the anomalous result should be disregarded – it should not be included when calculating a mean.)

4 Plot a graph to display these results.

5 Figure 4.3 shows the relationship between the concentration of a sucrose solution and its water potential.

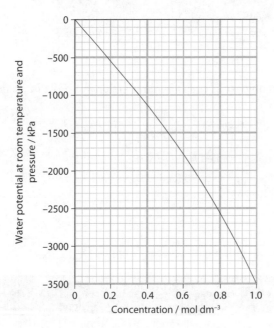

Figure 4.3 Relationship between concentration and water potential of a sucrose solution.

When a cell is just starting to become plasmolysed (known as incipient plasmolysis), the water potentials of the solutions outside and inside the cell surface membrane are equal. We can assume that, on average, each cell is at incipient plasmolysis when 50% of the cells in the tissue are plasmolysed.

Use the graph that you drew in **4**, and the graph above, to estimate the water potential of the cytoplasm of the epidermal cells of the flower petals.

6 The student wanted to obtain a more precise value for the water potential of these cells. Which **one** of the following would be the best way to do this?

A Repeat the experiment using glucose instead of sucrose.

B Repeat the experiment using a wider range of sucrose concentrations.

C Repeat the experiment at a higher temperature, to speed up the rate of osmosis.

D Repeat the experiment using smaller intervals of sucrose concentration between the range 0.5 and 0.8 mol dm⁻³.

Exercise 4.4 Comparing lipid composition of membranes

In Chapter 2, Exercise 2.4, you practised comparing data about the types of lipids found in different organisms. In this exercise, you will compare the types of lipids found in the cell membranes of normal red blood cells and those infected by the malarial parasite. First, though, you will check your understanding of the structure of a cell membrane and the roles of its various components.

Figure 4.4 A phospholipid molecule.

1 Figure 4.4 represents a phospholipid molecule.

   a Using this symbol for a phospholipid molecule, draw a diagram to show a phospholipid bilayer, as found in a cell membrane. Explain why the molecules arrange themselves like this when in a watery environment.

   b Explain why ions such as Na⁺ and Cl⁻ are unable to move freely through a phospholipid bilayer.

   c Return to the diagram you drew for **a**. Add a **channel protein** to your diagram.

   d Explain how channel proteins can help ions such as Na⁺ and Cl⁻ to move through the membrane.

The data below include some long and unfamiliar names. Don't let these put you off. A good way of dealing with them in your answers to use the full name once and then invent a shorthand for it.

When you are making a comparison, try to use comparative words, such as 'more'. When you are comparing numbers, you should calculate a difference (by subtracting one number from another) or calculate how many times greater one number is than another. In some cases, you could also calculate percentage difference, but because the numbers in this table are already percentages, that isn't really a good idea in this case.

2 Malaria is an infectious disease caused by a single-celled parasite called *Plasmodium*. This parasite enters red blood cells and replicates there. After infection, the composition of the lipids in the red blood cell membrane changes. Some of the differences between the uninfected and infected red blood cell membranes are shown in the table.

Molecule	Type of substance	Percentage in uninfected red blood cell membrane	Percentage in infected red blood cell membrane
phosphatidylcholine	phospholipid	31.70	38.70
sphingomyelin	phospholipid	28.00	14.60
palmitic acid	polyunsaturated fatty acid	21.88	31.21
oleic acid	monounsaturated fatty acid	14.64	24.60
arachidonic acid	polyunsaturated fatty acid	17.36	7.85

   a Explain the difference between:
   • a phospholipid and a fatty acid
   • a polyunsaturated fatty acid and a monounsaturated fatty acid.

   b Compare the phospholipid composition of the uninfected and infected red blood cell membrane.

   c Compare the fatty acid composition of the uninfected and infected red blood cell membrane.

3 Red blood cells do not contain endoplasmic reticulum. Suggest how the changes in the composition of the infected red blood cell membrane are brought about.

Exam-style questions

This question asks you to use your knowledge of the structure and function of cell membranes to interpret and explain data.

1 Figure 4.5 is a representation of the fluid mosaic model of membrane structure. The membrane shown is a cell surface (plasma) membrane.

The table shows the concentrations of several substances outside the cell (extracellular) and inside the cell (intracellular).

Substance	Extracellular concentration / mmol dm^{-3}	Intracellular concentration / mmol dm^{-3}
sodium ions, Na$^+$	150	15
potassium ions, K$^+$	5	150
amino acids	2	8
glucose	5.6	1.0
ATP	0	4

Figure 4.5 A cell surface membrane.

a Name the types of molecule labelled **A**, **B**, **C** and **D** on the diagram. [2]

b Outline how molecule **C** is involved in cell signalling. [3]

c Explain why sodium ions cannot diffuse through the part of the membrane made up of molecule **A**. [2]

d Sodium ions and potassium ions move through the membrane by active transport.

   i Give the letter of the part of the membrane through which these ions could move. [1]

   ii Describe the evidence in the table that supports the statement that these ions move through the membrane by active transport. [2]

e Glucose is able to move through gated channels in the membrane by facilitated diffusion.

   i Explain the meanings of the terms *gated channel* and *facilitated diffusion*. [2]

   ii Suggest **two** reasons why, despite glucose being able to move through the membrane by facilitated diffusion, the concentration of glucose is not the same on the two sides of the membrane. [2]

f Explain why no ATP is found outside the cell. [2]

[Total: 16 marks]

In Chapter 3, Exam question 2, you saw how the presence of *Helicobacter pylori* in the stomach can be detected by testing for urease activity. For this question, you will need to combine knowledge about enzymes with understanding of how substances can pass through membranes.

2 The presence of the bacterium *Helicobacter pylori* can lead to the development of stomach ulcers. This bacterium produces the enzyme urease, which breaks down urea to carbon dioxide and ammonia. Sodium acetate is also a substrate for this enzyme. A patient suspected to have *H. pylori* in their stomach can be asked to swallow a tablet containing sodium acetate labelled with ^{13}C. Their breath is then tested for $^{13}CO_2$.

The effect of pH on the activity of urease from *H. pylori* was measured in intact bacteria and in a homogenate made from the bacteria. A homogenate is produced by liquidising the bacteria, so that the enzyme is released from the cells.

Figure 4.6 shows the results.

Figure 4.6 The effect of pH on urease activity in intact bacteria and in a homogenate.

a Compare the effect of pH on urease in intact bacteria and urease in a homogenate. [3]

b It has been suggested that urea enters bacterial cells by facilitated diffusion, and that the urea channel in the bacterial cell membrane is activated by low pH.

Explain how this could account for the differences that you have described in your answer to **a**. [3]

c Before taking the urease breath test, patients are often asked to drink apple juice, which contains a variety of organic acids. Suggest why this is done. [2]

[Total: 8 marks]

You should be getting confident now in describing graphs. In this question, you also need to suggest explanations for a set of results and to consider whether these results support a particular hypothesis.

3 In birds, the main nitrogenous excretory product is uric acid, which forms salts called urates. Figure 4.7 shows an ion of urate.

Figure 4.7 A urate ion.

Urate is taken up by cells in the kidneys of birds.

Membrane-bound vesicles were isolated from turkey kidneys. One set of vesicles, set **A**, contained urate. The other set, **B**, did not. Both sets of vesicles were placed in a solution containing urate. The amount of urate taken up into the vesicles was measured over the next two minutes. The results are shown in Figure 4.8.

43

a With reference to Figure 4.8, describe the effect of concentration gradient on the uptake of urate. [3]

b With reference to the procedure that was used for this experiment, explain why the uptake of urate **cannot** be by active transport. [3]

c Do these results support the hypothesis that urate is taken into the vesicles by facilitated diffusion? Explain your answer. [2]

Figure 4.8 Uptake of urate into vesicles containing (**A**) or not containing (**B**) urate.

d It was found that urate was taken up more rapidly when there were excess potassium ions, K⁺, inside the vesicles. Suggest reasons for this. [2]

[Total: 10 marks]

4 a The cell surface membranes of the cells lining the walls of the small intestine contain ion channels through which chloride ions, Cl^-, can be actively transported out of the cells. When the channels are open, chloride ions accumulate outside the cells, causing water and sodium ions, Na^+, to also move out of the cells.

   i Explain what is meant by the terms *ion channel* and *active transport*. [2]

   ii Using the term *water potential*, explain how a build-up of chloride ions outside a cell causes water to move out of it. [3]

b The bacterium *Vibrio cholerae* causes cholera. When this bacterium gets into the small intestine, it produces a toxin that binds to receptors on the cell surface membranes of the cells in the intestinal lining. The cells then take up the toxin by endocytosis.

The uptake of the toxin sets off a cell signalling mechanism that results in the Cl^- channels remaining permanently open. The cells therefore lose a great deal of water, resulting in diarrhoea and dehydration.

   i Describe how a cell could take up the toxin by endocytosis. [2]

   ii Explain what is meant by a *cell signalling mechanism*. [3]

c The cell surface membranes also contain glucose–sodium co-transporter proteins. These use active transport to move glucose molecules and sodium ions into the cells from the lumen of the intestine. People with cholera are often treated by giving them drinks containing glucose and sodium ions. This results in the cells reabsorbing water from the small intestine, reducing diarrhoea and speeding recovery.

Suggest how a drink containing glucose and sodium ions can cause the cells in the intestine to reabsorb water. [3]

[Total: 13 marks]

You will often be provided with information in a question that requires you to work through it logically in order to arrive at an answer. In this question, you will use what you have learnt about the roles of cell membranes to explain events. Try sketching diagrams or flow charts to get things clear in your mind, before writing your answers.

Chapter 5
The mitotic cell cycle

Chapter outline

The questions in this chapter cover the following topics:

- the structure of chromosomes
- the stages of the cell cycle, including the interpretation of diagrams and micrographs
- the roles of mitosis
- telomeres and stem cells

Exercise 5.1 Interpreting a micrograph showing mitosis

You need to be able to recognise the stages of mitosis from micrographs. This exercise also gives you practice in calculating real dimensions when given the magnification of an image. Look back at Chapter 1 if you need reminding how to do this.

Figure 5.1 is a light micrograph of a stained root tip squash of broad bean, *Vicia faba*.

6 µm

Figure 5.1 Light micrograph of root tip squash of *Vicia faba*.

1 Count the number of chromosomes in cell **A**, and use your result to state the **diploid** number of chromosomes in *Vicia faba*.

2 Give the letter of a cell that is:

  a in interphase

  b in prophase

  c in early anaphase

  d in telophase.

3 Measure the maximum width of cell **C** on the micrograph. Use the scale bar to calculate the actual width of this cell. Show all of your working.

> **TIP**
>
> Remember that a diploid number must be an even number.

Exercise 5.2 Answering multiple choice questions on the cell cycle

Multiple choice questions can be tricky to answer. In this exercise, you think about how to maximise your chance of getting a multiple choice question correct.

This multiple choice question is about what happens during anaphase.

What happens during anaphase of mitosis?

A Chromatids line up on the equator of the spindle.

B Chromosomes are pulled to opposite ends of the cell.

C Spindle fibres pull chromatids towards the poles of the spindle.

D Nuclear membranes begin to reform.

Option **A** is not correct, because it is whole chromosomes (each made of two chromatids joined together) that line up on the equator. Option **B** is wrong, because each chromosome is pulled apart into its two chromatids during anaphase, and it is these individual chromatids that are pulled to opposite ends of the cell. **D** is not correct, because nuclear membranes do not reform until late telophase.

The correct answer is **C**. However, when this question was set as part of a test, many students answered **B**. This is probably because they were in a hurry, and gave the first answer that seemed to be correct, without taking the time to read all the options.

You may find the following approach helps you when answering multiple choice questions:

Step 1	Read the question very carefully (before looking at the options) to make sure you understand exactly what it is asking you. Many incorrect answers are a result of skim-reading the question too quickly.
Step 2	Next, read all of the options carefully, or study diagrams in detail.
Step 3	Decide if any of the options are definitely not correct.
Step 4	Now concentrate on the remaining options, and consider each one carefully. Think about the exact wording of each one (chromosomes or chromatids?) – or exactly what is shown in the diagrams if the options are illustrations – and make your decision.
Step 5	Never leave a multiple choice question unanswered. If you cannot decide between two options, just write down one of them.

Now apply this technique to the following multiple choice question.

1 Figure 5.2 shows the chromosomes in a cell in prophase of mitosis.

Figure 5.2

TIP

In deciding which answer is correct, ask yourself: what are the differences between the diagrams? Some show nuclear membranes and some do not – which is correct? Some show chromosomes made up of two chromatids and some show separate chromatids – which is correct?

In Figure 5.3, which diagram shows the cells that would be produced after cytokinesis?

A

B

C

D

Figure 5.3

2   Writing your own multiple choice questions can be a good way to help you to think clearly about the possible answers.

Here are two sets of options for multiple choice questions. Decide which will be the correct answer, and then write the question. Try out your questions on someone else in the class.

Option set 1

   A   centriole

   B   centromere

   C   chromatid

   D   chromosome

Option set 2

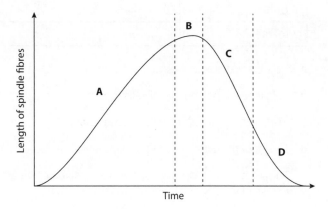

Figure 5.4

Exercise 5.3 Tally counts and testing a hypothesis

Tallies are a good way of counting a lot of objects. You simply draw a tally mark for each object counted, and put a cross through a group of four marks to represent the fifth. Later you can convert the tally marks to numbers. Before you answer 1b, make sure that you know which stages of the cell cycle are part of mitosis and which are not.

1 A student made a stained root tip squash of a bean plant, *Vicia faba*, following this procedure:

- She cut off the tip of a bean root, and placed it in acidified acetic orcein stain in a watch glass. This stain colours DNA red.
- She warmed the watch glass gently for five minutes to allow the acid to separate the cells in the root tip.
- She put the stained root tip onto a clean microscope slide and cut it in half, discarding the part nearest the tip – this part does not contain dividing cells.
- She added two drops of acetic orcein to the remaining root tip, and gently broke it apart and spread the root tissues out using a mounted needle.
- She covered the root tip with a coverslip, wrapped a piece of filter paper around it and very gently tapped it with the blunt end of a pencil until the tissue had spread out into a very thin layer.
- Finally, to intensify the stain, she moved the root tip squash preparation quickly through a Bunsen flame a few times, holding the slide with her fingers to make sure she did not let it get too hot.

She observed her preparation using a light microscope. She counted the number of cells in each stage of the cell cycle in several different fields of view and recorded her results in a tally chart as shown below.

Stage of cell cycle	Tally count
interphase	ℍℍ ℍℍ ℍℍ ℍℍ ℍℍ ℍℍ ℍℍ ℍℍ ℍℍ ℍℍ ℍℍ ℍℍ ℍℍ ℍℍ ℍℍ |||
prophase	ℍℍ ℍℍ ℍℍ |||
metaphase	ℍℍ ℍℍ	
anaphase	ℍℍ ℍℍ
telophase	ℍℍ
cytokinesis	|||

a How many cells did the student count in total?

b Calculate the percentage of cells that were in a stage of mitosis.

c Display the student's results as a **bar chart**.

d The student wanted to test this hypothesis:

The cell cycle of *Vicia faba* follows a diurnal (daily) rhythm, in which mitosis is more likely to take place at some times of day than at others.

Outline how the student could test this hypothesis. In your plan, you should refer to:

- the independent variable: what it is, how the student can vary it, and what values she should use
- the dependent variable: what it is, how the student can measure and record it
- variables that should be standardised (kept the same) and how this can be done
- whether repeats should be done
- how the results will be recorded, processed and displayed
- how the results can be used to draw a conclusion.

TIP

Remember:

- In a bar chart, the bars should not touch.
- Draw each bar very accurately, using a ruler and a sharp HB (medium hard) pencil.
- Do not shade the bars.

48

Exercise 5.4 Factors affecting telomere length

Investigating how a particular lifestyle factor affects humans is very difficult, because we cannot usually do controlled experiments. Instead, researchers measure particular variables in a large sample of people, and look for correlations between them. This means that we are rarely able to prove that one variable actually **causes** a change in another. In this exercise, you will practise describing and explaining a graph, and also discuss the strength of the evidence to support a conclusion made by researchers.

A chromosome is a very long molecule of DNA, and DNA molecules are made up of nucleotides linked together into long chains. Each nucleotide contains one of four bases: A, C, T or G.

Telomeres are protective caps of short, repeating DNA sequences on the ends of chromosomes. Each time the chromosomes replicate just before cell division, the telomeres get a little shorter. Eventually, they become so short that the cells can no longer divide. It is thought that loss of telomeres is a significant contribution to the effects of ageing, because tissues are not able to repair and renew themselves effectively.

1   A study was carried out to find the effects of age, obesity and smoking on the length of telomeres in humans.

Figure 5.5 shows the results of a study that measured the mean telomere length in the cells of 1122 women between the ages of 18 and 76. The length of the telomeres was measured in kilobases (kb). (The line was drawn after doing a calculation called linear regression, which uses the individual data points to predict the overall relationship between the two variables.)

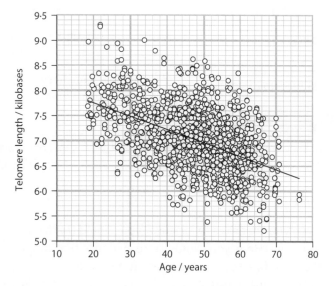

Figure 5.5 Results of a study into age and telomere length.

a   Describe the pattern shown in the graph.
b   Explain the reasons for the patterns that you have described in **a**.

Remember, when answering **a**:

• If you are asked to 'describe', you should not try to give any reasons or explanations. You are simply translating what you can see in the graph into words.
• Start by describing the general trend – what happens to the *y*-axis variable as the *x*-axis variable increases?

- Make a comment about how strong this trend is – in this case, you should comment on the wide variation around the line that has been drawn.
- Quote figures – for example, the range of telomere lengths at a particular age, the telomere length indicated by the line at age 18 and age 76.
- Use the figures to do a calculation that provides information about the changes with age – for example, the mean change in telomere length as a person ages by 10 years.
- For all the figures that you quote, remember to state the units.

2   Figure 5.6a shows the relationship between BMI and mean telomere length. BMI stands for body mass index, which is a measure of a person's mass in relation to their height. In general, a person with a BMI between 18.5 and 25.0 kg m^{-2} is considered to be of normal weight, while BMIs above or below that range indicate being overweight or underweight.

Figure 5.6b shows the relationship between smoking and mean telomere length.

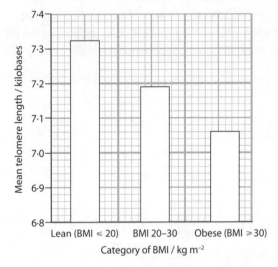

Figure 5.6a Results of a study into BMI and telomere length.

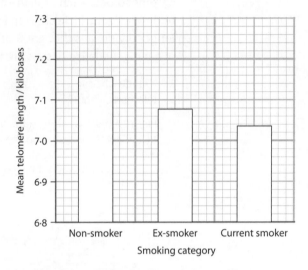

Figure 5.6b Results of a study into smoking and telomere length.

The researchers suggested that their results show that obesity and smoking accelerate ageing. Discuss the extent to which the data in Figures 5.6a and 5.6b support this idea.

Remember:

- When you are asked to 'discuss', you should try to make points on both sides of the argument. Here, you should state evidence that supports the researchers' suggestion, and also state the shortcomings in this evidence.
- To answer this question, you will need to pull together information from Figures 5.6a and b, and also use some of the information in the paragraph about telomeres and ageing at the beginning of the question.
- Jot down the points you want to make – you could have two columns, one for 'supports the suggestion' and one for 'does not support / more evidence needed' – and sort out your ideas into a sensible sequence before you begin to write your answer.

Exam-style questions

1 a A chromosome is a structure made up of a long molecule of DNA, associated with proteins. When a cell is not dividing, the chromosomes are not visible with an optical (light) microscope.

    i Name the type of proteins that are associated with DNA to form a chromosome. [1]

    ii Explain why chromosomes are not visible with an optical microscope when a cell is not dividing. [2]

b The diagram shows the structure of a chromosome, just before the cell enters mitosis.

    i Name the parts of the chromosome labelled **A** and **B**. [2]

    ii Make a copy of Figure 5.7, and label the parts of the chromosome where telomeres would be found. [1]

    iii Outline the function of telomeres. [2]

[Total: 8 marks]

2 a Outline the functions of mitosis in a multicellular organism such as a human. [3]

Figure 5.7 A chromosome.

b Figure 5.8 is a pie chart representing the mitotic cell cycle. The diagrams in Figure 5.9 show cells in various stages of the cell cycle.

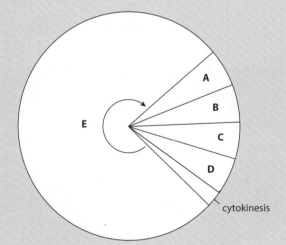

Figure 5.8 The cell cycle.

Figure 5.9 Cells at different stages of the cell cycle.

Copy and complete the table to identify the stage of the cell cycle shown in each diagram. [4]

Diagram	Letter of stage of cell cycle

c During a normal cell cycle, a cell will not continue with mitosis if the spindle fibres are not attached correctly to the centromeres. Several proteins, known as spindle checkpoint proteins, are involved in this control process. In the cells in cancer tissue, these spindle checkpoint proteins may not work properly.

Suggest how this can explain the observation that many cells in cancer tissue contain more or fewer chromosomes than normal cells. [3]

[Total: 10 marks]

3 The human heart is made of cardiac muscle tissue. This tissue contains a small proportion of stem cells. These cardiac stem cells are thought to be able to produce new cells to replace damaged cardiac muscle tissue.

a Explain what is meant by the term *stem cell*. [2]

b Chronic (long-term) heart failure occurs when the heart is not able to pump blood effectively. This may be caused by damaged cardiac muscle tissue.

Data were collected about the telomere length in cardiac stem cells in the hearts of people who had chronic heart failure and people with healthy hearts. The results are shown in Figure 5.10.

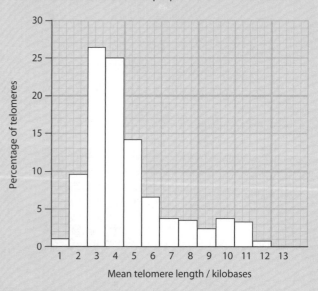

Figure 5.10 Telomere lengths in stem cells from healthy and diseased human hearts.

i Describe the distribution of telomere lengths in stem cells from healthy human hearts. [2]

ii Compare the telomere lengths in stem cells from people with chronic heart failure and people with healthy hearts. [3]

iii Suggest explanations for the differences you have described in your answer to **ii**. [4]

[Total: 11 marks]

Chapter outline

The questions in this chapter cover the following topics:

- the structure and replication of DNA
- the structure and roles of RNA
- how proteins are synthesised in cells
- mutations

Exercise 6.1 Answering multiple choice questions about DNA

In Chapter 5, we looked at an approach for answering multiple choice questions. Here are some more examples for you to try.

> **TIP**
>
> In the exam, you have 60 minutes to answer 40 multiple choice questions, which gives you an average of 1½ minutes for each one. But some questions are more complex than others, so it is a good idea to answer the straightforward ones first, and then go back and tackle the more complex ones that need more time.
>
> Set your phone or a timer to time one minute. Press 'start' and then sit motionless and silent until the minute is over. That's how long you should try to spend on a simple multiple choice question. You can allow more time for more complex questions.

Look at this question. Don't rush – the aim at this point is to get the right answer, however long it takes. Read the question, then follow the stages overleaf to help you to arrive at an answer.

1 The table shows the percentages of each type of base in the DNA from cells of different organisms.

Organism	Percentage of base			
	adenine	cytosine	guanine	thymine
human	30.9	19.8	19.9	29.4
grasshopper	29.3	20.7	20.5	29.3
yeast	31.3	17.1	18.7	32.9
sea urchin	32.8	17.3	17.7	32.1
wheat	27.3	22.8	22.7	27.1

What can be concluded from these data?

A Plants have less adenine and thymine than animals have.

B Small differences in the base sequences in DNA have large effects on the characteristics of an organism.

C There is approximately the same quantity of DNA in the cells of all organisms.

D The total percentage of purines is approximately the same as the total quantity of pyrimidines.

Step 1	First, look carefully at the **table of data**. Make sure you understand what it is showing.
Step 2	Now look at the **question**. Note that it is asking what can be 'concluded from these data', so you need to think about what the data are showing, not anything else that you might happen to know.
Step 3	Now for the **options**. Start with option **A**. It is about plants – which entries in the table are plants? There is only one, so we really can't conclude anything about plants. Discard that option.
Step 4	Now look at option **B**. You know that statement is true, but can we conclude it from the data?
Step 5	Now option **C**. Look at the headings of the table. Do the data tell us anything about the actual quantity of DNA in the cells in the organisms?
Step 6	Now look at option **D**. You'll need to remember which bases are **purines** and which are **pyrimidines**. (In case you've forgotten, A and G are purines, and C and T are pyrimidines.) Test it out on a couple of rows in the table.

So what is your final decision?

For the questions that follow, you might like to underline any words in the information or question that seem to be particularly important. There are also some suggestions in the margin that might help you.

TIP

What are the important words to concentrate on in this question?

2   Which statement describes the replication of DNA?

    A   It copies information from DNA to mRNA.

    B   It is semi-conservative.

    C   It produces tRNA.

    D   It takes place at a ribosome.

TIP

Try making a rough sketch of a small part of a DNA molecule before working through each option in turn.

3   A sample of DNA is analysed to determine the relative proportions of its components. What would be the results?

    A   equal proportions of phosphates, pentose sugars, adenine, guanine, cytosine and thymine

    B   equal proportions of purines and pyrimidines, and half the number of sugars and phosphates

    C   twice as many bases as phosphate and pentose sugars

    D   twice as many phosphates and bases as pentose sugars.

4   The list shows the events that take place during DNA replication.

    1   Free bases pair up with exposed bases on each DNA strand.

    2   The hydrogen bonds between the bases are broken.

    3   DNA polymerase links adjacent pentose and phosphate groups.

    4   Bonds form between complementary bases.

In what order do these events take place?

TIP

Sort the four events into the correct order yourself, before looking at the options.

    A   1, 4, 3, 2

    B   2, 1, 4, 3

    C   3, 2, 1, 4

    D   4, 1, 2, 3

TIP

You are not expected to know the molecular structures of the four bases, so you probably can't work the answer out from that.

But you should know that purines have a double ring structure, so you can tell which of the two bases is a purine.

You should also know that adenine and guanine are purines.

And lastly, you should know which bases pair together.

TIP

Try drawing a diagram of the original DNA – two strands, both all ^{14}N.

Then draw the two molecules that will be produced when this DNA replicates in ^{15}N – remembering that it replicates semi-conservatively.

Then draw the four molecules that will be produced when each of these two replicate in ^{15}N.

That should help you to see which curve is correct.

5 Figure 6.1 shows two bases, **P** and **Q**, linked by hydrogen bonds in a DNA molecule.

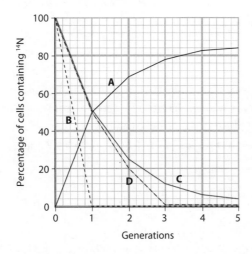

Figure 6.1 Two bases linked by hydrogen bonds.

What are bases **P** and **Q**?

	P	Q
A	adenine	thymine
B	cytosine	guanine
C	guanine	thymine
D	thymine	adenine

6 Nitrogen exists as two different **isotopes**, ^{14}N and ^{15}N. Bacteria were grown in a medium containing only ^{14}N, for many generations. They were then transferred to a medium containing only ^{15}N. Which curve in Figure 6.2 shows the percentage of the bacterial DNA strands that contain ^{14}N in the next five generations?

Figure 6.2 Graph showing ^{14}N content in several generations of bacteria.

Exercise 6.2 Writing good answers to exam questions

This exercise is about making the most of your knowledge to gain as many marks as possible in an exam question. Good examination technique is essential if you are going to get the best grade of which you are capable.

Read the question about normal and sickle cell haemoglobin and then read the answers that three different students wrote. None of the students got all three marks. There are questions for you to answer about each of the students' answers.

1 The sequences of DNA coding for the first seven amino acids in the gene for normal haemoglobin and the gene for sickle cell haemoglobin are as follows:

DNA for normal haemoglobin   CAC GTG GAC TGA GGA CTC CTC
DNA for sickle cell haemoglobin   CAC GTG GAC TGA GGA CAC CTC

The table below shows some of the DNA triplets that code for six different amino acids.

DNA triplet	Amino acid
CTC, CTT	glutamic acid
GTA, GTG	histidine
AAC, GAC	leucine
GGA, GGC	proline
TGA, TGG	threonine
CAA, CAC	valine

Use the information to describe the similarities and differences between the structure of a normal haemoglobin molecule and a sickle cell haemoglobin molecule.

[This question is worth 3 marks.]

Student X

The two kinds of haemoglobin have the same triplet code for their first 5 amino acids and the seventh amino acid. However, they differ in their sixth amino acid code CTC : CAC. This is the result of a substitution mutation. This shows that while the molecules remain the same, their base sequences can vary.

Student Y

The sickle cell haemoglobin has CAC instead of CTC, so it has a valine instead of a glutamic acid. This makes the haemoglobin molecules a different shape, so when the person is short of oxygen the haemoglobin molecules stick together and make the red blood cells into a sickle shape. This is very painful and the person is said to be having a sickle cell crisis.

Student Z

Both kinds of haemoglobin have a sequence of five amino acids that are identical, which is valine, histidine, valine, threonine and proline. The sixth amino acid is different; it is glutamic acid in the normal haemoglobin and valine in the sickle cell haemoglobin. This change in the primary structure will affect the way that the molecule folds, and will therefore affect its tertiary structure.

a Student X has not answered the question that was asked. Explain what this student has done incorrectly.

b Student Y has wasted time giving information that is correct, but that is not asked for by the question. Which information is this?

c Student Z has written the best answer, but there is one mistake. Correct the mistake.

Exercise 6.3 Making links across topic areas

Exam questions often require you to think about several different areas of the syllabus, moving from one topic to another. In this exercise, you will think about protein structure, the cell cycle and the involvement of DNA in protein synthesis.

1   With reference to the structure of haemoglobin, explain what is meant by each of the following terms:

    a   globular protein

    b   quaternary structure.

2   The gene for the α polypeptide of haemoglobin is found on chromosome 16, and the gene for the β polypeptide is found on chromosome 11.

    How many copies of the α polypeptide gene would be present in a cell at the following stages of the cell cycle:

    a   early interphase

    b   prophase?

3   The gene for the β polypeptide occurs in several different forms (alleles) with slightly different base sequences. This results in different amino acid sequences in the β polypeptide that is synthesised. One of these alleles, Hb^S, differs from the normal allele, Hb^A, in only one base, but the protein that is produced behaves so differently that it causes a genetic disease called sickle cell anaemia. This disease can be fatal if medical treatment is not available.

    Outline how a difference in a single base in DNA can result in a form of a protein that behaves very differently from the normal protein.

4   The allele Hb^S is especially common in populations of people living in areas where malaria is present.

    An investigation was carried out in a rural part of Kenya, where malaria is common, to find out whether children who had one copy of this allele and one copy of the normal allele (Hb^{A}Hb^S) had a better chance of survival than those who had two copies of the normal allele (Hb^{A}Hb^A) or two copies of the sickle cell allele (Hb^{S}Hb^S).

    The results are shown in Figure 6.3.

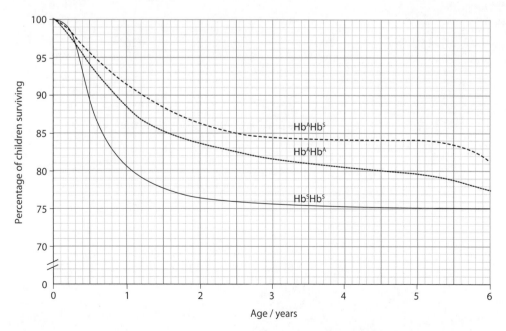

Figure 6.3 Survival curves for children with different genotypes for the haemoglobin β polypeptide gene.

> **TIP**
>
> There are five marks available for question **3**. You cannot second guess what the mark scheme would be, but you should try to make at least five different points in your answer.

57

a Describe the survival pattern of the children with two copies of the normal allele, Hb^AHb^A.

b Compare the survival pattern of the children with two copies of the sickle cell allele, Hb^SHb^S, with that of the children with two copies of the normal allele.

c These results support the hypothesis that having one copy of the sickle cell allele increases the chances of survival in an area where malaria is present. Suggest further investigations that could be carried out, or more information that could be obtained, to attempt to strengthen the evidence for this hypothesis.

Exam-style questions

The introduction to this question will get you thinking about enzymes, but in fact the answers you are asked to write are about protein synthesis and mutations. Only part **b** requires any information about enzymes, and even then it is quite a minor part of the question.

1 Tyrosinase is an enzyme that catalyses reactions involved in the production of melanin, a brown pigment in skin that gives protection from the damaging effects of sunlight.

Figure 6.4 outlines how tyrosinase is produced in human cells.

Figure 6.4 Tyrosinase production pathway.

a **i** Name process **P**. [1]

ii Name molecule **Q**. [1]

iii Name organelle **S**. [1]

iv Outline the importance of structure **R** in the synthesis of tyrosinase. [3]

b In some people, a mutation results in an altered base sequence of the gene for tyrosinase, *TYR*. In one such mutation, a nucleotide containing the base cytosine is deleted from the DNA molecule that makes up this gene.

Explain why a person with this mutation is unable to make melanin. [4]

Here is another question that crosses between several different areas of the syllabus. You may remember something about insulin from your previous studies, but don't worry if you do not – all the information that you need to know about it is given in the question.

2 Insulin is a protein synthesised in β cells in the pancreas. Insulin is a hormone that brings about actions in liver cells that reduce blood glucose concentrations. A lack of functioning insulin results in diabetes.

a The table shows the base sequence of part of the mRNA coding for the formation of insulin extracted from β cells.

GGUAUCGUGCAAUGUUGCACUUCCAUU

i Write the nine base triplets in the DNA from which this mRNA was transcribed. [2]

ii Write the anticodons of the tRNA that will form temporary bonds with the mRNA during translation at a ribosome. [2]

b Insulin does not enter liver cells, but brings about its effects by binding with a receptor on the liver cell membrane. This causes phosphate groups to bind with certain proteins within the cell which, in turn, leads to a series of events that increase the number of glucose transporter proteins in the cell membrane.

i With reference to the structure of the cell surface membrane, suggest why insulin molecules are not able to enter liver cells. [2]

ii State the type of molecule in a cell membrane that could act as a receptor for insulin. [1]

iii Explain how an increase in the number of glucose transporter proteins in the liver cell membrane can result in a decrease in blood glucose concentration. [2]

c In some people, a mutation in one triplet of the insulin gene causes leucine to be incorporated into the protein instead of valine. This insulin is unable to bind with its receptor.

i Explain what is meant by the term *mutation*. [2]

ii Explain how this mutation could result in a form of insulin that is unable to bind with its receptor. [3]

iii People with a chromosome containing this mutation do not normally show any symptoms of diabetes. Suggest why this is so. [2]

3 a i State how the structure of ribosomes differs between prokaryotic and eukaryotic cells. [1]

ii State how the distribution of ribosomes differs between prokaryotic and eukaryotic cells. [2]

b Figure 6.5 shows a ribosome, on which the synthesis of a protein is taking place.

This question contains one 4-mark section and one 5-mark section. These can be difficult to deal with. Common errors are to include material that goes beyond what the question is asking or saying the same thing more than once rather than moving on to something new in your answer. You should make sure that you give at least four or five (preferably five or six) different, strong, relevant points in your answer.

Figure 6.5 Protein synthesis on a ribosome.

Outline the roles of the ribosome in the synthesis of a protein. [4]

59

c An investigation was carried out to track the movement of amino acids through different organelles in a cell.

Pancreatic cells were provided with a small quantity of amino acids containing some tritium atoms, ^{3}H, instead of normal hydrogen atoms. Tritium is radioactive, and molecules containing it can be detected, so the amino acids containing tritium are said to be 'labelled'. After a short time, the pancreatic cells were provided with a large quantity of unlabelled amino acids.

Samples of the cells were extracted at particular times, and the levels of radioactivity in the rough endoplasmic reticulum, Golgi apparatus and secretory vesicles were determined. The results are shown in Figure 6.6.

Figure 6.6 Radioactivity in three organelles.

i Suggest why pancreatic cells were chosen for this experiment. [1]

ii Explain why the pancreatic cells were provided with a large quantity of unlabelled amino acids, after being given a small quantity of labelled amino acids. [2]

iii Use the information in Figure 6.6 to state the sequence in which the labelled amino acids moved through the three organelles. [1]

iv Explain the pattern shown by these results. [5]

Chapter 7
Transport in plants

Chapter outline

The questions in this chapter cover the following topics:

- drawing, labelling and describing the structure of stems, roots and leaves
- the structure of the two transport tissues in plants: **xylem** and **phloem**
- how the structures of xylem and phloem are related to their functions
- how water and mineral salts move through plants
- the investigation of water loss from leaves
- the adaptations of the leaves of **xerophytic** plants
- how organic molecules such as sucrose and amino acids move through plants

Exercise 7.1   Drawing, labelling and describing plant structures

In Chapter 1 you explored how to make diagrams of individual cells and groups of cells and how to carry out carry out magnification calculations. You also need to be able to draw plan diagrams of tissue groups using lower magnifications.

Figure 7.1 shows a transverse section through part of the stem of *Helianthus*, the sunflower.

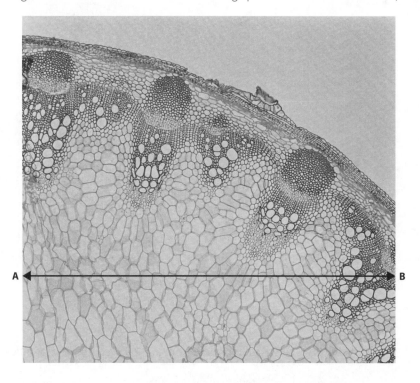

Figure 7.1 Transverse section through *Helianthus* stem. Magnification ×21.

1   The image has a magnification of ×10. Calculate the actual width of the entire specimen as shown along A–B on the image.

Before drawing a tissue map (plan diagram), consider the following:

- Take a very sharp HB pencil, ruler, eraser and piece of plain paper.
- Do not shade in regions and make sure that you use firm, solid lines.
- Draw a large diagram, at least 10 cm in width.
- Print labels neatly.
- Use a ruler to draw label lines accurately.
- Do not be frightened to take your time.

2 Now draw a plan diagram of Figure 7.1 using the following steps:

Step 1 Draw out the outline of the stem showing the epidermis as two lines. Ensure that the outline is a minimum of 5 cm wide.

Step 2 Draw out the vascular bundles clearly showing where the xylem, cambium and phloem tissues are. Do **not** draw individual cells.

Step 3 Draw out an outline of where the cortex tissue is found. Again do not draw individual cells.

Step 4 Add straight label lines and labels to show one example of xylem, phloem, cambium, cortex, **sclerenchyma fibres** and epidermis.

Step 5 Write a legend for your diagram: 'TS stem <u>Helianthus</u>' and state the magnification (×25).

Step 6 Now add a scale bar. You already know the actual width of the whole specimen. Determine the length of line that would represent 1 mm and draw it underneath your diagram. Compare your diagram with the answer.

3 Figure 7.2 shows a higher magnification of one of the vascular bundles from the *Helianthus* stem.

Figure 7.2 Vascular bundle from stem of *Helianthus*. Magnification ×21.

a Calculate the length of the vascular bundle labelled A–B in Figure 7.2.

b Draw a tissue map of Figure 7.2 (not showing individual cells), clearly labelling the sclerenchyma fibres, phloem, cambium, xylem, cortex and epidermis. Add a legend, magnification and scale bar that shows a 1 mm line.

Check your diagram with the answers and be critical!

4 a As well as drawing plan diagrams of tissues, you need to able to recognise particular cell types. Figure 7.3 shows a tissue plan diagram of a cross section of the centre of a buttercup (*Ranunculus*) root. Copy the photograph and add labels for: xylem, endodermis, cortex and phloem tissues. Include a scale bar representing 0.1 mm.

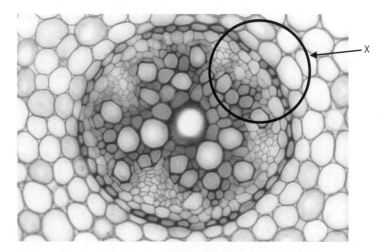

Figure 7.3 Photograph of a transverse section through *Ranunculus* root showing the stele. Magnification ×195

b Now draw a diagram showing individual cells for the area labelled X. Ensure that your diagram is about 4 cm in width. Identify and label the following cell types: xylem, phloem, endodermis, passage cell, pericycle and cortex.

5 Mark the student's response to a past paper style question below.

The light micrograph below shows a section of lower epidermis from a kidney bean plant.

Figure 7.4 Lower epidermis from leaf of kidney bean. Magnification ×233.

Make a copy of the diagram including labels to show: **guard cells**, **stomata**, epidermis cells, cell walls and cell nuclei. [4 marks]

63

Lower epidermis of kidney bean leaf

Figure 7.5 Student's drawing.

MARK SCHEME

- Diagram minimum of 4 cm width + sharp pencil + no shading;
- All cells correctly and clearly labelled using straight lines;
- Guard cells in proportion to epidermis cells and stomata are open;
- Epidermal cell walls smoothly drawn with accurate curves; all 19 nuclei drawn;

Exercise 7.2 Comparing two specimens

It is important to be able to look at biological specimens and compare them. Xerophytic plants have adaptations that enable them to survive in areas of low water. Figure 7.6 shows drawings of sections through the leaves of an oleander plant and a *Camellia*.

Figure 7.6 Drawing of transverse sections through leaves from **A** oleander and **B** *Camellia*.

1   Copy out the table below and complete it by comparing the structures in each leaf.

Structure	Oleander	Camellia
upper epidermis		
palisade mesophyll		
spongy mesophyll		
lower epidermis		

2   Suggest which plant is adapted to live in areas of very low water, and explain how the leaf is designed to minimise water loss.

Exercise 7.3 Identifying plant cell functions

There are many different types of plant cells with different structures and functions. You need to be able to recognise these and understand how they are adapted to their particular functions.

1   Complete the table below to match up the cell types with the statements given for functions, locations and structures. Some statements may be used several times.

The first cell type is done for you.

Cell type	Structure	Location	Function
xylem vessels	dead, hollow cells lignified cell walls which are impermeable to water cells joined end on end with no cross walls	associated with vascular bundles	transport of water from root to stem and leaf support of the stem
sieve tube element			
companion cell			
sclerenchyma			
collenchyma			
parenchyma			

STRUCTURES

- dead, hollow cells
- cell walls contain extra cellulose at the corners of cells
- living cells
- cells separated by sieve plates
- cells joined end on end with no cross walls
- **lignified** cell walls which are impermeable to water
- have cellulose cell walls
- no nucleus or ribosomes and only a thin layer of cytoplasm
- all typical cell organelles present

LOCATIONS

- associated with vascular bundles
- attached to **sieve tube elements** by **plasmodesmata**
- leaf mesophyll tissues
- found in corners of some stems
- found in leaf midrib
- root and stem cortex tissue

FUNCTIONS

- transport of water from root to stem and leaf
- support of the stem
- starch storage
- support of leaf
- transport of sucrose and amino acids
- carries out metabolic processes for attached sieve tube element
- photosynthesis

Exercise 7.4 Measuring transpiration rates

Plant **transpiration** rates can be measured using a **potometer** as shown in Figure 7.7.

1 A student was interested in comparing the effect of increasing wind speed on the rate of transpiration of two different plant species, laurel and rosemary. He set up the potometer as shown and investigated the distance that an air bubble moved along the capillary tube over a 10 minute period at each wind speed. This was repeated for both plants.

Figure 7.7 A potometer.

a Describe the precautions the student would need to take in order to ensure that there were no air bubbles in the potometer.

b Suggest how he could alter wind speed.

c In this experiment there are two independent variables; what are they?

d What is the dependent variable?

e Transpiration is affected by many variables. List all the variables that need to be controlled.

f What assumption do we make about the link between water movement in the capillary tube and transpiration?

In order to compare the transpiration rate of the two plants, the student wanted to calculate the rate of water loss in mm^3 per square centimetre of leaf. The table below shows the distance moved by the air bubble over a 10 minute period for the rosemary plant. The total surface area of the leaves was determined to be 52 cm^2.

g Copy out the table and use the following steps to complete the student's calculations:

Step 1 The volume of water lost is actually a cylinder of water where the length of the cylinder is the distance, d, moved by the air bubble, and the radius, r, is the radius of the capillary tubing, which in these experiments was 0.75 mm.

radius of capillary tubing, r

distance moved by air bubble, d

Figure 7.8 Calculating the volume of a cylinder of water in the potometer.

So volume for each wind speed is $\pi r^2 d$.

Step 2 Now calculate the water volume lost per minute. The experiment was run for 10 minutes, so divide the volume lost by 10. Fill in your answer in the table.

Step 3 To calculate the rate of water loss per square centimetre of leaf, divide your last answer by the surface area of the leaves (52 cm^2). Fill in your answer in the table.

Wind speed / arbitrary units	Distance moved by water / mm	Volume of water lost / mm^3	Rate of water loss / $mm^3\,min^{-1}$	Rate of water loss per cm^2 leaf area / $mm^3\,min^{-1}\,cm^{-2}$
0	8	14.13	1.41	0.03
10	15			
20	24			
30	27			
40	31			
50	33			

h The student repeated the experiment with the laurel plant. The time taken for the air bubble to move was five minutes, the total leaf surface area was 160 cm^2 and the radius of the capillary was 0.75 mm. Copy out and complete the table below.

Wind speed / arbitrary units	Distance moved by water / mm	Volume of water lost / mm³	Rate of water loss / mm³ min⁻¹	Rate of water loss per cm² leaf area / mm³ min⁻¹ cm⁻²
0	22			
10	36			
20	46			
30	57			
40	71			
50	85			

i Plot a graph to compare the rate of water loss per square centimetre of the two plants at different wind speeds. Ensure that you do the following:

- Use continuous axes with wind speed on the *x*-axis and rate of water loss per square centimetre on the *y*-axis.
- Plot both sets of data using the same axes. Draw appropriate curves or lines of best fit and label the lines for the two different plants with a key.

j Why is it appropriate to draw lines of best fit for these series of data?

k Another student criticised the data by pointing out that the time taken for the distance moved by the air bubble was different for the two different plants. Is the criticism valid?

Exam-style questions

1 Figure 7.9 shows a light micrograph of stomata from a *Tradescantia* plant.

Figure 7.9 Light micrograph of stomata from a *Tradescantia* plant.

a The magnification of the light micrograph is ×400. Calculate the length in µm of the stoma labelled **A** on the diagram. [2]

b Draw a copy of the area on the diagram labelled **B**. Add labels to clearly show the stomata, guard cells and lower epidermis cells. [4]

[Total 6 marks]

2   Figure 7.10 shows part of a cross section through a root of the buttercup, *Ranunculus*.

Figure 7.10 Part of a cross section through a root of the buttercup, *Ranunculus*.

a   Two of the pathways for water transport are shown on Figure 7.10 as **A** and **B**. State the names of these two pathways.   [1]

b   The cell walls of cells in the endodermis often contain the substance suberin. Explain the function of this substance.   [2]

Maize plants grown in heavily waterlogged soils often exhibit increased growth of a hollow root tissue called aerenchyma which is surrounded by an extensive coat of suberin. Figure 7.11 shows the development of aerenchyma and suberin in the roots.

Figure 7.11 Development of aerenchyma and suberin in maize roots.

c   Suggest why the development of the aerenchyma tissue and suberin is advantageous to plants growing in waterlogged soils.   [4]

[Total: 7 marks]

3   An investigation was carried out into the rate of transpiration and width of xylem vessels of Scots pine trees during a 24 hour period. The results are shown in Figure 7.12.

a   Describe the composition of xylem tissue and explain how it is designed to transport water throughout the plant.   [4]

Figure 7.12 Transpiration rate (thick line) and change in xylem diameter (thin line) of Scots pine tree over a 24 hour period.

b i Describe how xylem diameter and transpiration changed throughout the 24 hour period. [2]

ii Using your knowledge of the cohesion–tension theory, explain the association between xylem diameter and transpiration rate shown in Figure 7.12. [2]

iii Explain the changes in xylem diameter over the 24 hour period shown in Figure 7.12. [5]

[Total: 13 marks]

4 An investigation into the effect of rainfall on the size of stomata (mean area) and density of stomata on the lower surface of leaves of *Eucalyptus globulus* was carried out. The results are shown in the table below.

Parameter	High rainfall	Low rainfall
Mean maximum stomatal size / μm^2	169.30	125.70
Mean stomatal density/ mm^{-2}	238.80	229.60
Mean water loss / $mol\ m^{-2}\ s^{-1}$	1.66	1.25

a i Suggest how mean stomatal density could be determined in the laboratory. [4]

ii Compare the effect of rainfall on the development of stomata in *Eucalyptus* leaves. [1]

iii Explain the advantages to the *Eucalyptus* plant of changing stomatal patterns in response to the environment. [2]

b Figure 7.13 shows a diagram of part of a leaf from the xerophytic plant *Ammophila*.

Figure 7.13 Cross section through leaf from *Ammophila*. Magnification ×100.

    i   Calculate the length of the vascular bundle labelled **X**.   [1]

    ii   *Ammophila* is a xerophytic plant. Use the diagram to explain how the leaf is adapted to reduce water loss.   [4]

        [Total 12 marks]

5   An experiment was carried out into the absorption of mineral ions by the roots of barley seedlings. Root tissue was placed into two solutions of radioactive potassium ions, one of which also contained a respiratory inhibitor, potassium cyanide. The amount of potassium absorbed by the roots was measured at several intervals. The experiment was repeated with calcium ions. The results are shown in the table below.

Time / h	Quantity of ions absorbed / μmol			
	Potassium	Potassium + potassium cyanide	Calcium	Calcium + potassium cyanide
0	0	0	0	0
1	5	3	5	5
3	14	3	7	7
6	22	4	10	7
12	40	4	10	7

  a   Describe the effect of adding potassium cyanide on the absorption of potassium and calcium ions into the root tissue.   [2]

  b   Suggest and explain the processes by which potassium and calcium ions are absorbed by root tissue.   [4]

  c   Explain how the mineral ions are transported to the leaves.   [4]

        [Total: 10 marks]

6   Figure 7.14 shows a diagram of an electron micrograph of a **sieve tube element**.

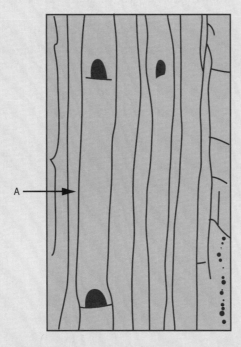

Figure 7.14 Diagram of an electron micrograph.

a **i** Calculate the length in micrometres of the sieve tube element labelled **A**.
Magnification ×145. [2]

ii Explain the differences between the structure of xylem vessels and **sieve tubes**. [3]

b An investigation was carried out into the effect of the presence of fruit on the speed of **translocation** of sucrose from tomato leaves.

A leaf on a tomato plant that had the fruit removed was given a pulse of radiolabelled $^{14}CO_2$ and the amount of radioactivity remaining in the leaf monitored over a 10 hour time period.

This was repeated with plants bearing fruits at 20 °C and 30 °C.

Figure 7.15 shows the results.

Figure 7.15 Graph to show effect of fruit on sucrose translocation from tomato leaves.

i Describe the effect of the removal of fruit on the speed of translocation of sucrose. [2]

ii Use your knowledge of the mass-flow hypothesis and sinks to explain the effect of temperature and removal of fruit on translocation of sucrose in the tomato plants. [4]

[Total: 16 marks]

Chapter 8
Transport in mammals

Chapter outline

The questions in this chapter cover the following topics:

- the structure of the mammalian circulatory system
- the structure of arteries, veins and capillaries in relation to their functions
- the structure and functions of blood, including oxygen transport
- the formation of tissue fluid and lymph
- the structure and function of the heart
- the cardiac cycle and its control

Exercise 8.1 Comparing the strength and elasticity of arteries and veins

1 A student carried out an experiment to investigate the effect of hanging increasing masses from **arteries** and **veins** on their length and elasticity.

The width of an artery taken from a sheep was measured using a ruler. A 50 g mass was then hung on the artery and the stretched length measured. The mass was removed and the recoiled length measured. This was then repeated with increasing masses until the artery snapped.

The experiment was then repeated for the vein.

The student's results are shown in Figure 8.1.

Aorta	Vein
0 g – 15 mm	0 g – 19 mm
50 g – 17 mm, 15 mm	50 g – 23 mm, 19 mm
100 g – 19 mm, 15 mm	100 g – 25 mm, 19 mm
150 g – 20 mm, 15 mm	150g – 27 mm, 24 mm
200 g – 21 mm, 15 mm	200g – 28 mm, 25 mm
250 g – 23 mm, 15 mm	250g – 31 mm, 28 mm
300 g – 26 mm, 15 mm	300g – 35 mm, 31 mm
350 g – 31 mm, 15 mm	350g – 38 mm, 35 mm
400 g – 35 mm, 15 mm	400g – 44 mm, 41 mm
450 g – 42 mm, 15 mm	450g – snapped!
750 g – 46 mm, 15 mm	
1 kg – 51 mm 16 mm	
1.5 kg 58 mm 18 mm	
2.0 kg 63 mm 23 mm	
3.0 kg – snapped!	

Figure 8.1 The lengths of arteries and veins with different masses.

a Design a results table to display the student's data.

b Plot a line graph to show the effect of increasing mass on the length of the artery and vein. You will need to plot four lines using the same axes for both the stretched lengths and recoiled lengths. We cannot be confident that intermediate points will fit the line, so join your points with straight lines.

c Calculate the maximum percentage increase in length for the artery:

((greatest stretched length − starting length) ÷ starting length)) × 100

Repeat this for the vein. Why is comparing percentage increase more valid than comparing increase in length?

d The student proposed that the maximum weight that the artery can withstand is 2.0 kg. Is this a correct assumption and how could the student improve the experiment to identify the breaking point?

e Figure 8.2 is a photograph of an artery and a vein.

Figure 8.2 Artery and vein. Magnification ×60.

i Make a plan drawing of the section, clearly labelling: the artery, vein and lumen.
ii Calculate the actual maximum diameters of the lumen of both blood vessels.
iii Compare the structure of the artery and vein. Copy out and complete the table below.

Structural feature	Artery	Vein
overall shape		
lumen		
tunica media (middle layer)		
tunica externa (out layer)		

f Use Figure 8.2 and your knowledge of blood vessel structure to explain the student's results.

Exercise 8.2 Methods for determining red blood cell counts

The measurement of the percentage (%) of an individual's blood that is composed of red blood **cells** is called the haematocrit test. It is often used to test for conditions such as anaemia where red blood cell count is low, or the use of performance enhancing drugs or blood doping, in sport, which often leads to a higher red blood cell count.

A simple method for determining red blood cell percentage by volume of blood is by centrifugation. A 7.5 cm long narrow glass capillary tube is loaded up with blood. The bottom of the capillary is sealed with clay and the blood centrifuged for five minutes at 10 000 rpm. An example of this is shown in Figure 8.3. The percentage of the blood that is composed of red blood cells is then determined by holding the capillary up against a haematocrit chart as shown in Figure 8.4.

Figure 8.3 Fractions of blood obtained by centrifugation.

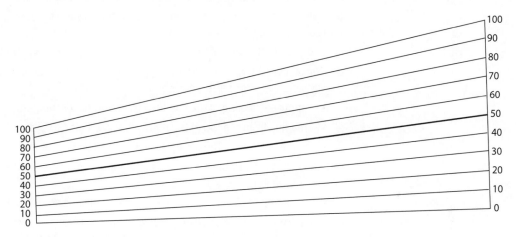

Figure 8.4 A haematocrit chart showing how the percentage of red blood cells is determined.

1 The three fractions that blood separates into contain:
 • mixed leukocytes and thrombocytes
 • erythrocytes (red blood cells)
 • plasma.
 Match each of each fraction with the letters A, B and C as shown in Figure 8.3.

2 To determine the percentage of blood that is composed of red blood cells, the capillary tube is held against the chart so that the bottom of the sample is at the zero line and the top is at 100%. The percentage of red blood cells is then read.
 Explain why using the chart means that the volume of blood in the capillary does not have to be a set volume.

3 Carry out a risk assessment for this method when used to determine the red blood cell concentration of human blood. Include the risks, the dangers they pose and what you would do to minimise the risk of harm.

4 The test must normally be carried out by two laboratory technicians in order to improve reliability. Eight students carried out an investigation into the reliability of the technique. They all performed haematocrit tests on five different samples of blood taken from women aged

between 19 and 35. One of the women had returned from a vacation spent at high altitude. The results are shown in the table below.

Blood sample	Percentage red blood cells / %							
	Student 1	Student 2	Student 3	Student 4	Student 5	Student 6	Student 7	Student 8
A	44	45	44	45	48	44	43	45
B	42	42	43	41	46	42	43	32
C	37	36	36	36	41	37	37	37
D	52	53	53	52	57	52	53	52
E	41	40	25	42	46	40	41	42

a Identify any values in the table that you would consider to be anomalous.

b Calculate the mean percentage of red blood cells (%) for each of the samples. Discard any readings that you consider anomalous.

c Explain whether any of the results appear to be due to a **systematic error**.

d Suggest what factors could be responsible for the anomalous values you have identified. Possible sources of error in the technique include:

- improper sealing of the capillary tube before centrifugation
- reading from the top of the meniscus of red blood cells
- centrifugation at the wrong speed (either too high or too low)
- leaving the sample for too long after centrifuging so that the red blood cells are not as compacted
- including the 'buffy coat' (leukocyte and thrombocyte fraction) in the reading.

e The partial pressure of oxygen at high altitude is reduced. Time spent at high altitude causes the body to synthesise more red blood cells. Identify the sample that was from the woman who had spent time at altitude, and explain the advantages and possible dangers of the change in her blood.

f Use the results in the table to suggest and explain what the minimum number of repeats should be when testing clinical samples. Would the same technician carrying out the repeats produce valid results?

5 There are many factors that can affect the haematocrit test.

Predict and explain whether the following events would cause a rise or fall in haematocrit:

a severe burns patient losing large amount of plasma due to capillary damage

b over hydration by drinking large volumes of water

c anaemia caused by a lack of iron in the diet

d immediately after a major trauma leading to extensive bleeding

e one day after a major trauma after bleeding has stopped

6 One of the students read that the size of individual red blood cells can vary and decided to investigate whether the percentage of red blood cells determined by the haematocrit test is correlated to the actual number of red blood cells.

a Explain why the red blood cell size could affect the value determined by the haematocrit.

To get an actual count of red blood cells, we must use a haemocytometer. A haemocytometer is a special microscope slide with two sets of ruled grids in the centre, with deep grooves either side.

b Reorder the following steps below into the correct sequence:

A The number of cells inside five of the 25 squares of the central grid are counted.

B Blood is placed into the space between coverslip and slide using a pipette.

C The haemocytometer is placed on the microscope stage and the central squares focused upon using the ×40 objective.

D A coverslip is placed over the counting chamber and the sides pressed down firmly until Newtonian rings appear. The gap between the slide and coverslip is exactly 0.1 mm.

Figure 8.5 shows five squares of a haemocytometer grid.

When counting red blood cells using a haemocytometer, you need to count the number of cells in five of the 25 medium-sized squares. When counting, any cells that touch the right and bottom edges are not included, whilst those that touch the top and left edges are included.

c Count the total number of cells in all five squares shown in Figure 8.5.

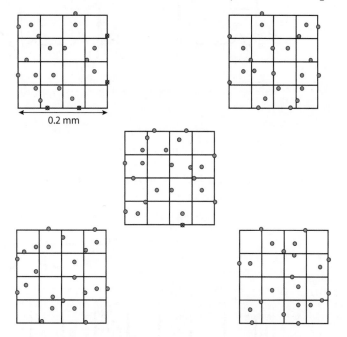

0.2 mm

Figure 8.5 Five square from haemocytometer central grid.

d The length of one side of each of these squares is 0.2 mm and the height of solution above the slide is 0.1 mm. Calculate the **total** volume of cell suspension over all five squares.

e Use the equation below to calculate your cell concentration:

cell concentration = number of cells in five squares ÷ volume of suspension in mm^3

Now convert this answer into cells per cubic decimetre by multiplying by 1 000 000, expressing your answer in standard form.

f Calculate the red blood cell count in cells per cubic decimetre for the following cell numbers counted from five squares:

A 76

B 125

C 52.

g The student took 30 different blood samples and carried out both a haematocrit test and cell counts on each sample. Explain what graph the student should plot in order to determine whether the two methods show a correlation with each other.

Exercise 8.3 Interpreting graphs of heart rate and blood pressure

Understanding how graphs relate to the topic under investigation and using them to extract numerical data are important skills. The topic of mammalian transport uses numerous graphical representations.

1 Figure 8.6 shows a typical electrocardiogram (ECG) from a healthy human. We can use ECG traces to calculate the heart rate.

   a First, calculate the time that one **small** square represents.

   b Now determine how many small squares one heart cycle takes (good places to use are the tops of the R waves).

1 large square = 0.2 s

Figure 8.6 Electrocardiogram trace from a normal, healthy human.

   c You should now calculate the time taken for one heart cycle by multiplying the answers to parts **a** and **b** together.

   d To determine the heart rate, determine how many heart cycles can fit into 60 s.

   Heart rate = 60 ÷ time taken for one heart cycle

   e Now calculate the heart rates of the ECG traces **A** and **B** shown in Figure 8.7.

Figure 8.7 Two ECG traces. **A** Fast heartbeat. **B** Slow heartbeat.

The transport of blood occurs by mass flow, meaning that blood will always flow from a higher pressure to a lower pressure. We can see how the pressures change in the different chambers of a heart during a heart cycle and predict when the blood is entering and exiting.

When interpreting these graphs do not try to commit every detail to memory! Remember two rules:

- Blood will try to flow from higher to lower pressure.
- Valves will prevent the blood flowing backwards by closing.

2 Figure 8.8 shows the pressure and volume changes occurring during two cardiac cycles in the left ventricle.

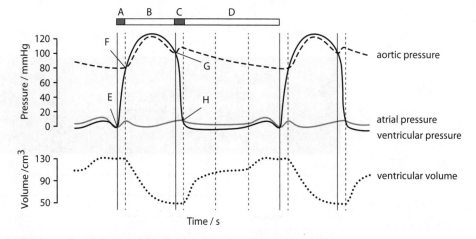

Figure 8.8 Pressure changes in aorta, left ventricle and atrium.

a Identify on the chart the period when the ventricle is filling. Look for an area where pressure is greater in the atrium than in the ventricle.

b Identify on the chart the period when the ventricle is emptying. Look for an area where the pressure in the ventricle is higher than in the aorta.

c Identify on the chart the period when the ventricle is undergoing a contraction but its volume is not changing. Use the graph to explain why the ventricle does not empty.

d Identify the letter where the bicuspid valve closes. Explain your answer.

e Identify the letter where the bicuspid valve opens. Explain your answer.

f Identify the letter where the semilunar valve closes. Explain your answer.

g Identify the letter where the semilunar valve opens. Explain your answer.

h Describe how the pressure generated by the right ventricle would differ from each other. Explain why the two ventricles generate different pressures.

You need to able to understand and use **haemoglobin** dissociation curves both quantitatively and qualitatively. Do not try to learn every possibly curve position for every situation – it is easier to work out what is happening.

3 Figure 8.9 shows oxygen dissociation curves for three mammals.

Figure 8.9 The oxygen dissociation curves for **A** llama, **B** human and **C** mouse haemoglobin.

a   At normal sea level, the partial pressure of oxygen in the lungs is approximately 12 kPa. Follow the following steps to determine the oxygen saturation of human haemoglobin in the alveolar capillaries at this value.

Using Figure 8.9:

Step 1   Place a ruler on the x-axis at 12 kPa and draw a line up to the human curve.

Step 2   Use the ruler to draw a line from this point on the curve to the y-axis. This is the oxygen saturation value at 12 kPa.

Step 3   Copy out the table below and enter this value in the table.

Species	Oxygen saturation of haemoglobin / %			Volume of oxygen bound to 1 g of haemoglobin / cm³			Volume of oxygen released to tissues / cm³	
	At 12 kPa	At 2 kPa	At 6 kPa	At 12 kPa	At 2 kPa	At 6 kPa	At atmospheric pressure (12 kPa)	At high altitude (6 kPa)
human								
llama								
mouse								

b   Now do the same to determine the oxygen saturation of human haemoglobin in capillaries in respiring tissues (2 kPa) and alveoli at high altitude (6 kPa). Fill in the data in the table.

c   1 g of fully saturated haemoglobin will carry 1.3 cm³ of oxygen. Calculate the volume of oxygen carried by human haemoglobin at 12 kPa, 2 kPa and 6 kPa. Enter your values in your table.

d   Now compare how much oxygen is delivered to tissues at normal and high altitudes.

For normal altitude:

Volume of oxygen released in tissue = volume of oxygen bound at 12 kPa − volume of oxygen bound at 2 kPa

For high altitude:

Volume of oxygen released in tissue = volume of oxygen bound at 6 kPa − volume of oxygen bound at 2 kPa

Enter your results in your table.

e   Repeat steps **a** through to **d** for llama and mouse haemoglobin.

f   Llamas live at high altitude. Mice are small mammals that maintain a constant body temperature. Explain the advantages to both these animals of their haemoglobin dissociation curves.

Exercise 8.4 Planning an experiment to investigate the effect of exercise on heart rate

1 Plan a method to investigate the effect of exercise on heart rate. You should copy out and complete the points in the text box below in order to structure your experimental plan.

Independent variable

Include:

- what it is
- how you will change it
- how many values will you use
- what range of values will you use
- how will you ensure it is standardised between repeats.

Dependent variable

Include:

- what it is
- how you will measure it accurately
- how you will decide whether you have enough repeats (sample size) to ensure reliability.

Standardised variables

Include:

- a list of all variables that could affect the dependent variable
- how you will ensure that they do not change.

Exam-style questions

1 Figure 8.10 shows a graph of how the hydrostatic pressure of the blood and oncotic pressure due to the presence of proteins in the plasma vary along the length of a capillary.

Figure 8.10 Hydrostatic and oncotic pressures in a capillary.

a **i** Use Figure 8.10 and your own knowledge to explain how tissue fluid is formed and returned in capillaries. [5]

    ii Kwashiorkor is a malnutrition disorder occurring in children who lack dietary protein. It results in the accumulation of excessive tissue, causing the appearance of a swollen belly. Use Figure 8.10 to explain why the tissue fluid accumulates. [3]

b Describe how excess tissue fluid that is not reabsorbed into the capillary is returned to the blood. [3]

[Total: 11 marks]

2 Figure 8.11 show the oxygen dissociation curves of human haemoglobin in the presence of a range of concentrations of carbon dioxide.

Figure 8.11 Haemoglobin dissociation curves of human haemoglobin with different partial pressures of carbon dioxide.

a Explain how the structure of the haemoglobin molecule generates an oxygen dissociation curve that is sigmoidal (S-shaped). [4]

b **i** The partial pressure of oxygen in the alveoli is 12 kPa. Use Figure 8.11 to determine the percentage saturation of normal haemoglobin in the alveoli. [1]

    ii 1 g of fully saturated haemoglobin carries 1.3 cm³ of oxygen. Calculate the volume of oxygen bound to 1 g of haemoglobin at a partial pressure of 12 kPa. [1]

    iii Use Figure 8.11 and your answer to **ii** to determine the volume of oxygen released to a rapidly respiring muscle. [3]

    iv Explain the advantage of the effect of CO_2 on the oxygen haemoglobin saturation curve. [3]

c Explain why the fetal oxygen dissociation curve is different to that of normal adult haemoglobin. [2]

[Total: 14 marks]

3 The table below shows the pressures inside the left ventricle and left atrium of a heart during one **cardiac cycle**.

Time / s	Atrial pressure / kPa	Ventricle pressure / kPa	Aortic pressure / kPa
0.0	1.4	1.2	11.7
0.1	1.8	3.9	11.6
0.2	1.4	11.9	11.5
0.3	1.5	16.0	15.8
0.4	1.5	6.7	14.7
0.5	1.4	1.2	14.5
0.6	1.5	1.3	12.5
0.7	1.4	1.3	12.1
0.8	1.4	1.3	11.7

a **i** One complete cardiac cycle takes 0.8 s. Calculate the pulse rate in beats per minute. [2]

ii State between which times the ventricle is emptying. [1]

iii State between which times the bicuspid valve is closed. [1]

iv State the time at which the ventricle is relaxing but not refilling. [1]

b Describe how the beating of a resting heart is controlled by electrical impulses. [5]

[Total: 10 marks]

4 Figure 8.12 shows a light micrograph of human blood cells.

Figure 8.12 Human blood cells. Magnification ×1100.

a **i** Make an accurate drawing of the blood cells. Clearly label: red blood cells, monocyte, neutrophil and lymphocyte. [4]

ii Calculate the diameter of the cell labelled **A**. [2]

b Explain how the structure of red blood cells maximises the transport of oxygen to tissues. [4]

[Total: 10 marks]

5 a Figure 8.13 shows the mechanisms for transporting carbon dioxide in the blood.

Figure 8.13 Diagram to show the transport of carbon dioxide in the blood.

  i State the names of substances **A** and **B**. [2]

  ii State the name of the enzyme that catalyses reaction X on the diagram. [1]

[Total: 3 marks]

6 Figure 8.14 shows how blood pressure, cross sectional area and blood velocity change in different blood vessels.

Figure 8.14 Diagram to show the total cross sectional area, blood velocity and pressure in different types of blood vessel.

a i Describe and explain how the blood pressures change as the blood moves from the aorta to the vena cava. [4]

  ii Describe and explain how the velocity changes as the blood moves from the aorta to the vena cava. [3]

b Varicose veins are veins that appear bloated and swollen with blood. They are often due to damaged valves in the veins. Suggest how damaged valves could lead to the appearance of varicose veins. [2]

[Total: 9 marks]

Chapter outline

The questions in this chapter cover the following topics:

- the structure of the human gas exchange system
- the distribution of tissues and cells within the gas exchange system
- the functions of these tissues and cells
- how gases are exchanged in the lungs
- how tobacco smoke affects the gas exchange system
- the effects of nicotine and carbon monoxide on the cardiovascular system

Exercise 9.1 Looking at smoking data

It is important to compare data in a valid way. The table below shows the number of smokers found in different countries. There are clearly more smokers in China than other countries – this is not a valid comparison though, as China has more people and so would naturally be expected to have more smokers. For epidemiological data that compares health statistics it is common to express findings as a fraction of the population (often in thousands) in order to give a proportional comparison.

Country	Total population	Estimated number of smokers	Number of smokers per 1000
Russia	142 467 651	78 357 208	
China	1 393 783 836	599 327 049	
Ukraine	44 941 303	19 774 173	
Vietnam	92 547 959	29 615 347	
Egypt	83 386 739	25 849 889	
Bangladesh	158 512 570	39 628 143	
Mexico	123 799 215	14 855 906	
India	1 267 401 849	101 392 148	

To calculate the number of people per 1000 population who smoke in China we must do the following:

- Calculate the proportion who are smokers (599 327 049 ÷ 1 393 783 836).
- Now scale it up to 1000 people by multiplying your answer by 1000.

1 a Now, copy the table and complete the last column giving the number of smokers per 1000 people for each country.

To visualise data it is often easiest to look at a graph. In this case, the independent variable is categoric – it has the names of the countries and we need to plot a bar chart.

b Plot a bar chart of the data – make sure that you place the independent variable on the *x*-axis and leave a gap between your bars.

When we look at epidemiological data it is often necessary to compare more than one set of data, which may be measured with different units or are in different magnitudes.

The table shows some historic data about the incidence of deaths from lung cancer and the number of cigarettes smoked per person per year during the 20th century. The two variables have different magnitudes and so it is difficult to plot the data meaningfully using one axis.

Year	Cigarettes smoked per person per year	Lung cancer deaths per 100 000 people
1900	900	N/A
1910	1100	N/A
1920	2300	20
1930	2700	25
1940	4000	40
1950	4300	100
1960	4200	175
1970	3900	185
1980	3100	175
1990	3000	150
2000	2900	135

2 **Step 1**   On a piece of graph paper, draw the x-axis, label it 'Year' and generate a continuous scale.

     Step 2   Draw the y-axis on the left hand side, label it 'Cigarettes smoked per person per year' and work out a continuous scale that uses most of the graph paper.

     Step 3   Now go to the right hand side of your graph and at year 2000 draw a second y-axis, this time labelled 'Lung cancer deaths per 100 000 people' and work out a different scale that again uses most of the graph paper.

     Step 4   Using the left hand y-axis, carefully plot the points for the frequency of smoking. As we cannot safely predict the intermediate points and the data are continuous, join the points with a ruler and a sharp pencil. Make a key for the line labelled 'Cigarettes smoked per person per year'.

     Step 5   Using the right hand y-axis, carefully plot the points for the frequency of lung cancer. As we cannot safely predict the intermediate points and the data are continuous, join the points with a ruler and a sharp pencil. Make a key for the line labelled 'Lung cancer deaths per 100 000 people'.

Exercise 9.2 Correlations and causal factors

A **correlation** is where there is a link between two variables but we cannot say for certain that one variable causes a change in the other. A positive correlation is where both variables increase together, a negative correlation is where one variable decreases as the other increases.

Correlation does not mean that one variable is causing a change in the other one. For example, over 90% of deaths occur when people are in bed. This is a positive correlation and certainly not causation – bed is not generally a dangerous place!

To show a **causal link** we need to do a full experiment where only one variable is changed compared to a **control group**. Most data about health effects on smoking tends to show correlations.

1   Now look at your graph from Exercise 9.1 question 2. We can often look for correlations when we plot graphs that have more than one set of data on them.

   a   Is there a positive or negative correlation between smoking and lung cancer deaths? Describe your answer in as much detail as possible.

   b   Does the research prove that smoking is a cause of lung cancer, and what experiment could be performed to prove that smoking is the actual cause of lung cancer?

2   As well as plotting two line graphs on the same axes to look for correlations, we can also produce a scattergram where we plot the two variables against each other. Figure 9.1 shows a scattergram where the cigarette consumption for states in the USA is plotted against the death rate from bladder cancer in that state. A line of best fit is drawn through the points.

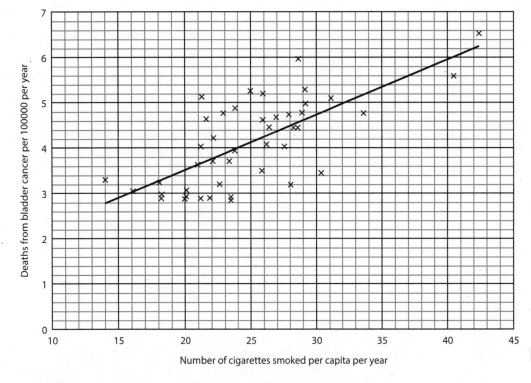

Figure 9.1 Scattergram to show number of cigarettes smoked per year per capita compared to deaths from bladder cancer per 100 000 in US states.

Each point represents the cigarette consumption plotted against the incidence of bladder cancer for that state.

   a   Does the graph show a positive or negative correlation between smoking and incidence of bladder cancer?

   b   Evaluate how strong the correlation is. For this you need to decide how much the angle of the line of best fit increases and how close all the points lie to it.

   c   Does the scattergram prove that smoking causes bladder cancer? What other evidence could researchers look for in order to be more secure in the link between smoking and bladder cancer?

3 The table below shows raw data for the incidence of leukaemia and kidney cancer in the different US states. Use scattergrams to decide whether or not there is a strong correlation between cigarette consumption and kidney cancer and leukaemia. Outline your reasons for why the data fit your conclusions.

State	Cigarettes smoked per capita	Deaths per 100 000 from kidney cancer	Deaths per 100 000 from leukaemia
AK	30.34	4.32	4.90
AL	18.20	1.59	6.15
AZ	25.82	2.75	6.61
AR	18.24	2.02	6.61
CA	28.60	2.66	7.06
CT	31.10	3.35	7.20
DC	40.46	3.13	7.08
DE	33.60	3.36	6.45
FL	28.27	2.41	6.07
ID	20.10	2.46	6.62
IL	27.91	2.95	7.27
IN	26.18	2.81	7.00
IO	22.12	2.90	7.69
KS	21.84	2.88	7.42
KY	23.44	2.13	6.41
LA	21.58	2.30	6.71
MA	26.92	3.03	6.89
ME	28.92	3.22	6.24
MD	25.91	2.85	6.81
MI	24.96	2.97	6.91
MN	22.06	3.54	8.28
MO	27.56	2.55	6.82
MS	16.08	3.54	8.28
MT	23.75	3.43	6.90
NB	23.32	2.92	7.80
ND	19.96	3.62	6.99
NE	42.40	2.85	6.67
NJ	28.64	3.12	7.12
NM	21.16	2.52	5.95
NY	29.14	3.10	7.23
OH	26.38	2.95	7.38
OK	23.44	2.45	7.46
PE	23.78	2.75	6.83
RI	29.18	2.84	6.35
SC	18.06	2.05	5.82

State	Cigarettes smoked per capita	Deaths per 100 000 from kidney cancer	Deaths per 100 000 from leukaemia
SD	20.94	3.11	8.15
TE	20.08	2.18	6.59
TX	22.57	2.69	7.02
UT	14.00	2.20	6.71
VT	25.89	3.17	6.56
WA	21.17	2.78	7.48
WI	21.25	2.34	6.73
WV	22.86	3.28	7.38
WY	28.04	2.66	5.78

Exercise 9.3 Comparative analysis of breathing

A spirometer is a piece of apparatus that can be used for investigating the volumes of air exchanged during breathing. A range of experiments can be performed with it, such as comparing the rates of oxygen uptake of individuals under different conditions.

1   A team of students set out to investigate lung volumes, breathing rates and the rate of oxygen consumption.

   They used a spirometer, which is shown in Figure 9.2. The spirometer can be used with or without the carbon dioxide absorber attached.

Figure 9.2 A spirometer set up to measure breathing volumes and rates.

   a   In the first experiment, the spirometer was set up without the carbon dioxide absorber. The student attached the mouthpiece and nose clip. They breathed in and out normally, took a full breath and then exhaled all the air. They then returned to normal breathing.

A graph showing the changes in lung volume is shown in Figure 9.3.

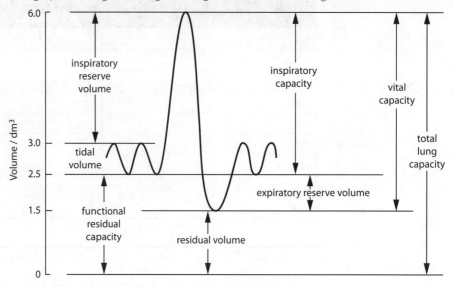

Figure 9.3 Graph showing changes in lung volume.

i The tidal volume is the amount of air exchanged during quiet breathing. Calculate the tidal volume (TV).

ii The inspiratory reserve volume (IRV) is the extra volume of air that can be inhaled, and the expiratory reserve volume (ERV) is the extra volume of air that can be exhaled. Calculate the expiratory and inspiratory volumes.

iii The vital capacity is the maximum amount of air that can be exchanged in one breath. It is equal to the IRV + ERV + TV. Calculate the vital capacity (VC).

iv The residual volume is the air that remains in the respiratory system after maximum exhalation. Calculate the residual volume.

v Determine the amount of air that is exchanged during one minute if the student is performing tidal breathing at a rate of 17 breaths per minute.

2 The student then inserted the carbon dioxide absorber filled with potassium hydroxide crystals and breathed in and out of the spirometer for two minutes. The resultant trace is shown in Figure 9.4.

TIP

Be careful converting from seconds to minutes. Remember that 0.5 of a minute is 30 s.

Figure 9.4 Spirometer trace obtained when potassium hydroxide is included in the carbon dioxide absorber.

a Use the graph to determine the approximate vital capacity from section **A** of the graph. To do this, follow these steps:

    Step 1   Measure the length of the 1 dm^3 scale bar in mm.

    Step 2   Determine how much volume in dm^3 that 1 mm represents (1 ÷ length in mm).

    Step 3   Use a ruler to measure the approximate length of the ERV + VC + IRV.

    Step 4   Multiply the length in mm by the amount that 1 mm represents.

b Now work out the breathing rate of the patient over section **B** on the diagram:

    Step 1   Count the number of breaths between points y and z.

    Step 2   Use the 10 s scale bar to determine how long period **B** lasts in minutes.

    Step 3   Calculate the rate in breaths per min (number of breaths ÷ time taken).

c You can now use the graph to calculate the mean volume of air exchanged per minute during tidal breathing:

    Step 1   Over section **B**, determine the volume of five different breaths and then calculate the mean tidal volume by adding them together and dividing by five.

    Step 2   Now multiply the mean tidal volume by the breathing rate.

d The spirometer was set up with potassium hydroxide in the carbon dioxide absorber. This removes exhaled carbon dioxide so that the trace falls. The amount that the trace falls represents the volume of oxygen used.

We can thus calculate the volume of oxygen used over section **B** by drawing a gradient line (x–z):

    Step 1   Calculate the volume of oxygen used in dm^3 by measuring line x–y.

    Step 2   Now calculate the rate of oxygen use. This is actually the gradient of the line x–y. Gradients in graphs are calculated by dividing the height (y-axis) by the length (x-axis).

3 Many medical conditions are known to affect the ability to exchange air. Peak flow meters are used to measure the forced vital capacity (FVC), which is the maximum amount of air that can be exhaled, and the forced expiratory volume in one second (FEV_1), which is the maximum amount of air that can be exhaled in one second.

The table below shows the FVC and FEV_1 values for a normal adult human and patients suffering with asthma, pulmonary fibrosis and **chronic obstructive pulmonary disease (COPD)**.

Patient	Volume of air exhaled / dm^3								
	Breath 1		Breath 2		Breath 3		Mean		
	FVC	FEV_1	FVC	FEV_1	FVC	FEV_1	FVC	FEV_1	FEV_1 /FVC ratio
Normal	4.80	3.85	4.75	3.78	4.78	8.82			
COPD	4.32	2.25	4.51	2.45	4.28	2.16			
Pulmonary fibrosis	3.78	3.01	3.67	3.02	3.75	3.10			
Asthma	4.75	3.09	3.45	3.01	4.73	2.95			

Copy out the table.

a Calculate the mean FVC and FEV_1 values for each condition, excluding any anomalous values, and enter your answers in the table.

b Calculate the ratio of FEV_1/ FVC and enter your values in the table.

c It has been suggested that the FEV_1/ FVC ratio could be used to diagnose respiratory disorders. Evaluate this suggestion.

d Use your knowledge of COPD to explain reasons for the FEV_1/FVC ratio.

Exercise 9.4 Comparing the structure of different parts of the airways

You need to understand the structure of the different parts of the airways and the functional roles of different cell types and tissues.

1   Copy out the table below and fill in the blank spaces using your own knowledge. Write in 'yes' or 'no' to show presence or absence.

Region of airway	Cartilage	Smooth muscle	Ciliated epithelial cells	Goblet cells
trachea				
bronchus				
terminal bronchus				
respiratory bronchiole				
alveolar duct				
alveoli				

2   Copy out the table below and write in the functions of the different cell and tissue types.

Cell / tissue type	Function
cartilage	
smooth muscle	
ciliated epithelia	
goblet cells	

3   We can compare the composition of gases at different points in the airway.

The value of atmospheric pressure at sea level is 100 kPa. This pressure is made up of the partial pressures of all the gases present in the air:

$$\text{total atmospheric pressure} = p\text{N}_2 + p\text{O}_2 + p\text{CO}_2 + p \text{ (other gases)}$$

$$100 \text{ kPa} = 78 \text{ kPa} + 21 \text{ kPa} + 0.03 \text{ kPa} + 0.97 \text{ kPa}$$

$$(100\% = 78\% + 21\% + 0.03\% + 0.97\%)$$

Region	$p\text{N}_2$ / kPa	$p\text{O}_2$ / kPa	$p\text{CO}_2$ / kPa	$p\text{H}_2\text{O}$ / kPa	p(others) kPa
inhaled	78.60	20.90	0.04	0.06	0.40
alveolar	74.90	13.60	5.30	6.00	0.20
exhaled	74.50	15.70	3.60	6.00	0.20
pulmonary artery	76.39	5.33	6.00	N/A	N/A
pulmonary vein	76.39	12.67	5.33	N/A	N/A

   a   Compare the composition of inhaled, alveolar and exhaled air.

   b   Use your knowledge of gas exchange to explain the differences in the partial pressures of oxygen and carbon dioxide in the different airway regions.

   c   Explain the differences in the partial pressure of nitrogen gas in the airway regions. At atmospheric pressure, little nitrogen gas will dissolve into the blood.

Exam-style questions

1 Figure 9.5 shows two magnifications of a section through part of an airway.

Figure 9.5 Tissue maps showing the wall of a region of the airways.

a The part of airway that the section was taken from was the:

    A bronchus

    B terminal bronchiole

    C respiratory bronchiole

    D alveolar duct.   [1]

b Explain the functions of the goblet cells and ciliated epithelial cells.   [4]

c Asthma is often caused by allergic responses and causes sufferers to have breathing difficulties. Figure 9.6 shows a cross section through a section of airway from a healthy person and a section of airway from a patient with severe asthma.

Figure 9.6 Regions of airways from **A** a healthy person and **B** a person with severe asthma.

    i Draw up a table and use it to compare the differences in the airways of the normal and asthmatic patients.   [4]

    ii Use Figure 9.6 to explain why people with asthma often have lower oxygen concentrations in their blood.   [3]

    iii The drug salbutamol is used to induce the smooth muscles of the airways to relax.

93

Figure 9.7 shows the structures of the hormone adrenaline and the drug salbutamol.

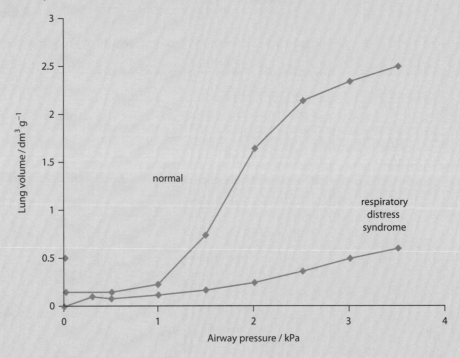

Figure 9.7 The structures of adrenaline and salbutamol.

Suggest how salbutamol makes breathing easier during an asthma attack. [3]

[Total: 15 marks]

2 Respiratory distress syndrome is a condition that occurs in young babies. It is characterised by problems in breathing and low oxygen levels in the blood. Figure 9.8 is a graph showing the amount of pressure that has to be generated in order to increase the volume of the lungs in healthy babies and those with respiratory distress syndrome.

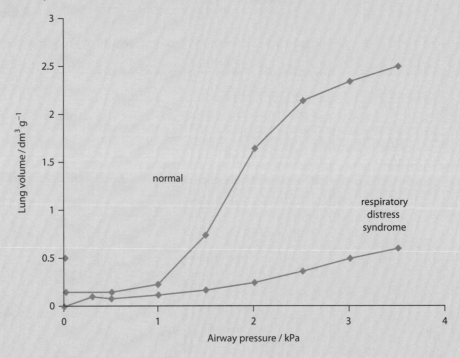

Figure 9.8 The effect of airway pressure on lung volume in healthy babies and babies suffering from respiratory distress syndrome.

a **i** Describe the effect of increasing airway pressure on the lung volume of normal babies. [2]

ii Compare the effect of increasing airway pressure on the lung volumes of normal babies and babies with respiratory distress syndrome. [2]

b Pulmonary surfactant is a substance that is released by cells in the alveoli. It contains proteins and fatty acids and reduces the surface tension of the alveolar fluid.

Figure 9.9 shows the structure of DPPC, one of the molecules found in the surfactant fluid.

Figure 9.9 Diagram of DPPC – a molecule found in pulmonary surfactant.

    i State the group of molecules to which DPPC belongs. [1]

    ii Draw out a copy of DPPC and clearly label the hydrophobic and hydrophilic regions. [1]

    iii Suggest how DPPC reduces the surface tension of aqueous solutions. [2]

c Babies who suffer from respiratory distress syndrome are often found to be short of pulmonary surfactant. Suggest and explain why these babies suffer from breathing difficulty and low oxygen concentration in the blood. [3]

[Total: 11 marks]

3 Figure 9.10 shows the **alveoli** from a non-smoker and a smoker suffering from **emphysema**.

  a **i** Explain how cigarette smoking can result in emphysema. [4]

      ii Use Figure 9.10 to explain why patients suffering from emphysema suffer from severe fatigue and are unable to perform arduous physical tasks. [4]

Figure 9.10 Alveoli from smoker and non-smoker.

b The expiration of a patient with chronic obstructive pulmonary disease was investigated. The patient was asked to take one deep breath and exhale as fully as possible. The cumulative amount of air from this breath was measured over the time of the breath and the results are shown in Figure 9.11.

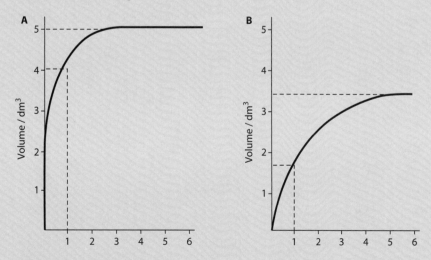

Figure 9.11 Volume of one exhaled breath over time in **A** a healthy patient and **B** a patient suffering from emphysema.

    i Compare the exhaled breath from the patient with chronic obstructive pulmonary disease with that of the healthy person. [2]

    ii Use your knowledge of chronic obstructive pulmonary disease to explain the results shown in Figure 9.11. [3]

[Total: 13 marks]

4 a Explain how carbon monoxide inhalation can lead to short-term and long-term damage to health. [6]

  b An 'anti-smoking' vaccine has recently been trialled on smokers. The vaccine stimulates the body to produce **antibodies** against **nicotine**. When nicotine is absorbed into the blood, antibodies bind to it and prevent it passing over the blood–brain barrier and entering the brain.

In one trial, 201 smokers with no other ongoing health issues were injected with the anti-nicotine vaccine.

The smokers were divided up into two groups, half of which received a placebo drug. The smokers reported how often they had smoked over the 26 weeks of the trial.

Some smokers were found to have a high response to the vaccine, producing a high concentration of antibodies, whilst others had a lower response.

The percentage of patients reported as giving up smoking is shown in the table below.

Level of response to vaccine	Percentage of patients receiving vaccine who did not smoke between weeks 19–26 of trial
high	24.6
low	12.6
placebo group	13.0

    i Suggest and explain why the vaccine might help to prevent people smoking. [2]

    ii Critics of the vaccine have suggested that the vaccine could cause some people to smoke more cigarettes. Explain why it could lead to a higher consumption of cigarettes. [2]

    iii Explain how the placebo group should be treated. [2]

    iv Evaluate the claim that the vaccine is a success and will help to reduce smoking [4]

[Total: 16 marks]

Chapter 10
Infectious diseases

Chapter outline

The questions in this chapter cover the following topics:

- what is meant by infectious and non-infectious diseases
- the organisms that can cause some infectious diseases
- how cholera, measles, malaria, TB and HIV/AIDS are transmitted
- the ways in which biological, social and economic factors influence the prevention and control of cholera, measles, malaria, TB and HIV/AIDS
- the factors that influence global patterns of malaria, TB and HIV/AIDS
- how penicillin acts on bacteria and why antibiotics do not affect viruses
- how bacteria become resistant to antibiotics
- the consequences of antibiotic resistance and how we can reduce its impact

Exercise 10.1 Types of infectious disease

This exercise tests your knowledge of the causes and features of various **infectious diseases.**

1 The table below summarises infectious diseases, **pathogens** and clinical features.

Copy out and complete the table using the information in the boxes below.

Disease	Name of pathogen	Type of pathogen	Method of transmission	Clinical features

Disease

- cholera
- malaria
- TB
- measles
- HIV/AIDS

Name of pathogen

- *Vibrio cholerae*
- *Plasmodium vivax, P. falciparum, P. ovale, P. malariae*
- human immunodeficiency virus
- *Mycobacterium tuberculosis, M. bovis*
- measles virus

Type of pathogen

- bacterium
- protoctist
- virus
- bacterium
- virus

Method of transmission

- water borne, food borne
- insect vector – *Anopheles* mosquito
- semen and vaginal fluids, infected blood and blood products, across the placenta, via breast milk
- airborne droplets or undercooked meat/unpasteurised milk.
- airborne droplets

Clinical features

- severe diarrhoea, weight loss, dehydration
- fever, anaemia, nausea, headaches, shivering, sweating
- flu like symptoms initially as the disease progresses, pneumonia, other infections, cancers, weight loss
- cough, chest pain, coughing up blood, fever, shortness of breath
- fever, rash, cough, sore eyes

Exercise 10.2 HIV/AIDS

This exercise focuses on the epidemiology of HIV and AIDS. It looks at different sets of global data regarding the incidence and prevalence of HIV and associated diseases.

Figure 10.1 shows the prevalence of HIV in South Africa in men and women of different age groups.

Figure 10.1 Recorded HIV cases in South Africa.

You may be asked to describe the patterns shown by a set of data. In exam questions, this may be for more than one mark, so you will need to add more detail than just a simple trend. Consider the question 'Describe how the percentage of individuals who are HIV positive changes with age.' To answer this fully, break the answer up into several sections:

1 **a** Describe how the percentage of males **and** females with HIV changes with different age groups.

    b Describe any 'turning points' where an increase or decrease in a trend changes direction.

    c Now give a quantitative increase or decrease. Don't just quote data points, manipulate them. Use the graph to calculate the increase in percentage from the 0–14 age group in females to the 30–34 age group.

    d Compare the male and female trends. Is the incidence of female HIV always higher and by approximately how much? Are there ages where the female incidence in not higher?

    e If standard deviation bars are shown, use them. If the standard deviation bars (or ranges) show an overlap, the difference between male and female incidence is not very significant. State which age ranges show a more significant difference in female incidence compared to male incidence.

After describing the data you will often be asked to suggest an explanation. The word *suggest* means that you need to use your knowledge of the course to think of a reason that fits with the data – do not always expect to have a 'ready-made' answer.

Again, break up the graph into different sections:

2 **a** Suggest reasons for the general increase in incidence followed by decrease.

    b Suggest reasons for the generally higher incidence of HIV in women between the ages of 20–24. For this, think about the data. The data were gathered from blood samples that were taken when people attended doctors and hospital clinics, usually for reasons unrelated to HIV infection. The data may not be a true representation of the actual incidence of infection.

If you are asked to evaluate data, you need to look at things that support the conclusion and things that go against it.

3 Figure 10.2 shows the global prevalence of HIV infection and the incidence of new cases of TB in 2003. Figure 10.3 shows the prevalence of HIV and incidence of TB in patients in South Africa between 1980 and 2000.

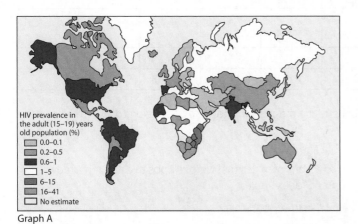

HIV prevalence in the adult (15–19) years old population (%)
- 0.0–0.1
- 0.2–0.5
- 0.6–1
- 1–5
- 6–15
- 16–41
- No estimate

Graph A

Incidence rate per 100 000 people for all forms of TB
- 0–24
- 25–49
- 50–99
- 100–299
- 300 and more
- No estimate

Graph B

Figure 10.2 A HIV prevalence in the adult population and **B** estimated TB incidence rate in different countries.

Figure 10.3 Prevalence of TB and HIV in South Africa between 1980 and 2006.

Many people have claimed that HIV is a cause of TB. Look at Figures 10.2 and 10.3 in order to evaluate this claim, and use some of your own knowledge of the diseases.

You should consider:

- Are there any correlations?
- Is there evidence for a direct causal link?
- How big is the sample size?
- Do many variables change?
- Are there any data that seem to conflict with the conclusion?

4 Pie charts are often used in order to see how proportionate data is. The table below shows a set of data for the reporting of new cases of HIV in a region of the USA.

Reported group	Number of new cases of HIV		Proportion of new cases of HIV		Angle on pie chart	
	Male	Female	Male	Female	Male	Female
homosexual contact	3436	0	0.6			
heterosexual contact	1260	1699				
injection drug use	802	352				
homosexual contact and injection drug use	172	0				
other	57	21				
total	5726	2072				

a Use the following steps to construct a pie chart to show the proportions of HIV in males in each of the groups:

Step 1 Copy out the table above.

Step 2 Work out the proportions of males that were HIV positive and reported homosexual contact, for example:

$$(3436 \div 5726) = 0.6$$

Step 3	Work out the angle that this proportion represents on a pie chart: $0.6 \times 360° = 216°$.
Step 4	Carry out calculations for all the male reported groups and enter these in the table.
Step 5	Use a compass to draw a circle of approximate radius 4 cm. Use a protractor and ruler to measure out an arc of 216 ° from the centre.
Step 6	Repeat this for all the categories and label each sector.

b Now use the data to plot a pie chart for female HIV cases.

c Look at your two pie charts and compare the proportions of male and female HIV cases.

d How could health care professionals use the data to target prevention of HIV transmission in the community?

5 Figure 10.4 shows the number of diagnoses of HIV and AIDS in the UK between 1981 and 2010 and the number of deaths from AIDS related disorders. Haart (highly active antiretroviral therapy) is the name for the treatment regime for HIV infection using combined antiretroviral drugs such as AZT.

Figure 10.4 Graph of New HIV diagnoses, new AIDS diagnoses and deaths from AIDS between 1981 and 2010.

a Use the graph and your own knowledge to suggest reasons for the changes in AIDS diagnoses, new HIV diagnoses and deaths over the period 1981 to 2010.

You should look carefully at how the graphs change in relation to each other and the introductions of HIV testing and Haart treatment.

b AZT is one drug that is often used to treat HIV. The chemical structure of AZT is shown in Figure 10.5, along with the structure of the nucleotide thymidine. Use Figure 10.5 and your own knowledge of DNA structure to suggest how AZT slows down the activity of the viral enzyme reverse transcriptase.

101

AZT   Thymidine

Figure 10.5 Structure of AZT and thymidine.

c   Suggest why AZT can have many side effects.

Exercise 10.3 Cholera

This exercise looks at the symptoms of cholera and how the bacterium causes them. Cholera is often treated by oral rehydration therapy (ORT), and this exercise should also help you to gain an understanding of how this works and the ethics of testing new therapies.

1   The cholera bacterium, *Vibrio cholera*, releases a toxin that causes intestinal epithelial cells to actively pump out chloride ions into the lumen of the intestine. This causes water loss from the blood and intestinal epithelial cells. This is shown in Figure 10.6.

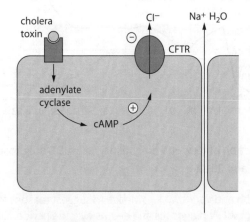

Figure 10.6 The action of cholera toxin on intestinal cells.

Use your knowledge of osmosis to explain why cholera infection leads to dehydration.

2   People infected by cholera suffer from severe diarrhoea, which causes dehydration. In an effort to rehydrate patients, they are often given oral rehydration salt solutions to drink. These solutions consist of a mixture of ions and glucose measured out in carefully controlled concentrations. Figure 10.7 shows a packet of oral rehydration therapy.

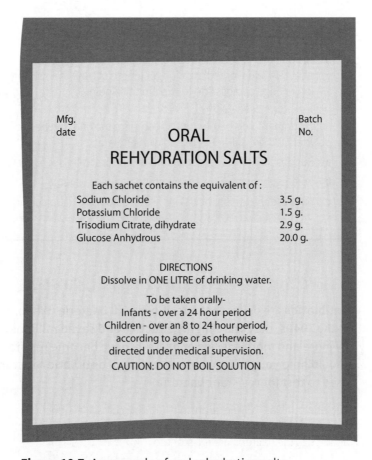

Figure 10.7 An example of oral rehydration salts.

Calculate the molar concentrations of sodium chloride, potassium chloride and glucose found in the oral rehydration salts when dissolved in 1 dm³ of water.

3   ORT helps the intestinal epithelial cells to take up water and pass it into the blood. It is critical that the oral rehydration salts are made up to the volume shown on the label. If too much or too little water is added the diarrhoea is not improved or sometimes found to be worse.

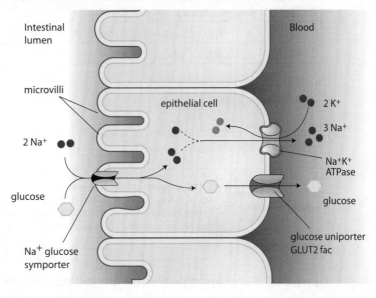

Figure 10.8 Sodium–glucose symporter in intestinal epithelial cells.

a   Use Figure 10.8 to explain how ORT works and explain why it is so important to add the correct volume of water.

b   Ground up rice powder is often used instead of glucose. This was often found to be more effective and worked for a longer length of time than simply using glucose. Use your knowledge of digestion to explain this finding.

4   An experiment was carried out to compare the effectiveness of standard ORS with the rice powder ORS on children infected with cholera.

a   Suggest four factors that should be controlled in such an experiment.

b   Suggest how the experiment could be made reliable.

c   Suggest any ethical decisions that would have to be considered.

Exercise 10.4 Antibiotic resistance

Antibiotics are drugs that specifically kill bacteria. When they were initially developed in the 1940s, they were highly effective and saved millions of lives. As time has gone by more and more species of bacteria have become resistance to them. This exercise should help you gain an understanding of antibiotic resistance and the techniques used to test for resistant bacteria.

Bacteria, such as those responsible for tuberculosis, are becoming resistant to many different antibiotics. When a patient is admitted with tuberculosis, it is important to identify which antibiotics the bacteria are resistant to.

1   a   Copy out the table below and fill in whether or not each statement is true or false.

Statement	True / false
Antibiotics cause bacteria to mutate.	
Horizontal transmission of antibiotic resistance can occur between different species of bacteria.	
Conjugation occurs in vertical transmission of antibiotic resistance.	
Antibiotics should be used to treat measles.	
Penicillin is not effective against *M. tuberculosis*.	
Overuse of antibiotics is one of the causes of MRSA.	

b   Why is it important to identify the correct antibiotic to use from the point of view of the patient and the general population?

2   In order to test antibiotic resistance, there are several tests that can be performed. One of these tests is the antibiotic disc method. The stages in this are shown in Figure 10.9.

Figure 10.9 Stages in carrying out the disc method for measuring antibiotic resistance.

a State the variables that are controlled when carrying out the disc method.

b Explain why a sterile technique is essential throughout.

c Explain why the bacterial plate is examined by placing it on a black background using reflected light. Figure 10.10 shows examples of these plates.

After measuring all the zones of inhibition around the antibiotic discs, the measurements are compared with standard tables to ascertain whether the bacteria are susceptible, resistant or intermediate to a particular antibiotic. When the investigation is carried out, two quality control plates are created simultaneously using standard *E.coli* and *S. aureus* bacteria. These quality control plates are treated exactly the same as the plate with the bacteria under investigation. The table below shows the reference diameters of the zones of inhibition for different antibiotics.

Drug	Diameter of zone of inhibition / mm			Quality control strains / mm	
	susceptible	intermediate	resistant	*E.coli*	*S. aureus*
amoxicillin	≥ 17	14–16	≤ 13	16–22	27–38
chloramphenicol	≥ 18	13–17	≤ 12	21–27	19–26
ciprofloxacin	≥ 21	16–20	≤ 15	30–40	22–30
erythromycin	≥ 23	14–22	≤ 13	N/A	22–30
nalidixic acid	≥ 19	14–18	≤ 13	22–28	N/A
norfloxacin	≥ 17	13–16	≤ 12	28–35	17–28
co-trimoxazole	≥ 18	≤ 12	≤ 10	23–29	24–32
tetracycline	≥ 19	15–18	≤ 14	18–25	24–30

d What is the purpose of the quality control strain plates?

e Figure 10.10 shows antibiotic disc test plates for two patients. Also shown are the quality control plates.

The magnification of the plates is × 0.75.

Use a ruler to determine the **true** diameters of the zone of inhibition for each plate. Draw out the table below to display your results and write in the final columns whether or not the bacteria are S – susceptible, I – intermediate, R – resistant, or N – not known, for both patients. Record 'N' for not known if the control plates suggest that an antibiotic was not working.

Drug	Diameter of zone of inhibition /mm				Resistance state of bacteria (R, I, S, N)	
	E. coli	*S. aureus*	Patient 1	Patient 2	Patient 1	Patient 2
(1) amoxicillin						
(2) chloramphenicol						
(3) ciprofloxacin						
(4) erythromycin						
(5) nalidixic acid						
(6) norfloxacin						
(7) co-trimoxazole						
(8) tetracycline						

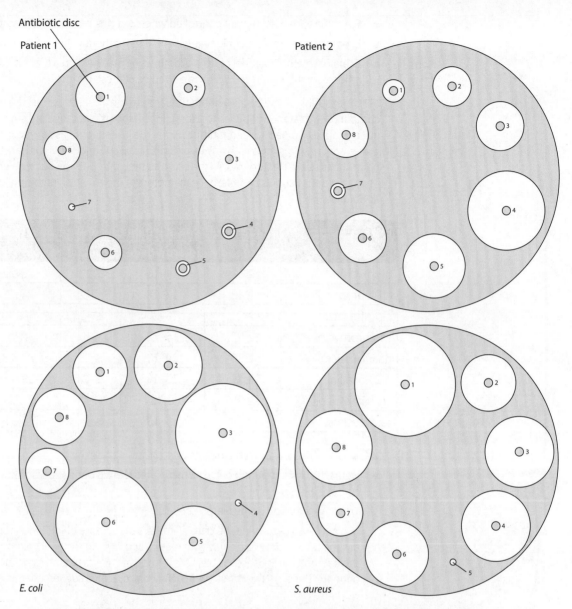

Figure 10.10 Antibiotic resistance test plates on bacteria taken from two patients infected with *M. tuberculosis, and two quality control plates (E. coli and S. aureus).* The number by each disc corresponds to the number given to each antibiotic in the table.

f Some of the zones of inhibition for patient 2 had isolated bacterial colonies growing within them. Suggest what these colonies could be caused by.

3 The MIC or Minimal Inhibitory Concentration technique is a method for identifying the minimum concentration of antibiotic that will kill a particular strain of bacteria. It is used for identifying the level of resistance the bacteria have developed to different antibiotics. The method is shown in Figure 10.11.

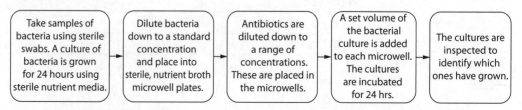

Figure 10.11 Minimal Inhibitory Concentration method for determining antibiotic resistance in bacteria.

The results of an MIC test on a strain of *M. tuberculosis* are shown in Figure 10.12.

Antibiotic	Concentration of antibiotic / µg dm^{-3}											
	128	64	32	16	8	4	2	1	0.5	0.25	0	0 (sterility control)
Amoxicillin	●	●	●	●	●	●	●	●	●	●	●	○
Chloramphenicol	○	○	○	○	○	○	○	○	○	○	○	○
Ciprofloxacin	○	○	○	○	○	○	○	●	●	●	●	●
Erythromycin	○	○	○	○	○	○	○	○	●	●	●	○
Nalidixic acid	○	○	○	○	○	●	●	●	○	●	●	○
Norfloxacin	○	●	○	○	○	○	○	○	○	●	●	○
Co-trimoxazole	○	●	●	●	○	●	●	●	●	●	●	○
Tetracycline	○	○	○	○	○	○	○	○	○	○	●	○

Figure 10.12 The results of Minimum Inhibitory Concentration test on a strain of *M. tuberculosis*. Shaded ovals show where bacteria are growing.

a Explain how 10 cm³ of each concentration of antibiotic solution could be made by serial dilution, starting with a 128 µg dm^{-3} stock solution.

State which antibiotic test:

b would need repeating due to contamination of the stock broth

c has one well which received cross-contamination

d has an MIC of 1.0 µg dm^{-3}

e has an MIC of 0.25 µg dm^{-3}

f lacked live bacteria in all samples

g has bacterial resistance at all concentrations tested

h had a well missed out when bacteria were added

i has an MIC of 128 µg dm^{-3}.

j Explain the roles of the tests with no antibiotic and the sterility control. .

Exam-style questions

1 a Figure 10.13 shows the number of recorded cases of malaria and the rainfall in a region of South Korea over a 12 month period.

   i Give the name of **one** of the species of the parasite that causes malaria. [1]

   ii Describe the change in number of recorded cases of malaria over the 52 week period. [2]

   iii Use the data in Figure 10.13 and your own knowledge of the life cycle of the malaria parasite to explain the change in number of recorded cases of malaria over the 52 week period. [5]

b Artemisinin is a drug that was first used to treat malaria in the 1990s. By 2013, 392 million treatment courses were being used. In 2007, The WHO called for artemisinin to only be prescribed as part of a multiple drug package where patients received a high dose of the drug alongside another one or two anti-malaria drugs. By 2015, large numbers of cases of malaria parasite resistance against artemisinin in South-East Asia were reported. Figure 10.14 shows the proportion of cases of malaria that were resistant to artemisinin in different countries.

Figure 10.13 Incidence of malaria and rainfall during a 52 week period in South Korea.

Figure 10.14 Incidence of malaria parasite resistance in South-East Asia.

    i Use the information in Figure 10.14 to suggest the country in which artemisinin resistance began. [1]

    ii The WHO blamed poor treatment practices, inadequate patient adherence to prescribed anti-malarial regimens, and the widespread availability of substandard forms of the drug as causes of the drug resistance.

       Explain how these factors could have contributed to the development of the drug resistant malaria parasite. [5]

c Describe and explain **two** other measures that could be taken to reduce the spread of malaria. [4]

[Total: 18 marks]

2 a i One of the microbial agents responsible for the disease tuberculosis (TB) is:

   A tuberculosis virus

   B *Vibrio cholerae*

   C *Mycobacterium bovis*

   D *Plasmodium falciparum*.   [1]

   ii Outline the method of transmission and the clinical features of tuberculosis.   [5]

b Figure 10.15 shows the effect of GDP, a measure of national wealth, on the prevalence of
   tuberculosis in different European Union countries.

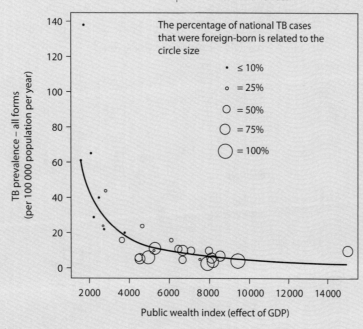

Figure 10.15 Effect of GDP on prevalence of TB in EU countries.

   i Use the information in Figure 10.15 to describe the effect of GDP on the prevalence
      of TB.   [3]

   ii Explain the effect of GDP on tuberculosis prevalence.   [4]

c Tuberculosis is treated with a 6–9 month course of several antibiotics. In some countries,
   people who refuse to receive treatment for the full course may be placed into detention
   and forcibly treated. Explain the reasons why it is important to ensure that treatment is
   completed.   [6]

                                                                   [Total: 19 marks]

3 In 2010, a major earthquake occurred in Haiti causing the destruction of many buildings and
   much of the infrastructure of essential services, such as water and electricity supplies. In the
   aftermath of the earthquake, thousands of people entered refugee camps. Several weeks after
   the earthquake, a cholera epidemic began that lasted several years.

   a i Name the organism that causes cholera.   [1]

      ii Outline the clinical features of cholera infection.   [2]

      iii Suggest and explain why the cholera epidemic occurred after the earthquake.   [6]

b The number of cases of cholera in Haiti that occurred after the earthquake, between 2010 and June 2014, and the cholera fatality rate are shown in the table below.

Year	(Oct–Dec) 2010	2011	2012	2013	June 2014	Total
cases	185 351	352 033	101 722	58 650	7451	705 207
deaths	4101	2927	927	572	32	8559
fatality rate / %	2.2		0.9	1.0	0.4	1.2

 i Calculate the fatality rate for 2011. [1]

 ii Suggest and explain the WHO measures that caused the reduction in the number of cases and in the fatality rate during the years after the earthquake. [3]

 iii Explain why more economically developed nations generally have a much lower incidence of cholera. [3]

[Total: 16 marks]

4 Figure 10.16 shows a diagram of the HIV virus.

Figure 10.16 The structure of HIV.

a Explain how the structure of the HIV virus enables it to infect cells. [4]

b Figure 10.17 shows the estimated global population infected with HIV, the annual increase in new HIV infections and the death rate from AIDS.

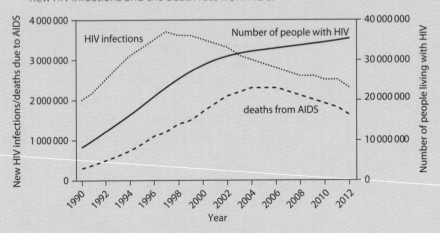

Figure 10.17 Estimated global population with HIV and deaths from AIDS between 1990 and 2012.

i Explain the difference between HIV and AIDS. [2]

ii Compare and contrast the trends in new HIV infections and the number of people living with HIV between 1990 and 2012. [2]

iii Suggest and explain the trend in number of people living with HIV between 1990 and 2012. [4]

Figure 10.18 shows the projected age pyramids for the population of Botswana both with and without AIDS.

Figure 10.18 Predicted population age pyramid for Botswana with and without AIDS to 2020.

iv Use Figure 10.18 to describe the projected effect of AIDS on the population profile of Botswana in 2020. [3]

v Explain the differences in the population age pyramids with AIDS and without AIDS. [3]

vi Use Figure 10.18 to suggest and explain the socioeconomic difficulties that Botswana may face in 2020. [4]

[Total: 22 marks]

5 Puerperal fever was a common cause of death of women following childbirth in the 19th century and early 20th century. It is caused by bacterial infection.

Ignaz Semmelweis investigated the transmission of puerperal fever in two clinics in Vienna in the 19th century. In one ward, childbirth was supervised by medical students who had often carried out prior anatomical dissections. In the second ward, childbirth was supervised by midwives who did not carry out other duties.

Semmelweis reached the conclusion that the medical students were transferring bacteria to the women after pathological anatomical dissections. He formulated a hypothesis that hand washing in chlorine solutions would reduce the spread of infections.

The table below shows results of the research of Ignaz Semmelweis on the causes of puerperal fever. The numbers of maternal deaths are shown at different times.

a **i** Calculate the death rate from puerperal fever after pathological anatomy (1823–33). [1]

ii Use the table below to explain how Semmelweis reached his conclusion that medical students were transferring the infections from pathological anatomy investigations. [2]

iii Evaluate the hypothesis that hand washing in chlorine solutions prevented infections. [3]

	Births	Maternal deaths	Death rate / %
before pathological anatomy (1784–1823)	71 395	897	1.25
after pathological anatomy (1823–33)	28 429	1509	
Ward 1, male medical students, no chlorine washings (1841–7)	20 042	1989	9.92
Ward 2, female midwives, no chlorine washings (1841–7)	17 791	691	3.38
Ward 1, male medical students, since chlorine washings (1891–1959)	47 938	1712	3.57
Ward 2, female midwives, since chlorine washings (1891–1959)	40 770	1248	3.06

b In the 1940s, antibiotics became available to treat bacterial infections. Figure 10.19 shows the death rate of mothers from bacterial infection following childbirth in the UK.

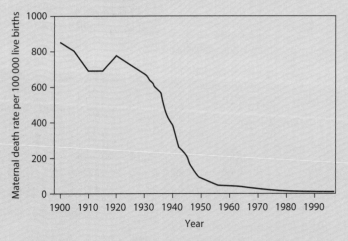

Figure 10.19 The rate of maternal death after childbirth in the 20th century.

i Explain why the data are expressed as number of deaths per 100 000 live births. [1]

ii Use Figure 10.19 to describe the impact of antibiotics on maternal death rate between 1940 and 1950. [2]

iii Describe the processes by which bacteria such as MRSA have become resistant to many different antibiotics since the widespread use of antibiotics beginning in the 1940s. [6]

iv Explain what measures should be taken to reduce the rate at which bacteria are becoming resistant to antibiotics. [3]

[Total: 18 marks]

Chapter 11
Immunity

Chapter outline

The questions in this chapter cover the following topics:

- the roles of phagocytes, B-lymphocytes and T-lymphocytes in the immune response
- the structure and function of antibodies
- myasthenia gravis, an example of an autoimmune disease
- active, passive, natural and artificial immunity
- vaccination
- monoclonal antibodies

Exercise 11.1 Writing a good answer on the immune response

Questions worth five marks can be tricky to answer in an examination. You will normally be given around 12 lines to write on, and a really good, well-focused answer should be able to include at least five relevant points within that space. It's often a good idea to take a few minutes to plan your answer before you begin to write. Try to use appropriate subject-related terminology where you can.

1 Three students were asked to answer the following question:

Explain the roles of phagocytes (macrophages), B-lymphocytes and T-lymphocytes in the immune response. [5]

a Read the answers written by the three students.

Student X

T-lymphocytes start the immune response. They are activated by specific antigens. T-helper cells release cytokines which stimulate specific B-cells to divide into plasma cells and produce antibodies and also stimulate macrophages to carry out phagocytosis. T-killer cells patrol the tissues and if they encounter non-self antigens on the surface of host cells they bind to the cell and release toxins like hydrogen peroxide to kill the host cell and the pathogen inside it. They also cause the lysis of these cells. B-lymphocytes are activated when they recognise complementary specific antigens from a pathogen which they recognise as non-self. They divide by mitosis (clonal expansion) into plasma cells and memory cells. Plasma cells produce antibodies which cause pathogens to agglutinate, neutralise toxins etc. Memory cells remain in the body for a second encounter with the same antigen.

Phagocytes carry out phagocytosis, engulf harmful bacteria by endocytosis, fuse with the pathogen, and enter body in a phagocytic vacuole and digest them with hydrolytic enzymes of lysosomes. Also they cut the pathogens out to display their antigen on their surface for antibodies (humoral response).

Student Y

Macrophages are phagocytes that have as a function to uncover the antigen (foreign cell) receptor, for lymphocytes to know how to attack the foreign cell. T-lymphocytes can be either helper, which stimulate B-lymphocytes to produce antibodies or killer, which attach to pathogens and secrete toxins. They normally use the receptor uncovered by macrophages.

Student Z

Macrophages, B-lymphocytes and T-lymphocytes are produced in the bone marrow. They are used to detect and destroy foreign bodies / antigens that come into contact with the body's immune system. Receptors on antibodies detect these antigens and cause B-lymphocytes to be secreted (memory and plasma cells) and T-helper and killer cells. The memory cells detect the non-self matter during the first immune response and plasma cells are used to secrete more antibodies to destroy the antigens. T-lymphocytes continue the process by destroying, and antigens and the memory cells remain in the event of these antigens entering again so that a rapid secondary immune response is met.

    i   Rank the three answers in order, with the one that you think will gain most marks first.

    ii   Write a brief commentary on each answer, stating clearly what is good about each one, and what could be improved.

  b Write your own answer to the question.

Exercise 11.2 Choosing the appropriate type of graph

Graphs are drawn to display data in a form that helps people to understand the relationship between the variables on the *x*-axis and the *y*-axis. You will already have drawn many bar charts, line graphs and histograms (frequency diagrams), and this exercise gives you practice in deciding when to use each of these methods of displaying information.

Line graphs are used when there is a continuous variable on both the *x*-axis and the *y*-axis. A continuous variable is one that goes up steadily – there is a continuous range of numbers, and the data can be of any value within that range. Each point is plotted as a small cross (or a dot with a circle around it), and the points are then joined with ruled straight lines between points, or a best fit line is drawn. See example in Figure 11.1.

Bar charts are used when there is a discontinuous variable on the *x*-axis and a continuous variable on the *y*-axis. A discontinuous variable is one where there are distinct categories that are separated from one another. The bars are drawn so that they do not touch. See example in Figure 11.2.

Histograms, also called **frequency diagrams**, are used when the variable on the *x*-axis is a series of categories that are continuous, and the *y*-axis shows the frequency of each category. The bars are drawn touching one another. See example in Figure 11.3.

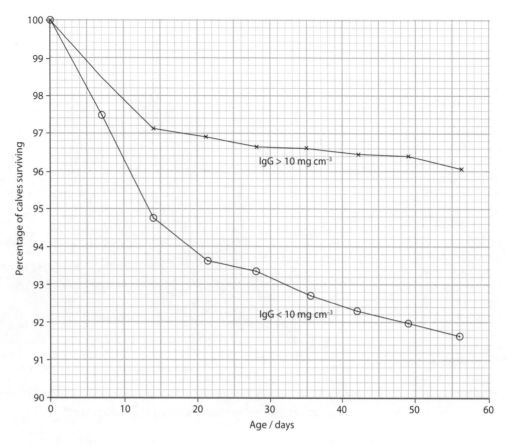

Figure 11.1 Line graph showing the survival rates of calves with two levels of IgG antibodies in their blood in the first 56 days after birth.

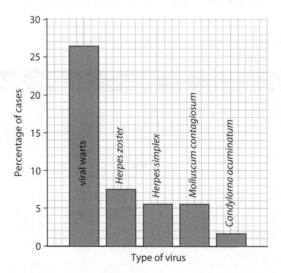

Figure 11.2 Bar chart showing the frequency of different viral infections of the skin, in patients treated with immunosuppressant drugs after a kidney transplant.

In the example in Figure 11.3, the numbers on the x-axis scale are shown on the lines between the bars. These numbers show where the range for the next bar begins. So, for example, the histogram shows that there are 16 calves with a level between 4.20 and 4.39 g 100 cm^{-3}. You may also see histograms where the numbers are placed between the lines, so that they align with the centre of each bar; this is also acceptable.

TIP

There is not always a sharp dividing line between these types of graph. There are occasions when either a line graph or a histogram would be suitable, and others when either a bar chart or a histogram would be suitable. This is the case in some of the questions below, so don't worry too much if you are having trouble deciding between two alternative types of graph. Consider the question carefully, make your decision and then justify it.

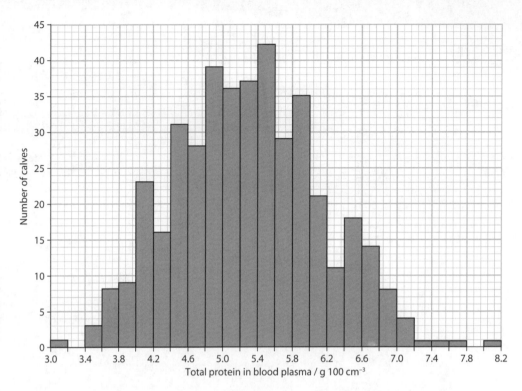

Figure 11.3 Histogram showing the number of calves with different levels of total protein (including antibodies) in their blood 24 hours after birth.

1   A study was carried out to find out if a person's sociability affected how likely they were to get a cold.

A sample of 334 people were given tests to determine how sociable they were. Each person was assigned to one of five categories, 1 to 5, with category 1 having the highest sociability and category 5 having the lowest sociability.

The percentage of people in each category getting a cold during the experimental period was recorded. The results are shown in the table below.

Sociability score	Percentage of people getting a cold
1	34
2	28
3	27
4	22
5	18

a   Decide on the best way to display these results graphically, and give your reasons.

b   Draw the graph to display the results.

2   Researchers measured the numbers of a type of lymphocyte called an NK cell in different parts of the bodies of mice that had been injected with an antigen. They recorded the NK cells as the percentage of the lymphocytes in that part of the body. The results are shown in the table below.

Part of body	Percentage of lymphocytes that were NK cells
spleen	2.1
blood	4.0
lung	5.4
liver	3.2
bone marrow	0.8

   a Decide on the best way to display these results graphically, and give your reasons.

   b Draw the graph to display the results.

3 The table shows the number of reported cases of *Haemophilus influenzae* (Hib) infection in Canada between 1985 and 2004.

Year	Number of cases of reported cases of Hib
1985	410
1986	543
1987	518
1988	690
1989	516
1990	407
1991	385
1992	291
1993	133
1994	80
1995	72
1996	81
1997	82
1998	58
1999	19
2000	24
2001	47
2002	46
2003	56
2004	91

   a Decide on the best way to display these results graphically, and give your reasons.

   b Draw the graph to display the results.

Exercise 11.3 Displaying and analysing data about colostrum

This exercise gives you more practice in choosing the right kind of graph to draw. There is also a calculation to do, a question that asks you to think back to earlier work on movement across cell membranes, and others that check your understanding of how antibodies confer immunity.

1 Colostrum is a type of milk produced by female mammals just after giving birth. Newborn mammals normally have very poorly developed immune systems, and are unable to make sufficient quantities of antibodies to protect themselves against infections. Colostrum contains relatively large quantities of a type of antibody called immunoglobulin G, or IgG.

a What type of immunity is provided by the antibodies in colostrum? Choose from:

active, natural   active, artificial   passive, natural   passive, artificial

b The ability of the small intestine of a newborn calf to absorb antibodies from the milk it drinks from its mother decreases rapidly after birth. The table shows the percentage of antibodies that can be absorbed at birth and up to 30 hours afterwards.

Time after birth / hours	Percentage of antibodies in milk that are absorbed
0	32
6	15
12	7
18	3
24	1
30	0

i Display these results, using the most appropriate type of graph.

ii Antibodies are proteins. Using your knowledge of how molecules are transported across cell membranes, suggest how antibodies are absorbed into the cells lining the small intestine, in a very young calf.

iii Farmers are advised to give calves colostrum from a bottle feeder if the calf has not drunk from its mother within three hours of birth. Use the information in the text and table above to explain the reasons for this.

c The milk of cows was analysed just after giving birth (colostrum) and on the second day afterwards. The results are shown in the table below.

Component of milk	Time after birth / days	
	0	2
fat / %	6.7	3.9
protein / %	14.0	5.1
antibodies / %	6.0	2.4
lactose / %	2.7	4.4
minerals / %	1.11	0.87
vitamin A / µg 100 cm^{-3}	295	113

i Display these data as a bar chart, with 'Component of milk' on the x-axis. Draw two bars touching one another for each component, representing the values for the two different times after birth. You will need to use a key to identify the two types of bar. You may also like to use two different y-axes.

ii Explain why these results should be shown as a bar chart, and not as a histogram or a line graph.

iii A young calf may drink as much as 2.5 dm³ of milk in one feeding session.

Calculate the percentage difference between the quantity of antibodies it would receive in one feeding session immediately after birth and two days after birth. Show all of your working.

Exercise 11.4 Determining the effectiveness of a vaccine

This exercise, like the previous ones, asks you to choose the right kind of graph to draw. You will also need to use your knowledge about how the immune system responds to infection, and – in part (d) – apply knowledge about the effectiveness of vaccination programmes in a new context.

1   Infection with a rotavirus is a major cause of childhood death worldwide. Some children with this infection have mild diarrhoea for a short period of time, but others have severe diarrhoea, accompanied by vomiting and fever, which often results in death. More than 80% of children are infected with this virus before they are 5 years old, but severe and potentially fatal symptoms are normally seen only in children aged between 3 and 35 months.

   a   A child who has had a rotavirus infection is not totally protected against further infections, but these will only be very mild.

      i   Using your knowledge of the immune system, explain how surviving a first infection with a rotavirus gives protection against future infections.

      ii   Name the type of immunity that you have described in your answer to **i**.

      iii Suggest why children who have survived a rotavirus infection may still be infected again, even though only mildly.

   b   Research to develop a safe, effective vaccine against rotavirus began in the 1970s in the USA. Trials determined that a vaccine containing attenuated viruses was safe and effective, particularly if given in three oral doses at the ages of 2 months, 4 months and 6 months.

      i   Use your knowledge of the immune response to suggest why three doses of the vaccine were given.

      ii   Suggest why the vaccine was given at these ages.

   c   Some parents reported that their children suffered mild illness after being given the vaccine. Research was carried out to test whether these claims were true. Children were given either the vaccine or a placebo (a substance that did not contain the vaccine). The children, the parents and the researchers did not know whether a particular child had been given the vaccine or the placebo. The percentage of children developing a fever during the next five days was recorded.

      The results are shown in the table below.

Dose	Percentage with temperature above 38 °C	
	Given vaccine	Given placebo
1 (at 2 months)	22	6
2 (at 4 months)	11	8
3 (at 6 months)	13	12

      i   Display these data using the type of graph you think is most appropriate. Justify your choice.

      ii   Discuss the extent to which these data support the parents' concern that the vaccine caused fever.

   d   New versions of the rotavirus vaccine have now been developed. Only two doses are now required, and symptoms of fever after vaccination are much milder and much rarer. The vaccine is now given routinely to many children in developed and developing countries all over the world. However, rotavirus continues to be a common infection in small children.

      Suggest why vaccination programmes for rotavirus have not succeeded in eradicating the associated disease.

Exam-style questions

1 Figure 11.4 shows two types of white blood cell (leucocyte).

As you near the end of your course, it is important to keep revisiting earlier work. In this question, you are asked to link knowledge you have gained in your study of the immune system with knowledge relating to cell structure and function.

Figure 11.4 Two types of leucocyte.

   a Identify cells **A** and **B**.   [2]

   b Name organelles **P**, **Q** and **R**.   [3]

   c Explain why cell **A** contains a relatively large number of organelle **P**.   [3]

   d Explain why cell **B** contains a large quantity of **R**.   [3]

[Total: 11 marks]

2 **a** Figure 11.5 shows how some of the different types of blood cell are formed.

     i Name the part of the body in which the process shown in Figure 11.5 takes place.   [1]

     ii With reference to Figure 11.5, explain the meaning of the term *stem cell*.   [2]

This is a relatively straightforward question, as long as you know and understand the facts and concepts in this section of the syllabus. It is worth taking time to plan your answer to **b iii** before starting to write.

Figure 11.5 Formation of blood cells.

b For the production of monoclonal antibodies, plasma cells derived from B-lymphocytes are fused with a cancer cell.

   i Explain why neither B-lymphocytes nor plasma cells alone could be used to produce monoclonal antibodies. [2]

   ii Name the type of cell that is produced by the fusion of a plasma cell and a cancer cell. [1]

   iii Describe how monoclonal antibodies can be used in the diagnosis of disease. [4]

[Total: 10 marks]

Here is another question that requires you to use knowledge from several different areas of the syllabus. The question also contains information that may be new to you, about nerve cells and muscles. You will need to read the information at the start of the question carefully, as it is needed to work out some of the answers.

3 Myasthenia gravis (MG) is an autoimmune disease involving damage to the neuromuscular system. The immune system produces antibodies that bind with proteins at neuromuscular junctions.

At a normal neuromuscular junction, the arrival of a nerve impulse causes acetylcholine to be released, which diffuses across a very narrow cleft to the muscle cell membrane, where it binds with a receptor. This event triggers the opening of sodium ion channels, resulting in an influx of sodium ions into the muscle cell. This leads to contraction of the muscle.

In one, relatively uncommon, form of MG, the antibodies bind with proteins that form part of the receptor for acetylcholine on the muscle cell membrane. These are large proteins with a quaternary structure. The binding of the antibodies blocks the receptor.

a Explain the meaning of each of the following terms:

   i autoimmune disease [2]

   ii quaternary structure. [2]

b The normal function of the neuromuscular junction is an example of cell signalling.

   i Outline the process of cell signalling. [3]

   ii Suggest how the opening of sodium ion channels results in an influx of sodium ions into the muscle cell. [3]

c People with MG have acetylcholine receptor-specific T-lymphocytes in their blood.

   Suggest how these cells may increase the quantity of antibodies that bind with the acetylcholine receptor. [4]

[Total: 14 marks]

Once again, this question touches on many different parts of the syllabus. In **a**, you can practise doing a calculation with numbers in standard form. Take care in **d**, where there are two command words – make sure that you respond to each of these in your answer.

4 Chronic lymphocytic leukaemia (CLL) is a type of cancer that occurs when the processes that produce blood cells, in the bone marrow, result in the formation of large numbers of abnormal B-lymphocytes. These lymphocytes do not work as they should, and there are so many of them that not enough functioning blood cells are produced.

a The table shows information about the numbers of lymphocytes in a healthy person and a patient with CLL.

Person	Lymphocyte count /number of cells dm^{-3}
healthy person	3.5×10^9
patient with CLL	6.1×10^{10}

Calculate the percentage difference between the lymphocyte count of the healthy person and the patient with CLL.

Show your working. [3]

b B-lymphocytes, but not other cells, have a protein called CD20 in their cell surface membranes (see Figure 11.6). This protein is known as the B-lymphocyte antigen. The function of the protein is not known, but it is thought that it may function as a Ca^{2+} channel.

   i Explain how a protein such as CD20 could function as a Ca^{2+} channel. [3]

   ii With reference to the CD20 protein, explain what is meant by the term *antigen*. [2]

Figure 11.6 The CD20 protein in a membrane.

iii It was found that the percentage of lymphocytes with the CD20 protein in their membranes was 95.7% in the patient with CLL, and 7% in the healthy person. Explain this difference. [2]

c A monoclonal antibody, rituximab, is used in the treatment of CLL. Rituximab binds with the CD20 protein.

Figure 11.7 shows the structure of rituximab.

Figure 11.7 A rituximab molecule.

i Explain how the structure of an antibody such as rituximab is related to its function. [3]

ii A patient with CLL was given rituximab intravenously. The initial dose was 50 mg, followed by a further 150 mg after 24 hours, and a further 500 mg after 48 hours. The total lymphocyte count in blood samples taken at intervals during and after this treatment was recorded and then calculated as the percentage change in count compared with the count at time 0. The results are shown in Figure. 11.8.

Figure 11.8 Percentage change in lymphocyte count following treatment with rituximab.

Describe **and** explain the changes in the total lymphocyte count during and after treatment with rituximab. [4]

[Total: 17 marks]

Chapter 12
Energy and respiration

Chapter outline

The questions in this chapter cover the following topics:

- the need for energy in living organisms
- the role of ATP as a the universal energy currency
- how energy from complex molecules is transferred to ATP in the process of respiration
- the different energy values of respiratory substrates
- how to use simple respirometers
- how to use a redox dye to investigate respiration in yeast
- how the structure of a mitochondrion is adapted for its functions
- respiration in aerobic and anaerobic conditions
- how rice plants are adapted for growing with their roots submerged in water

Exercise 12.1 Anaerobic respiration in yeast

This exercise should help you to gain an understanding of how to compare data by identifying anomalous values and comparing means whilst taking into account how the raw data vary.

1 Below is the method used by a student carrying out an investigation into the effect of different sugars on the anaerobic respiration of yeast.

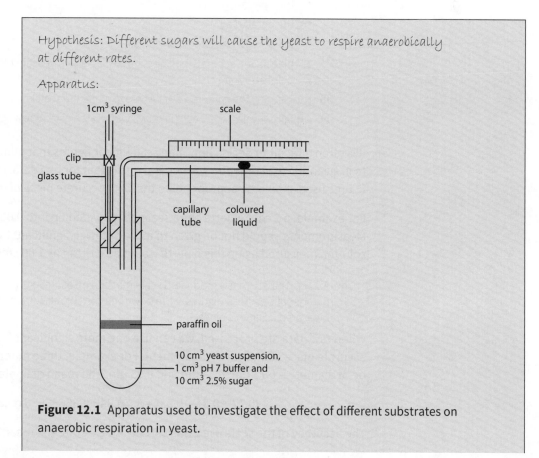

Hypothesis: Different sugars will cause the yeast to respire anaerobically at different rates.

Apparatus:

1cm³ syringe

scale

clip

glass tube

capillary tube

coloured liquid

paraffin oil

10 cm³ yeast suspension, 1 cm³ pH 7 buffer and 10 cm³ 2.5% sugar

Figure 12.1 Apparatus used to investigate the effect of different substrates on anaerobic respiration in yeast.

Method: The apparatus was set up as shown in the diagram. Using a 10 cm³ pipette, 10 cm³ of 10% yeast suspension in water was placed into a boiling tube. Using a separate 10 cm³ pipette, 10 cm³ of 2.5% glucose solution was placed into a separate tube and 1 cm³ of pH 7 buffer added. All solutions were made up with boiled water that had been cooled. Both boiling tubes were placed into a water bath at 30 °C for ten minutes. The solutions were then mixed and the bung placed into the boiling tube, which was then placed into the water bath. The coloured liquid was set to the start of the scale. The distance moved by the liquid in five minutes was then measured. This was repeated ten times with glucose.

The experiment was repeated with 2.5% sucrose solution, 2.5% maltose solution and with distilled water.

The results were recorded in a table.

a   i   Copy out the table below. Identify the independent, dependent and controlled variables and the methods used to change, measure or control them in the experiment, and write them in the table. There is more than one controlled variable.

124

Variable type	Named variable	Method of changing, measuring or controlling
independent		
dependent		
controlled		

   ii   Explain the purpose of the following:
   • the syringe
   • the paraffin oil
   • using boiled water to make up all solutions
   • placing the separate boiling tubes of sugar and yeast in the water bath for 10 minutes before mixing.

   iii   Explain why the coloured dye will move along the scale.

   iv   Explain why an experiment is set up with water instead of a sugar.

It is often difficult to decide how many significant figures that numbers should be recorded to in scientific experiments. The general rule is that for raw data, the number of significant figures used should be appropriate to the least accurate piece of measuring equipment.

For example, a 1 cm³ pipette has a scale on it divided up into 0.01 cm³ increments. Measurements should not be given to more or fewer significant figures. So, 1 cm³ of a solution measured using this pipette would be written as 1.00 cm³.

   b   A 10 cm³ pipette has a graduated scale that can measure to 0.1 cm³. Using the correct number of significant figures, write down the correct measurement of 5 cm³ of water when measured using this pipette.

When raw data are processed, we can use one more significant figure than the least accurate piece of measuring equipment. For example, three mitochondria were found to be of diameters 0.77 µm, 0.84 µm and 0.93 µm. The mean diameter of the mitochondria is:

$$(0.77 + 0.84 + 0.93) \div 3 = 0.8466666666666 \text{ recurring}$$

The accuracy of the scale used was 0.01 µm so we state the mean diameter as 0.847 µm.

i The masses of six separate samples of starch from different potatoes were found to be 25.27 g, 28.43 g, 22.46 g, 21.00 g, 23.45 g and 27.45 g. The balance was accurate to 0.01g. The mean mass of starch from the five different potatoes is:

A 24.67666

B 24.677

C 24.676

D 24.67

E 24.7.

2 The student's table of results for an experiment is shown below.

Number of repeated experiment	Distance moved by coloured dye in 5 minutes			
	Glucose	Sucrose	Maltose	Water
1	6.9 cm	7.42 cm	3.22 cm	0.22 cm
2	7.34 cm	7.38 cm	3.4 cm	0.10 cm
3	7.2 cm	7.54 cm	3.46 cm	0.12 cm
4	8.1 cm	8.5 cm	2.9 cm	0.3 cm
5	7.54 cm	8.32 cm	2.65 cm	0.31 cm
6	0.2 cm	7.65 cm	2.91 cm	0.2 cm
7	7.1 cm	19.21 cm	3.1 cm	0.01 cm
8	7.8 cm	6.43 cm	2.77 cm	0.22 cm
9	7.98 cm	6.5 cm	2.8 cm	0.1 cm
10	7.52 cm	7.3 cm	3.01 cm	0.3 cm
mean	6.768 cm	8.62 cm	3.01 cm	0.19 cm

When drawing a table, there are certain rules that should be followed:

- Ensure that all raw data are shown in a single table with ruled lines and border.
- Place the independent variable in the first column.
- Place the dependent variable in columns to the right (for quantitative observations) **or** descriptive comments in columns to the right (for qualitative observations).
- Place processed data (e.g. means, rates, **standard deviations**) in columns to the far right.
- Do not place calculations in the table, only calculated values.
- Ensure that each column is headed with informative description (for qualitative data) or physical quantity and correct SI units (for quantitative data); units should be separated from the physical quantity using either brackets or a solidus (slash).
- Do not place units in the body of the table, only in the column headings.
- Ensure that raw data are recorded to the number of decimal places and significant figures appropriate to the least accurate piece of equipment used to measure them.
- Ensure that all raw data are recorded to the same number of decimal places and significant figures.
- You can add processed data that are recorded to up to one decimal place more than the raw data.

a The scale used to measure the distance the coloured oil travelled was accurate to 0.1 cm. Copy out the table below and identify which features of the student's table are correct.

Table feature	Correct (Y/N)	Description of errors
All raw data in a single table with ruled lines and border.		
Independent variable in the first column.		
Dependent variable in columns to the right (for quantitative observations) or descriptive comments in columns to the right (for qualitative observations).		
Processed data (e.g. means, rates, standard deviations) in columns to the far right.		
No calculations in the table, only calculated values.		
Each column headed with informative description (for qualitative data) or physical quantity and correct SI units (for quantitative data); units separated from physical quantity using either brackets or a solidus (slash).		
No units in the body of the table, only in the column headings.		
Raw data recorded to a number of decimal places and significant figures appropriate to the least accurate piece of equipment used to measure them.		
All raw data recorded to the same number of decimal places and significant figures.		
Processed data recorded to up to one decimal place more than the raw data.		

b Draw a new table that takes into account all the features listed above. Do not add the mean values yet though.

When processing the data it is often useful to calculate a mean value. To generate an accurate mean value, however, we need to look closely at the raw data and identify any data points that appear to not fit the general pattern and are, in other words, **anomalous**. In biological experiments, it is important to note that many outlying data points may just be due to natural variation, and we must be absolutely certain that a point is not due to natural variation before we class it as an anomaly. In the student's table, the value of 0.2 cm in the glucose column does appear to be a long way from the trend of other results and appears to be anomalous.

c Now, calculate the mean distance moved by the coloured dye in five minutes when glucose is the substrate. Do not include the value of 0.2 cm in your calculation. Write this in your table.

d Now calculate the mean distances for the coloured dye movement for all the other substrates, taking into account any clearly anomalous values.

We can now compare the mean values of the substrates. Mean values do not, however, tell the whole story. The mean distance moved by the dye when the substrate is glucose is higher than the mean distance moved when the substrate is sucrose. This does not necessarily mean, however, that every time that the yeast has glucose as a substrate the dye moves further than when sucrose is used. To help compare different means and get an idea of how reliable a set of data is, it is useful to see how much variation around the mean the raw data shows.

The **range** is simply the minimum value to maximum value; in the case of the distance for glucose this would be from 6.9 cm to 8.1 cm, if we discount the anomaly. The range can, however, include outliers, and a better measure is **standard deviation**, which tells us how much the majority of the data is spread about the mean.

Many sets of data will produce a symmetrical pattern when plotted as a frequency diagram; this is called a **normal distribution**. Examples of this are shown in Figure 12.2. The larger the standard deviation, the wider the spread of data about the mean. When looking at repeats in experimental data, a low standard deviation suggests that the data points are all close to the mean and that the mean is **reliable**. If the standard deviation is high, it shows that there is a lot of variation about the mean and our data are less reliable.

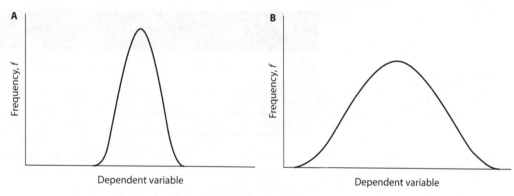

Figure 12.2 Normal distributions showing **A** small and **B** large standard deviations.

To calculate standard deviation you can either use your calculator, a spreadsheet or do it manually. If you do choose to do it using a calculator, however, you still need to know how to perform the calculation!

3 **a** Follow the steps below to calculate the standard deviation for the distance moved by the coloured dye when glucose is the substrate:

    Step 1   Copy down the table below.

    Step 2   Write down all the distances (x) that the dye moved when glucose was used as a substrate, in the left hand column.

    Step 3   For each distance, subtract the mean distance ($x - \bar{x}$) and enter that number in the second column. Don't worry if some are negative.

    Step 4   Square each number in the second column and write that in the third column ($(x - \bar{x})^2$). There should be no negative numbers in this column.

Distance moved by coloured dye (x) / cm	Distance moved by coloured dye minus the mean distance ($x - \bar{x}$) / cm	$(x - \bar{x})^2$
6.9	$(6.9 - 7.49) = -0.59$	0.35

Step 5 Calculate $\Sigma\,(x-\bar{x})^2$. To do this, add together all the $(x-\bar{x})^2$ values. The Greek capital letter sigma, Σ, means 'sum of'.

Step 6 To now calculate the standard deviation, use the formula below:

$$\text{standard deviation} = \sqrt{\frac{\Sigma(x-\bar{x})^2}{n-1}}$$

where n is the number of samples.

Step 7 Divide your value for $\Sigma(x-\bar{x})^2$ by $(n-1)$. In this case $n=9$. Then find the square root of this number. You will now have the standard deviation.

Step 8 We can now state the mean distance moved by the coloured dye when glucose was used as a substrate, along with its standard deviation in the form:

Mean ± 1 standard deviation

b Now calculate the standard deviations for the movement of the coloured dye when sucrose, maltose and water were used as substrates. Copy down the table below and write in your answers.

Substrate	Mean distance moved by coloured dye / cm	Standard deviation / cm
glucose		
sucrose		
maltose		
water		

c Describe the differences between the mean values of each substrate. Take into account the size of the standard deviations for each and explain whether or not the mean values are reliable.

Exercise 12.2 Energy density and calorimetry

Different substrates can be used to generate ATP through respiration. The majority of the energy released from aerobic respiration comes from oxidation of hydrogen to water via the Krebs cycle and electron transport chain. The more hydrogen present per molecule, the more energy that molecule will have available per gram of substance. Calorimetry experiments aim to quantify the energy density of different substrates. This exercise should help you understand how calorimeters work, how experiments are designed to give accurate readings and how we can calculate the energy densities of different respiratory substrates.

Figure 12.3 shows a simple method for demonstrating the energy content of a substrate.

A known mass of substrate is placed on a metal mounted needle. A volume of 25 cm³ of water is placed into a clamped boiling tube and a thermometer placed in the water. The temperature of the water is measured (t_1). The food is ignited using a Bunsen burner and then moved under the boiling tube so that the heat energy from the burning food is used to heat the water. The maximum temperature that the water reaches is then recorded (t_2).

The energy density of the substrate is calculated using the following formula:

$$\text{energy density} = \frac{\text{temperature rise } (t_2 - t_1) \times 4.2 \times \text{mass of water}}{1000 \times \text{mass of substrate}}$$

Figure 12.3 A simple calorimeter.

The specific heat capacity of water is 4.2. It takes 4.2 J to raise the temperature of 1 g of water by 1 °C. The number '1000' is present to convert from J to kJ. As water at normal temperature has a density of 1 g cm^{-3}, we normally assume that the volume in cm^3 is the same as the mass in g.

The units should be:

- energy density: kJ g^{-1}
- temperature rise: °C
- mass of water: g
- mass of substrate: g
- specific heat capacity of water: kJ g^{-1}°C^{-1}.

1   The table below shows some calorimetry results that compare the energy density of starch, casein and stearic acid.

Substrate	Mass of substrate/ g	Start temperature / °C	Max temperature / °C	Energy density /kJ g^{-1}
starch (carbohydrate)	1.3	5	67	
casein (protein)	1.2	7	72	
stearic acid (lipid)	0.8	4	92	

a   Use the formula to calculate the energy density of each substrate. Ensure that you state the units for energy density.

b   The published energy densities for carbohydrates, proteins and lipids are 15.8 kJ g^{-1}, 17.0 kJ g^{-1} and 39.4 kJ g^{-1}, respectively. Compare the published data with the data obtained using the equipment shown above. List and explain all the sources of inaccuracy that could occur when using this experiment that might account for the differences in the results from published data.

c   State why saturated fats such as stearic acid have higher energy densities than unsaturated fats such as oleic acid.

Figure 12.4 shows a different calorimeter. This apparatus is designed to give a far more accurate value of energy content than the apparatus shown in Figure 12.3.

Figure 12.4 A more accurate calorimeter.

2 Copy out and complete the table below to explain how each listed feature of the calorimeter helps to ensure that the energy value for each substrate is close to the true value.

Feature	How feature improves accuracy
foil covered glass vacuum jacket	
stirrer	
heating element inside the apparatus	
oxygen supply	
500 cm³ water volume	
coiled tubing through which exhaust gas passes	

Exercise 12.3 Mitochondria experiments

There are a lot of biochemical and physiological data regarding mitochondria, which can show us how processes such as the electron transport chain occur. This exercise should help you to fully understand the mechanisms of **oxidative phosphorylation** and some of the experimental methods used.

1 Mitochondria are isolated by homogenising liver tissue in an isotonic pH 7.4 buffer solution at 4 °C. They are separated from other cell organelles by centrifugation and then re-suspended in the same isotonic buffer at 4 °C. The suspension is placed into a small cavity slide and an oxygen probe lowered into the suspension. The oxygen probe measures the concentration of oxygen in the suspension. Different substances can then be added to the suspension and the effect of them on the oxygen concentration examined.

a Explain why the mitochondria are placed in isotonic pH 7.4 buffer at 4 °C.

b In the first experiment, pyruvate was added as a substrate, and ADP and inorganic phosphate (P$_i$) added at repeated intervals. The oxygen levels were monitored and the results are shown in Figure 12.5 below.

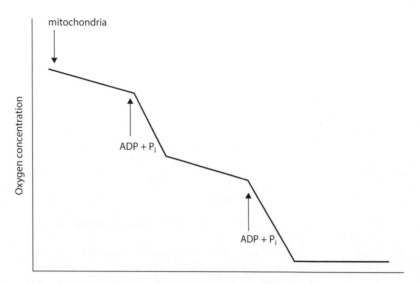

Figure 12.5 The effect of addition of ADP and inorganic phosphate (Pi) on oxygen concentration.

    i   Explain why pyruvate was added rather than glucose.

    ii Describe and explain the effects of addition of ADP + P_i on the concentration of oxygen.

2   In a further experiment, the effects of addition of the respiratory inhibitor rotenone were investigated. Rotenone inhibits the activity of the first set of electron carriers in the inner mitochondrial membrane, as shown in Figure 12.6.

Figure 12.6 Diagrams of the **A** electron transport chain showing the sites of action of the inhibitors rotenone, cyanide and oligomycin, and **B** Krebs cycle showing the role of the intermediate sugar succinate.

As in the first experiment, ADP and P_i were added to the mitochondrial suspension followed by a mixture of ADP, P_i and rotenone. The Krebs cycle intermediate sugar, succinate, was then added. The results are shown in Figure 12.7.

Figure 12.7 Effect of addition of ADP, P_i, rotenone and succinate on oxygen concentration.

a Explain why the first addition of ADP + P_i was carried out.

b Use Figures 12.6 and 12.7 to explain the effect of rotenone on oxygen uptake and the effect of succinate addition.

3 In two final experiments, the effects of the respiratory inhibitors oligomycin and cyanide were investigated. Oligomycin inhibits the movement of H^+ ions through the ATPase channel. Cyanide inhibits the enzyme cytochrome oxidase at the end of the electron transport chain, preventing it from releasing electrons on to oxygen.

DNP is a substance that makes the inner mitochondrial membrane permeable to H^+ ions so that they will diffuse into the matrix and dissipate their energy as heat. It 'decouples' the movement of H^+ ions into the matrix from ATP synthesis.

Mitochondria were treated as in previous experiments. ADP and P_i were added to the mitochondrial suspensions followed by either ADP, P_i and oligomycin or ADP, P_i and cyanide. In both cases, DNP was then added to the mitochondrial suspension. The results are shown in Figure 12.8.

Figure 12.8 The effect of addition of **A** oligomycin and **B** cyanide with DNP on oxygen concentration.

Compare and explain the effects of oligomycin and cyanide addition with and without DNP.

Exercise 12.4 Measuring respiratory quotient (RQ) and using a respirometer

The **respiratory quotient (RQ)** is a ratio of the volume of oxygen used by an organism compared to the amount of carbon dioxide released. The RQ for the complete aerobic respiration of glucose is 1, since from the equation for aerobic respiration, 6 molecules of oxygen are used for every 6 molecules of carbon dioxide produced.

$$6O_2 + C_6H_{12}O_6 \rightarrow 6CO_2 + 6H_2O$$

$$RQ = \frac{CO_2}{O_2}$$
$$= \frac{6}{6}$$
$$= 1$$

Other substrates, however, do not have an RQ of 1. This exercise should help you to understand how we can carry out practical work to determine the RQ of respiring organisms.

Figure 12.9 shows a diagram of a **respirometer**.

Figure 12.9 A typical respirometer.

An investigation was carried out into how respiratory substrates change during the germination of barley seeds over a seven day period.

- 5 g of barley seeds were soaked in water for 12 hours.
- After 12 hours of soaking in water the barley seeds were washed with a solution of sodium hypochlorite bleach. All glassware was also soaked with the sodium hypochlorite. The barley seeds were placed into the metal cradle in boiling tube B. A sample of 5 g of identically treated boiled barley seeds was placed into the metal cradle in boiling tube A. A volume of 10 cm³ of potassium hydroxide solution was placed into both boiling tubes as shown in Figure 12.9.
- The coloured oil in the U-tube was set so that it was at an equal height on both arms of the tube.

- The tap on boiling tube A was closed and the distance moved by the coloured liquid recorded after 15 minutes.
- This was repeated five times in total.
- The potassium hydroxide was then replaced with water and the experiment repeated five more times.
- This was repeated for seven days in total.
- After three days the seeds were seen to be germinating. At this point, all respirometer work was carried out, with the seeds in the dark.

1 a Explain why the seeds and apparatus were washed with sodium hypochlorite bleach.

  b Explain the purpose of the 1 cm³ syringe.

  c List the variables that should be controlled.

  d Explain why, after day 3, the respirometer experiment was carried out in the dark.

  e Explain why an equal mass of boiled barley seeds was placed into boiling tube A.

  f Explain the purpose of the potassium hydroxide.

2 The volumes of oxygen used are calculated from the distances the dyes moved in the presence of potassium hydroxide. Oxygen will be removed by the barley seeds, and carbon dioxide will be released. The potassium hydroxide removes the carbon dioxide, so we see a reduction in volume which is the volume of oxygen removed.

Day	Mean distance moved by dye /cm		Volume of O_2 used in 15 min / mm³	Volume of carbon dioxide released in 15 mins/ mm³	RQ
	In presence of sodium hydroxide.	In presence of water.			
0	6.3	−4.1			
1	7.3	0.1			
2	7.7	0.9			
3	6.7	1.1			
4	6.5	1.6			
5	6.7	1.8			
6	7.1	0.2			
7	7.8	0.0			

a Follow the steps below to calculate the volumes of oxygen used on different days:

  Step 1   Copy out the table above.

  To calculate the volume of oxygen used, we need to assume that the U-tube manometer is a cylinder where the height is the distance moved by the coloured dye.

radius, *r*, of U tube / cm

distance, *d*, moved by oil / cm

Figure 12.10 Diagram showing dimensions of a cylinder.

The formula for the volume of a cylinder is:

$$\pi r^2 d$$

Step 2 For day 0, the distance, d, moved in the presence of potassium hydroxide was 6.3 cm.

Convert this to millimetres:

6.3 cm = 63 mm

Step 3 The radius of the U-tube was 0.1 cm.

Convert this to millimetres:

0.1 cm = 1 mm

Step 4 Now calculate the volume of the cylinder of oxygen:

Volume = $\pi r^2 d$

Volume = $3.14 \times (1)^2 \times 63 = 197.82$ mm³

b Now calculate the volumes of oxygen used by the respiring barley seeds on all the days. Write your answers in your table.

Determining the volume of carbon dioxide released by the respiring barley seeds is slightly harder. We have to look at the movement of the dye when the barley seeds are in the presence of water (with no potassium hydroxide to remove the carbon dioxide) and compare this with the movement of the dye when the barley seeds are in the presence of potassium hydroxide.

If the coloured dye has moved towards the respiring barley seeds in tube B:

In Figure 12.11, the distance x is the distance moved by the coloured dye in the presence of sodium hydroxide and represents the volume of oxygen. Distance y is the distance moved by the coloured dye in the presence of water, and represents the combined effect of oxygen removal and carbon dioxide release. The fluid has moved towards the respiring seeds in tube B, so that means more oxygen has been removed by the seeds than carbon dioxide has been released. The volume of carbon dioxide is the distance $x - y$.

Figure 12.11 Calculating volume of carbon dioxide released when the coloured dye moves towards the respiring seeds in tube B.

c Calculate the volumes of carbon dioxide released by the seeds by following the steps below:

Step 1 On day 1, the distance moved in the presence of potassium hydroxide, x, is 7.3 cm.

Convert this to millimetres:

7.3 cm = 73 mm

Step 2 The distance moved in the presence of water, y, is 0.1 cm.

Convert this to millimetres:

0.1 cm = 1 mm

Step 3   Distance moved due to carbon dioxide release = $x - y$

$= 73\,mm - 1\,mm$

$= 72\,mm$

Step 4   Now calculate the volume of carbon dioxide released:

Volume of cylinder $= \pi r^2 d$

Volume of cylinder $= 3.14 \times 72 \times (1)^2 = 226.08\,mm^3$

d   Now calculate the volumes of carbon dioxide released on days 2–7 and write your answers in your table.

If the coloured dye has moved away from the respiring barley seeds in tube B:

In Figure 12.12, the distance x is the distance moved by the coloured dye in the presence of sodium hydroxide and represents the volume of oxygen. Distance y is the distance moved by the coloured dye in the presence of water, and represents the combined effect of oxygen removal by the respiring seeds and carbon dioxide release. The fluid has moved down, so that means more carbon dioxide has been released than oxygen removed. The volume of carbon dioxide is the distance $x + y$.

x + y, volume of carbon dioxide released

x, volume of oxygen used (distance moved by dye in presence of potassium hydroxide)

y, distance moved by dye in presence of water

Figure 12.12 Calculating volume of carbon dioxide released when the coloured dye moves away from the respiring seeds in tube B.

e   Calculate the volume of carbon dioxide released on day 0.

The change in volume for day 0 is listed as −4.1. The negative sign is to show the opposite direction of movement – we ignore this when carrying out the calculation.

Step 1   Distance x moved by dye in the presence of potassium hydroxide = 6.3 cm. Convert this to millimetres.

Step 2   Distance y moved by the dye in the presence of water = 4.1 cm. Convert this to millimetres.

Step 3   Calculate the distance moved due to carbon dioxide release, $x + y$.

Step 4   Use this distance to calculate the volume of carbon dioxide released on day 0.

Volume of a cylinder $= \pi r^2 d$

Step 5   Add the value to the table.

3 **a**   Now use the formula given at the start of this exercise to calculate the respiratory quotients for each day and write your answers in your table.

   b   Plot a suitable graph to show how the RQ values change over the seven day period.

   c   Describe the changes in RQ values over the seven day period and suggest explanations for the changes. Typical RQ values are: aerobic respiration of carbohydrate 1.0, lipids 0.7, protein 0.9; anaerobic respiration of carbohydrate <1.

Exam-style questions

1 **a** The table below lists four different stages of aerobic respiration and some statements about aerobic respiration. Place ticks in the boxes if the statements are correct, and crosses for those that are wrong.

Statement	Glycolysis	Link reaction	Kreb's cycle	Oxidative phosphorylation
NAD is reduced				
FAD is oxidised				
decarboxylation occurs				
occurs in the cytoplasm				
occurs in the matrix of the mitochondria				

[5]

b Explain why ATP is frequently described as the 'energy currency of the cell'. [4]

[Total: 9 marks]

2 Figure 12.13 shows an electron micrograph of a mitochondrion.

Figure 12.13 An electron micrograph of a mitochondrion. Magnification × 62 000.

a Calculate the length in µm, between **A** and **B**, of the mitochondrion in Figure 12.13. [2]

b In a study into the effect of endurance training on muscle cells, the density of the cristae within the mitochondria was measured. It was found that after six months of endurance training, the density had increased by 43% compared to control groups. Use your knowledge of aerobic respiration to explain how this change could benefit endurance athletes. [4]

[Total: 6 marks]

3 Mitochondria were extracted from liver tissue and placed into ice-cold isotonic solution with excess quantities of pyruvate and inorganic phosphate (P_i). ADP was added and the change in oxygen concentration of the solution measured. This was repeated until ADP addition had no more effect. The results are shown in Figure 12.14.

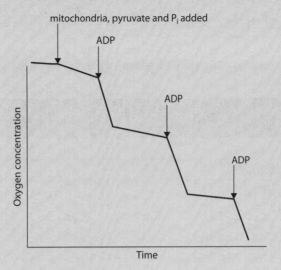

Figure 12.14 Effect of addition of ADP on oxygen concentration.

a Using your knowledge of **chemiosmosis**, explain the change in oxygen concentration after addition of ADP. [4]

b In a further experiment, mitochondria from a specialised adipose tissue called 'brown fat' were investigated. This tissue is found to be prevalent in hibernating animals. The results are shown in Figure 12.15.

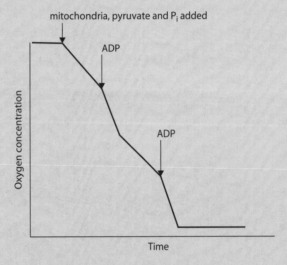

Figure 12.15 Effect of addition of ADP to mitochondria from brown fat on oxygen concentration.

i Compare the results from the mitochondria extracted from brown fat with the liver mitochondria. [2]

ii The inner membranes of mitochondria from brown fat cells possess high concentrations of an H⁺ protein channel called UCP-1. UCP-1 is not attached to ATP synthase. Suggest and explain how the UCP-1 protein helps hibernating animals survive cold conditions. [5]

[Total: 11 marks]

4 The respiratory quotient (RQ) is a measure of the amount of oxygen consumed by an organism compared to the amount of carbon dioxide released. It is calculated using the following formula:

$$RQ = \frac{\text{volume of carbon dioxide released}}{\text{volume of oxygen consumed}}$$

The RQ for the aerobic respiration of glucose is 1.

The equation for the oxidation of the fatty acid oleic acid is:

$$C_{18}H_{34}O_2 + 25.5\,O_2 \rightarrow 18CO_2 + 17H_2O$$

a Calculate the RQ for the aerobic respiration of oleic acid. [1]

b An investigation was carried out into the effect of fasting on the RQ of two students. One of the students was given no food (fasting) for 12 hours whilst the other ate a normal balanced diet. The students were then made to exercise at increasing intensities in rooms set at the same temperature and humidity. The volumes of oxygen used in their bodies and carbon dioxide produced were measured and the RQ calculated for the different exercise intensities. Intensity was measured as power output. The results are shown in Figure 12.16.

Figure 12.16 Effect of fasting on RQ during different intensities of exercise.

i The temperature and humidity of the room were kept the same. Suggest two other factors that would need to be controlled. [1]

ii Compare the effects of increasing exercise intensity on the RQ of the two students. [3]

iii Using your knowledge of RQ values for different substrates explain the results in Figure 12.16. [4]

iv Migratory birds such as Canada geese have a much higher ratio of saturated fatty acid to glycogen for their energy reserves than flightless birds such as ostriches. Using your knowledge of the energy density of different substrates, suggest and explain reasons for this difference. [3]

[Total marks: 12]

5 Black mangrove trees are found in muddy coastal regions. The soil is waterlogged and the roots spend time submerged. Figure 12.17 shows the root system of a black mangrove tree.

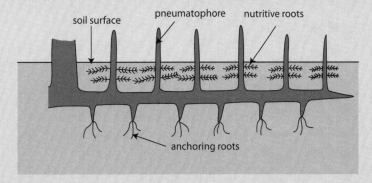

Figure 12.17 Root system of the black mangrove tree.

The mangrove trees develop three types of root:

- anchoring roots, which help stabilise the tree
- nutritive roots, which absorb mineral ions from the soil
- pneumatophores, which are roots with large numbers of lenticels that protrude out of the mud and water.

a Explain how the root system of the black mangrove enables it to grow in the shifting, waterlogged soil. [5]

b Describe and explain the how rice plants are adapted to grow whilst partially submerged in water. [5]

[Total: 10 marks]

6 Figure 12.18 shows an outline of some stages of respiration.

Figure 12.18 Outline of stages of aerobic respiration.

a i Name molecules **Y** and **Z**. [2]

ii Name stages **A**, **B** and **C**. [1]

iii State the exact location in the cell where stages **B** and **C** occur. [1]

b i Explain how reduced NAD and reduced FAD are used to generate ATP. [5]

ii Assuming that each reduced NAD can produce 2.5 molecules of ATP and each reduced FAD can produce 1.5 molecules of ATP, calculate the total number of ATP molecules produced from one molecule of glucose. [1]

c In the absence of oxygen, stages B and C in Figure 12.18 stop. Explain why in anaerobic conditions animals covert pyruvate into lactate. [3]

[Total: 13 marks]

Chapter outline

The questions in this chapter cover the following topics:

- the absorption of light energy in the light dependent stage of photosynthesis
- the transfer of energy to the **light independent stage** of photosynthesis and its use in the production of complex organic molecules
- the role of chloroplast pigments in the absorption of light energy
- how the structure of a chloroplast fits it for its functions
- how environmental factors influence the rate of photosynthesis
- how C4 plants are adapted for high rates of carbon fixation at high temperatures

Exercise 13.1 The effect of different colours of light on the light dependent reactions

The **light dependent reactions** of photosynthesis include the **photolysis** of water to give hydrogen ions, electrons and oxygen and the synthesis of ATP. Light energy causes the excitation and loss of electrons from the **primary pigments** of photosynthesis. The electrons on the pigments are replaced by those from the water. The electrons pass through a range of electron carrier molecules and are eventually added to NADP along with H^+ ions to produce reduced NADP. The substance DCPIP can act as a substitute for NADP. DCPIP is blue in its oxidised state and colourless when reduced.

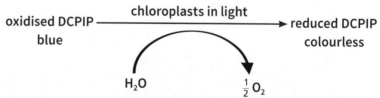

$$\text{oxidised DCPIP} \xrightarrow{\quad \text{chloroplasts in light} \quad} \text{reduced DCPIP}$$

oxidised DCPIP — chloroplasts in light → reduced DCPIP
blue   colourless

H_2O $\frac{1}{2} O_2$

This exercise should help you to understand how to use DCPIP to investigate photosynthesis and use the **standard error** of the means to compare mean values.

1 **Chloroplasts** were isolated from spinach leaves, suspended in an isotonic pH 7.4 buffer and kept at 4 °C. Ten test tubes were placed into an ice-cold water bath and chloroplast suspension and DCPIP added to each. The tubes were exposed to light of different colours by placing sheets of coloured cellophane in front of a lamp. The distances of the lamps to the tubes were kept constant as shown in Figure 13.1.

Figure 13.1 Diagram to show position of lamp and light filter.

The contents of each tube and the light colour each tube was exposed to are shown in the table below. Ticks and crosses represent the presence or absence of substances.

Tube	Light colour	Wavelength range of light / nm	5 cm³ chloroplast suspension	5 cm³ DCPIP
1	white	390–780	✗	✓
2	white	390–780	✓	✗
3	none (foil wrapped)	none	✓	✓
4	white	390–780	✓	✓
5	violet	390–455	✓	✓
6	blue	455–495	✓	✓
7	green	495–575	✓	✓
8	yellow	575–600	✓	✓
9	orange	600–625	✓	✓
10	red	625–780	✓	✓

Tubes 1, 2, 3 and 4 acted as controls or were used to make comparisons.

The tubes were exposed to the appropriate light and the time taken for the DCPIP to decolourise recorded. Each of tubes 4–10 were replicated five times. The results are shown in the table below.

Tube number	Colour of light	Time taken for DCPIP to decolourise / s					Mean	sd
		1	2	3	4	5		
1*	white	-	-	-	-	-	-	-
2**	white	-	-	-	-	-	-	-
3***	None (foil wrapped)	-	-	-	-	-	-	-
4	white	33	36	41	32	39	36.2	3.6
5	violet	72	68	79	67	68	70.8	5.0
6	blue	85	92	91	84	82	86.8	4.4
7	green	274	225	265	268	245	255.4	20.2
8	yellow	167	152	143	168	156	157.2	10.5
9	orange	96	89	102	96	97	96.0	4.6
10	red	65	59	71	73	71		

* DCPIP remained blue.
** remained green colour of chloroplast suspension.
*** remained starting colour of mixed blue DCPIP and green chloroplast suspension.

a **i** Explain the purpose of each of tubes 1, 2, 3 and 4.

ii Calculate the mean time taken and standard deviation for DCPIP to decolourise in red light.

The experiment suggests that the mean times taken for the DCPIP to decolourise in different colours of light are different. If we repeated each colour again would the times taken to decolourise the DCPIP be the same? We can never be certain of this but we can carry out a calculation to determine whether our mean value is close to the true mean value. This calculation works out the standard error of our mean (S_M). S_M tells us how certain we can be that our mean is the true mean. The formula for S_M is:

$$S_M = \frac{s}{\sqrt{n}}$$

where S_M is the standard error
S is the standard deviation
n is the sample size.

We can be 95% certain that if we carried out another experiment the result would be within two times our value of S_M. This range around the mean is known as the **95% confidence limit**.

Follow the steps to calculate the 95% confidence limits of the mean time taken to decolourise DCPIP in violet light:

Step 1   Calculate the standard error using the formula given above:

$$S_M = \frac{5.0}{\sqrt{5}}$$
$$= \frac{5.0}{2.2}$$
$$S_M = 2.3$$

Step 2   Now calculate $2 \times S_M$:
$$S_M = 2 \times 2.3 = 4.6$$

This means that we can be 95% confident that the mean from a second sample would lie between:

70.8 ± 4.6, which means that the 95% confidence limits are between 66.2 and 75.4.

   b   Calculate the standard error and 95% confidence limits for the mean times taken for DCPIP to colourise for all the colours of light.

We can use the confidence limits as **error bars** on graphs. If error bars overlap, there is no significant difference in mean values. If the error bars do not overlap, we cannot definitely state that the difference is significant but we do know that there is a possibility that it is. This is shown in Figure 13.2.

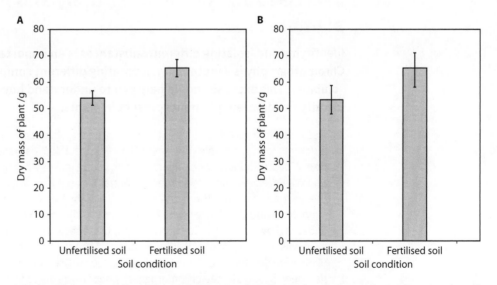

Figure 13.2 Errors bars that **A** do not overlap and **B** do overlap. Where they overlap, the difference in mean is not significant.

   c   Plot an appropriate graph of light colour against mean time taken for DCPIP to decolourise. You will need to think what type of variables you have – categoric or continuous – before you select the correct graph. When you draw the x-axis, it will be helpful if the order of the colours corresponds to the increasing wavelength

d Add error bars onto the each mean plot. The upper error bar should be $2 \times S_M$ above the mean, and the lower error bar should be $2 \times S_M$ below the mean.

e Look at your graph. State which mean values show an overlap of error bars and are not significantly different from each other.

f Describe and explain the pattern shown by the graph.

2 It was suggested that the different cellophane filters not only altered the wavelength (colour) of light passing through but also the absorbance of light by the filters. The relative percentage transmission of light was measured for each colour using a light meter. The data are shown in the table below. 'White' light was set at 100% transmission when passed through a clear filter.

Colour of light	Relative transmission of light / %
white	100
violet	23
blue	38
green	72
yellow	80
orange	75
red	58

a Plot an appropriate graph to determine whether transmission of light had a significant effect on DCPIP decolourisation.

b Think carefully about the experiment. Evaluate how effective the method was at generating accurate data and identify the major sources of error. Suggest improvements that could give more accurate results.

Exercise 13.2 Chromatography and photosynthetic pigments

Identifying and isolating different substances is an important practical tool in biology. Chromatography is a method for separating different compounds on the basis of their solubility. This exercise should help you to understand how we use chromatography to identify the different pigments present in plants.

1 A scientist carried out an investigation into the effects of ageing and illumination levels on the pigments found in maple tree leaves. Three types of leaves were taken from the same maple tree: old leaves that were changing colour, young leaves from the sun exposed upper branches and young leaves from the shaded lower parts of the tree. Pigment was extracted by cutting up the leaves and placing them into a mortar with six drops of propanone (an organic solvent) and a pinch of sand. The leaves were then ground until a dark coloured extract was formed. A pencil line was drawn on a strip of chromatography paper 1.5 cm from the base. A fine glass capillary tube was used to place spots of extract on the pencil line. Each time a spot was placed it was allowed to dry before the next one was placed on the same spot. When a dark coloured spot had been produced, the chromatography paper was placed into a boiling tube so that the end below the dark spots was submerged in propanone solvent. The chromatogram was allowed to run until the solvent almost reached the end of the chromatography paper.

The R_f value of a chemical is a measure of its solubility in nonpolar solvents. For a particular solvent, the R_f should be approximately the same every time. It is calculated using the formula:

$$R_f \text{ value} = \frac{\text{distance moved by substance}}{\text{distance moved by solvent}}$$

a Calculate the R_f values for each of the pigments **A**, **B**, **C** and **D**. Always measure from the origin line to the centre of the spot. Use the table below to identify each one.

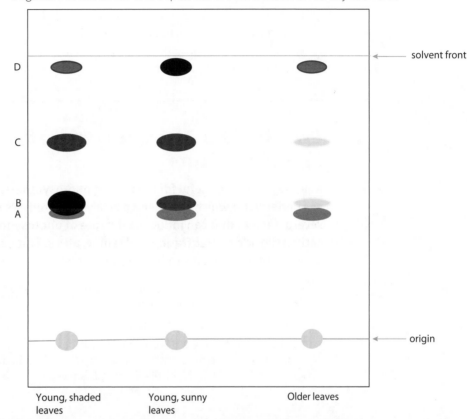

Figure 13.3 Chromatogram showing pigments in different leaves.

Pigment	R_f value
anthocyanin	0.31
carotene	0.96
chlorophyll *a*	0.70
chlorophyll *b*	0.48
pheophytin	0.85
xanthophyll	0.44

b Explain why the pigment spot is dried between applications.

c Compare the differences in pigments shown on the chromatogram in Figure 13.3 for each of the leaves. Darker, larger spots suggest a higher concentration of pigment.

d There have been several hypotheses proposed to explain why different concentrations of pigments are found in leaves. Some of these hypotheses are:

Carotene protects **chlorophyll** from over oxidation in bright light.

Chlorophyll *b* absorbs wavelengths of light that reach the woodland floor.

Xanthophyll is an **accessory pigment** that absorbs wavelengths of light not absorbed by chlorophyll.

In autumn, or the fall, chlorophylls *a* and *b* are broken down so that leaves turn brown, red and yellow, the colours of carotene and xanthophyll.

Discuss which of these hypotheses could be consistent with the results shown in Figure 13.3.

e Explain whether or not it is acceptable to make valid, quantitative conclusions when comparing the leaves.

f Suggest how the experiment could be extended to generate quantitative data in order to compare concentrations of the pigments.

g Review the original method and carry out a risk assessment. State the risks and what strategies could be used to minimise the risks.

Exercise 13.3 Measuring the rate of photosynthesis in aquatic plants

Aquatic plants are useful for measuring photosynthesis rates as they produce oxygen gas underwater which can then be easily collected. We can use them to investigate several factors that can influence the rate of photosynthesis, such as light intensity, carbon dioxide concentration and temperature. This exercise should help you to understand Spearman's rank correlation test, a statistical test for correlations.

1 Plan an investigation into the effect of increasing light intensity on the rate of photosynthesis of *Cabomba aquatica*, a pond weed.

The apparatus you have available is:

a photosynthometer (see Figure 13.4), glass beaker, thermometer, pair of sharp scissors, paper clip, 10 cm³ syringe, stop watch, ruler graduated in millimetres, anhydrous sodium hydrogen carbonate (dry), balance, distilled water, 1 dm³ volumetric flask, a bench lamp, a metre ruler, clamp and stand, sources of hot and cold water.

Figure 13.4 A photosynthometer set up to measure the volume of oxygen produced by an aquatic plant.

Plan your experiment under the following headings:

HYPOTHESIS

Your hypothesis should be a testable prediction of the effect of changing light intensity on rate of photosynthesis. State how you think changing light intensity will affect the rate, and draw a sketch graph of what you predict your results will be like if the hypothesis is correct.

METHOD

When outlining your method break it up into parts as shown below:

Independent variable: name the independent variable and give full details of how you will change it. You should state the range you will use, the increments, explain why you have chosen the range and increments and how you will decide on the number of repeats.

Dependent variable: name the dependent variable and give full details of how you will measure it. In this case you will need to explain how to measure the length of a bubble of oxygen using the scale and the syringe. The method should generate accurate, quantitative results. Explain why the measure you have chosen is a measure of photosynthesis rate.

Control variables: state all the variables that you will control, explain why they need controlling and how you will control them. Do not list everything you can think of, only list relevant things.

Detailed method: In your method give practical details and the precautions you will take. For instance, 'the *C. aquatica* stem is cut using the sharp scissors at an angle in order to help it release oxygen bubbles. It is then placed cut end upwards in …'. This should include details of how you will make up any concentrations of solutions that you will need. You will also need to explain the role of the syringe.

2   The results from a similar investigation into the effect of changing light intensity on rate of photosynthesis are listed in the table below. It looks from the data like there is a negative correlation between the distance of the lamp from the sample and the size of the bubble of oxygen, in other words, as distance increases, the length of the oxygen bubble decreases. To find out if this correlation is significant, we need to do carry out a statistical test. **Spearman's rank correlation** is used to find out if there is a significant correlation between two sets of variables when they are not normally distributed and may not be in a linear relationship. Follow the steps below to determine whether the correlation is significant.

   a   Formulate a **null hypothesis**. In statistical tests, we make the assumption that there is no significant association or correlation between the two variables; e.g. in an experiment to see if addition of fertiliser increases plant dry mass, a null hypothesis would be 'there is no significant correlation between concentration of fertiliser and dry mass of plant.'

Distance of lamp from *C. aquatica* / cm	Rank for distance of lamp, r_1	Mean length of oxygen bubble formed after five minutes illumination / cm	Rank for mean length of bubble, r_2	Difference in ranks, D $(r_1 - r_2)$	D^2
5		26.4	1		
10		20.3	3		
15		20.5	2		
20		21.6			
25		18.4			
30		18.4			
35		14.0			
40		8.2			
45	2	1.6			
50	1	1.6			

   Formulate a null hypothesis for the results in the table above.

   b   Rank the distances of the lamp from the plant in order, with the largest as '1'. Write the ranks into your table. The first two are completed for you.

Two of the mean lengths of oxygen bubble are both 18.4 cm, and we will need to give them the same rank. We give them an average rank as follows:

18.4 and 18.4 would nominally rank '5' and '6'.
The average rank will be:
$(5 + 6) \div 2 = 5.5$
Both values of 18.4 are ranked 5.5, the next rank awarded will be 7.

   c   Rank the mean length of oxygen bubble, again with the largest ranked as '1'. The first three are done for you.

   d   Calculate the difference in ranks, D, for each pair of results and write your answer in your table.

   e   Calculate the square of the difference in rank of each pair, D^2. Write your answer in your table. Now calculate the sum of the squared differences in rank (ΣD^2).

   f   Use the formula below to calculate the Spearman's rank correlation coefficient.

If the coefficient is positive, the correlation is positive; if it is negative, the correlation is negative:

$$r_S = 1 - \frac{6\Sigma D^2}{n^3 - n}$$

where
r_s is Spearman's rank correlation coefficient
ΣD^2 is the sum of the differences between the ranks of the pairs
n is the number of pairs.

We now need to decide the probability that the null hypothesis is correct. To determine this, we compare the value of the coefficient with a critical value in a table. In most statistical tests in biology, we use a probability of 0.05 as our baseline.

If our coefficient is larger than the critical value, this means there is only a probability of <0.05 (or 5%) that our null hypothesis is correct. This means that the correlation is significant and we reject the null hypothesis. There is a probability of less than 0.05 that the correlation is due to chance.

If our coefficient is smaller than the critical value, this means there is a probability of >0.05 (or 5%) that our null hypothesis is correct. This means that the correlation is not significant and we do not reject the null hypothesis. There is a probability of greater than 0.05 that the correlation is due to chance.

   g   Use the critical values in the table below to determine whether or not there is a significant correlation between distance of the lamp and length of bubble. Use the terms *probability*, *null hypothesis*, *chance*, *reject* and *significant* in your answer.

n	5	6	7	8	9	10	11	12	14	16
critical value of r_s	1.00	0.89	0.79	0.76	0.68	0.65	0.60	0.54	0.51	0.51

3   Test the following sets of data to determine if there are significant positive or negative correlations. In each case formulate a null hypothesis and give a full explanation in terms of probability and chance:

   a   The association between the concentrations of chlorophyll *b* in the leaves of a tree with increasing height.

Distance from base of tree / m	Chlorophyll concentration / µmol m^{-2} leaf area
0.0	645
0.5	524
1.2	524
2.3	627
3.5	345
4.6	350
4.9	253
5.1	145

b The association between the number of ladybirds per 0.25 m^2 quadrat in a maize field and the dry mass of maize seeds.

Quadrat number	Number of ladybirds	Dry mass of maize seeds / g
1	8	225
2	4	178
3	5	201
4	2	101
5	7	223
6	9	254
7	3	154
8	7	227
9	6	213
10	8	244

Exercise 13.4 Free response questions

An important exam skill is to be able to answer open essay-style questions. You need to read questions carefully, look at the mark allocation and think of the relevant points that are creditworthy. Marks are awarded for scientifically accurate, A-level standard answers. This exercise looks at three candidates' answers to a question.

Look at the three candidates' answers to the questions below. Use the mark scheme to decide how many marks each would get. Read the answers carefully and think how easy each was to mark. Remember, even if more points are made, you cannot get more than the maximum number of marks.

1   Describe how chloroplasts use light energy to manufacture ATP. [8]

a   Plants use chlorophyll to photosynthesise. Chlorophyll is what gives them a green colour and it is found in the chloroplasts. Chloroplasts can absorb plenty of carbon dioxide, water and light energy to photosynthesise. The chloroplasts can also move towards light so that they can maximise the amount of light absorbed. Because plants are green, they reflect green light and cannot use it in photosynthesis. The light is used to oxidise chlorophyll molecules and the electron is passed on to electron transport chains where it is used to make ATP and reduced NADP. To replace the chlorophyll's electron, water releases an electron that sticks onto the chlorophyll and can then be used again. This is called photolysis. The waster product of photolysis is oxygen gas, which we can use to breathe. This all takes place on the chloroplast membranes.

b Chloroplasts are designed for photosynthesis. There are two main stages of photosynthesis – the light dependent stage and the light independent stage. The light dependent stage is where ATP and reduced NADP are made. The thylakoid membranes, in the grana, are where the light dependent reaction occurs. Light energy is absorbed by collections of primary and accessory pigments that are bound together in two photosystems: photosystem 1 (PS1) and photosystem 2 (PS2). Chlorophyll a is the primary pigment and sits at the reaction centre of the photosystems surrounded by molecules of accessory pigments such as carotene and chlorophyll b. Chlorophyll a absorbs light in the red and blue areas of the spectrum. Chlorophyll b and carotene also absorb extra wavelengths of light and pass the energy on to chlorophyll a. The light energy is used to oxidise the chlorophyll by ejecting an electron. The electron is passed on to electron transport chain proteins which use the energy of the electron to pump H^+ ions into the centre of the thylakoids. The H^+ diffuses back out into the stroma of the chloroplast through H^+ channels attached to ATP synthase enzyme. The movement of the H^+ ions provides energy to phosphorylate ADP + Pi into ATP. The electrons can pass through carriers from PS2 to PS1 through non-cyclic photophosphorylation and from PS1 back to PS1 via electrons through cyclic photophosphorylation.

c Chlorophyll is found in two photosystems – PSI and PSII – that are located in the thylakoid membranes of the chloroplast. The chlorophyll absorbs light from the red and blue end of the spectrum and is oxidised. An electron is passed along a series of electron carriers and uses its energy to make ATP from ADP + Pi. The electron moves from PSII to PSI and then to the enzyme NADP reductase to combine with hydrogen ions to make reduced NADP. The ATP and reduced NADP are used to make sugars in the Calvin cycle, which takes place in the stroma. Photolysis occurs as well, which releases oxygen that can be used in respiration. DCPIP can be used to measure the rate of electron release from chlorophyll. Plants also have other pigments such as carotene, pheophytin and xanthophyll, which can also absorb light.

Mark scheme

1 chlorophyll *a* is a primary pigment
2 carotenoids / chlorophyll *b* is an accessory pigment
3 in grana / thylakoids
4 reference PSI and PSII; A P700 and P680
5 primary pigment / chlorophyll *a*, in reaction centre
6 chlorophyll *a* / primary pigment is oxidised / loses electron
7 chlorophyll *a* absorbs red (ignore orange) and blue (ignore purple)
8 accessory pigments (accept named, e.g. carotene) absorb other wavelengths
7 electron is transferred to electron transport chain / electron carriers
8 H^+ diffusion into stroma
9 reference to ATP synthase
10 ADP + P_i → ATP / ADP is phosphorylated; P_i not just P

2 Explain why **photorespiration** reduces plant growth rates. Describe how some plant species have evolved to reduce photorespiration. [7]

a Photorespiration is a wasteful process that is caused by the enzyme rubisco binding to oxygen instead of carbon dioxide. This leads to less RuBP being regenerated, so the Calvin cycle will slow down. C4 plants are able to make malate that transports carbon dioxide into the mesophyll cells, where it can enter the Krebs cycle.

b Photorespiration reduces plant growth. It is due to the enzyme rubisco binding to oxygen so that the plant now respires instead of photosynthesises. The plant will now use up its glucose faster, so that it does not grow as well. Maize is a plant that does not do photorespiration because its palisade mesophyll cells are found in a tight band and so do not pick up oxygen.

c Typical C3 plants often undergo photorespiration when oxygen levels are high. The enzyme rubisco has an active site that will bind carbon dioxide and oxygen. If it binds oxygen, the enzyme combines RuBP with oxygen to make one molecule of GP and 1 molecule of a 2C sugar. This means that less RuBP is regenerated and levels fall so that the Calvin cycle occurs more slowly. Some plants, known as C4 plants, have a specialised anatomy to prevent oxygen from coming into contact with RuBP. Bundle sheath cells are kept inside a tight circle of mesophyll cells so that oxygen cannot reach them. In the mesophyll cells, CO_2 is combined with a sugar called PEP to make oxaloacetate, which is then transported into the bundle sheath cells where it breaks down into pyruvate and CO_2. The CO_2 can then enter the Calvin cycle.

Mark scheme

1 rubisco will bind oxygen
2 RuBP + oxygen does not produce 2 × GP / produces 1 × GP + 1 × glycolate
3 RuBP levels decline / loss of carbon / equivalent
4 reference to C4 plants / named example, e.g. maize
5 bundle sheath cells / rubisco are kept away from air
6 tight mesophyll cells wrapped around bundle sheath (accept from diagram)
7 CO_2 + PEP → oxaloacetate in mesophyll cells
8 (oxaloacetate) converted to malate in mesophyll cells
9 malate transferred to bundle sheath cells
10 (malate) breaks down into pyruvate and CO_2
11 CO_2 enters the Calvin cycle

Exam-style questions

1 Figure 13.5 shows apparatus that can be used to measure the rate of photosynthesis of algae. The algae can be trapped inside a gel bead made out of sodium alginate. The beads can be placed into a boiling tube containing a solution of sodium hydrogen carbonate. As the algae photosynthesise, they release oxygen which becomes trapped in the alginate beads and causes the beads to rise.

Figure 13.5 The apparatus available to carry out an investigation into the effect of carbon dioxide concentration on rate of photosynthesis.

a i Describe how you could use the apparatus above to investigate the rate of photosynthesis at different concentrations of sodium hydrogen carbonate (a source of carbon dioxide). You will be provided with a stock of 10% sodium hydrogen carbonate solution and distilled water and may assume that you have access to normal school or college laboratory equipment such as boiling tube racks. [7]

   ii State the dependent variable. [1]

b Alginate beads were used to investigate the effect of three light colours, red, yellow and blue, on the rate of photosynthesis. The results are shown in the table below. A hypothesis was made:

   Red and blue light will cause faster photosynthesis than yellow light so the alginate beads will rise faster.

| Light colour | Time taken for beads to rise 10 cm / s | | | | | | | | | | |
	1	2	3	4	5	6	7	8	9	10	Mean
red	96	126	134	145	156	156	165	166	173	376	146.3
yellow	210	225	243	244	247	259	254	273	281	286	252.2
blue	122	144	157	157	167	168	175	179	181	185	163.5

   i Explain how the mean values have been calculated to generate a reliable mean. [1]

   ii The standard error for the results was calculated.

   The standard error for red is 7.6.

   The standard error for yellow is 7.2.

   The formula for standard error is:

   $$S_M = \frac{s}{\sqrt{n}}$$

   Calculate the standard error for blue. Show all your working. [3]

   iii State what the standard deviation shows. [2]

   iv Plot a graph to show the effect of light colour on the mean time taken for the alginate beads to rise 10 cm. Add error bars. [4]

   v Explain whether or not the data support the hypothesis. [2]

[Total: 20 marks]

2 a Describe the process by which carbon is fixed continuously in the palisade mesophyll cells in **C3 plants**. [8]

b Predict and explain the changes in carbon dioxide concentration at different heights in a tropical rain forest over a 24 hour period. [7]

[Total: 15 marks]

3 Figure 13.6 shows the effect of increasing light intensity on the net rate of release of oxygen of two woodland plants, a 'sun plant' and a 'shade plant'. The 'sun plant' is a tall tree, while the 'shade plant' grows on the woodland floor.

Figure 13.6 Effect of increasing light intensity on net oxygen release from sun and shade plants.

a i Compare the effect of increasing light intensity on the sun plant and the shade plant. [3]

ii Explain the effect of increasing light intensity on the sun plant. [4]

iii Suggest and explain a reason for the difference in the effect of increasing light intensity on the two plants. [2]

b Figure 13.7 shows the effect of increasing temperature on the net assimilation rate of carbon dioxide of barley and maize plants. Barley was grown at different temperatures in ambient (normal atmospheric) and high levels of carbon dioxide. Maize was grown at different temperatures in ambient carbon dioxide.

Figure 13.7 Effect of increasing temperature on the net assimilation rate of carbon dioxide of maize and barley plants.

i Use your knowledge of photorespiration to explain the effect of increasing carbon dioxide and temperature on the net carbon dioxide assimilation rate of barley. [4]

ii Explain the difference in the effect of increasing temperature on net uptake of carbon dioxide in maize at ambient carbon dioxide concentrations compared with the effect on barley. [5]

iii Use Figure 13.7 to suggest and explain why C4 plants tend to be found in hotter, more arid regions than C3 plants. [4]

[Total: 22 marks]

4 a Outline the roles of chlorophyll *a* and the accessory pigments in photosynthesis. [5]

b Different types of algae are found at different depths in the ocean. The algae found at different depths have different combinations of accessory pigments. Figure 13.8 shows the ranges of depth at which different algae are found and the approximate depths that different light colours penetrate through the water.

Figure 13.8 Depth of penetration of different light colours and depth ranges of different types of algae.

Figure 13.9 shows the absorption spectra of different photosynthetic pigments. The table shows the different pigments found in the different types of algae.

Figure 13.9 Absorption spectrum of photosynthetic pigments.

Type of algae	Pigments present
green	chlorophyll *a*, chlorophyll *b*, carotenoids
brown	chlorophyll *a*, chlorophyll *b*, carotenoids, phycocyanin
red	chlorophyll *a*, phycocyanin, phycoerythrin, carotenoids

Use Figures 13.8 and 13.9 and the table above to explain the depth ranges of the different types of algae. [4]

[Total: 9 marks]

5 Figure 13.10 shows the structure of a chloroplast.

Figure 13.10 Drawing from an electron micrograph of a chloroplast.

a Name the structures labelled **A**, **B** and **C** in Figure 13.10. [3]

b Carbon fixation of isolated chloroplasts was investigated. Chloroplasts were placed into an isotonic buffer solution and illuminated. Radiolabelled $^{14}CO_2$ was added and the relative amounts of radiolabelled GP and RuBP measured every minute for 10 minutes. The light was switched off and the relative amounts of GP and RuBP were again measured every minute for 10 minutes. The results are shown in Figure 13.11.

Figure 13.11 Effect of light and dark on amount of radiolabelled GP and RuBP.

Use your knowledge of the Calvin cycle to:

i Explain the changes in the amounts of radiolabelled GP and RuBP in the light. [4]

ii Explain the changes in the amounts of radiolabelled GP and RuBP after the light was switched off. [3]

[Total: 10 marks]

Chapter outline

The questions in this chapter cover the following topics:

- the importance of homeostasis and how the nervous and endocrine systems coordinate homeostasis in mammals
- the structure of the kidneys, and their role in excretion and osmoregulation
- how blood glucose concentration is regulated
- what is meant by negative feedback
- how cell signalling is involved in the response of liver cells to adrenaline and glucagon
- the principles of operation of dip sticks to test for the presence of glucose in urine
- the factors that cause stomata to open and close
- how abscisic acid causes guard cells to close stomata

Exercise 14.1 The action of the drug metformin in the control of blood glucose concentrations

Type 2 diabetes is caused by the inability of the liver and muscle cells to respond to insulin. It is not treated by injection of **insulin**, since insulin levels in people with this condition are often normal or higher than normal. The drug metformin is often used to help to lower blood glucose levels. This exercise looks at some results of experiments with metformin on rats and should help reinforce your ability to carry out statistical tests and understand secondary signalling.

1 An experiment was carried out where two groups of 12 rats were injected with either water or the drug metformin which had been dissolved in water. After 60 minutes, half of the rats from each group were injected with either saline solution or **glucagon** dissolved in saline. Blood glucose concentration was then measured every 10 minutes for 30 minutes.

   a This is quite a complicated experiment, so it can help to represent it in a flow chart. Copy out Figure 14.1 and fill in the blanks.

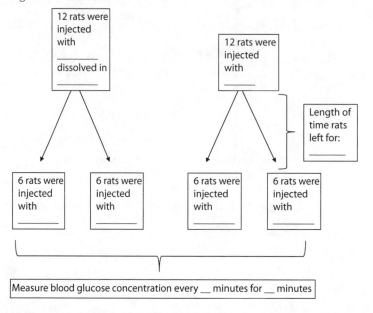

Figure 14.1 Experimental design flowchart.

b List the independent variables (there are two).

c Suggest three factors that should be controlled.

d Explain why the rats were also injected with water and saline rather than metformin and glucagon.

e Explain why patients with type 2 diabetes can be found to have higher than normal concentrations of insulin in their blood.

The results of the experiment are shown in Figure 14.2.

Figure 14.2 Blood glucose concentrations of rats after treatments with metformin and glucagon.

Describing complex data patterns is an important skill and it is important to look for different parts of a graph and be clear what you are comparing. Look carefully at the graph in Figure 14.2 and answer the following:

2 a Compare the effects of injection with water and metformin on blood glucose concentration from time 0 minutes to time 60 minutes. Here you are looking for differences between the two treatments with water and the two treatments with metformin.

b The glucagon and saline were injected at 60 minutes. There are three main comparisons to make:

- First, compare water + glucagon with water + saline. This shows us the normal effect of glucagon in the absence of metformin. It is a baseline effect of glucagon.
- Second, compare the rats injected with water + glucagon with those injected with metformin + glucagon. This shows us whether metformin affects glucagon action.
- Third, compare the rats with metformin + saline with the rats with metformin and glucagon. This shows us how much blood glucose concentration will rise when adding glucagon with or without metformin.

c Look at your comparisons. Now make a valid conclusion about whether or not metformin affects blood glucose concentration and how it might causes this.

d Suggest how you could make your conclusion more valid and what information you would require to do so.

3 At the end of the experiment, the effects of metformin and glucagon on the production of cyclic AMP (cAMP) in rat liver cells were also investigated. Liver tissue was removed from the same rats and the cAMP levels measured. The results are shown in the table below. Note that cAMP is expressed as its mass as a proportion of total cellular protein mass.

Substances injected	Mass of cAMP / pmol µg⁻¹ cellular protein							
	1	2	3	4	5	6	mean	s.d.
water followed by saline	9	10	8	6	7	10	8.3	1.6
water followed by glucagon	65	68	53	54	58	61	59.8	6.0
metformin followed by saline	5	7	12	9	7	6	7.7	2.5
metformin followed by glucagon	24	23	18	16	17	18	19.3	3.3

a Draw a graph to show the effects of the different treatments on the rat liver cells on mean cAMP mass. In Chapter 13 you learned how to calculate and use the standard error of the mean and 95% confidence limits. Calculate the standard error and 95% confidence limits and use them to add error bars to your graph.

b Explain what the data now show us about the effects of metformin and glucagon on cAMP production. Does it suggest evidence that glucagon utilises a secondary messenger system? Does it suggest that one of the ways in which metformin reduces blood glucose is to reduce the response of liver cells to glucagon?

4 a You need to be able to understand the role of cAMP as a secondary messenger. The table below contains a set of statements about the action of the hormone glucagon. Place the statements in the correct order.

A	G protein is activated and in turn activates an enzyme, adenylate cyclase, to convert ATP into cAMP.
B	Phosphorylase kinase activated by protein kinase.
C	Protein kinase activated by cAMP.
D	Glucagon binds to glucagon receptor on surface of liver cell membrane.
E	Glucose diffuses out of liver cells through GLUT2 transporter channels.
F	Glycogen phosphorylase activated by phosphorylase kinase.
G	Glycogen phosphorylase converts glycogen into glucose.

b Now use the statements to explain why metformin can reduce blood glucose concentration.

Exercise 14.2 Osmoregulation and isotonic drinks

There are many sports drinks available that are described as isotonic. Many of them suggest that rehydration is far more effective if drinks contain fluid that is isotonic to normal body fluids rather than being pure water. In this exercise, you will review an experiment that investigates the effect of different sodium chloride concentrations in drinks on urine output, revisit molar solutions and gain a better understanding of the process of osmoregulation.

1 Imagine that you are going to plan an experiment into the effects of consuming drinks of different sodium chloride concentrations on the reabsorption of water by the kidneys after athletes have performed strenuous exercise. First you would need to make up a range of drinks with different concentrations of sodium chloride.

a Take a look back at Chapter 2, Exercise 2.2, to refresh your memory on how to calculate the concentrations of different solutions. The table below shows the different concentrations of the drinks that could be used in this investigation. The concentrations are given as percentage by total volume of solution. Copy out the table and write down the mass of sodium chloride required to make up 1 dm³ of each solution.

b Calculate the molarity of each solution and enter it into your table.

The molecular masses you will need are:

Sodium: 23

Chlorine: 35.5

Concentration of sodium chloride solution / % by volume	Mass of sodium chloride dissolved in 1 dm³/ g	Concentration of sodium chloride solution / mol dm^{-3}
0.0		
0.3		
0.6		
0.9		
1.2		
1.5		
1.8		

2 In this experiment, 18 male students aged between 18 and 21 and all of the same approximate fitness were asked to pedal on a bicycle for one hour at the same power output. After this hour, the students were given a drink of a particular sodium chloride concentration between 0% and 1.2%. The students all had the same fluid intake for four hours prior to the experiment.

0.9% concentration of sodium chloride is isotonic to normal body fluids.

Five different salinity drinks were used and three students received each salinity. The volume of drink was the same in all cases = 1000 cm³. Three students received no drink. The total volume of the students' urine was then measured over the next three hours. The results are shown in the table below.

Concentration of saline / % by volume	Volume of urine produced over 3 hours / cm³			
	Student 1	Student 2	Student 3	Mean
0.0	348	374	325	349.0
0.3	325	359	345	343.0
0.6	254	275	288	272.3
0.9	201	245	242	229.3
1.2	204	195	202	200.3
no drink	143	129	133	235.0

a State the independent and dependent variables.

b State four of the variables that were controlled.

c Describe the effect of increasing the concentration of sodium chloride in the drink on the volume of the urine.

d Suggest an explanation for the pattern you have described. You should think about water potentials, osmoreceptors, salt loss and diffusion of salts into the blood.

e Drinking solutions with very high concentrations of sodium chloride can lead to a high concentration of sodium chloride in the blood. Predict and explain the effects of drinking hypertonic, 1.8%, sodium chloride solution on the body.

3 Place the following statements about osmoregulation in order:

Letter	Statement
A	**Osmoreceptors** in hypothalamus detect the lower water potential and impulses are sent to the posterior pituitary.
B	Blood water potential becomes lower (more negative).
C	ADH binds to receptors in membranes of **collecting duct** cells.
D	Phosphorylase enzyme is activated.
E	ADH released into blood.
F	Water passes through aquaporins into lumen of collecting duct.
G	Vesicles containing aquaporins move to the cell surface membrane and fuse with it.
H	Blood water potential rises and ADH release stops.
I	High rates of sweating lead to evaporation of water.

Exercise 14.3 Measuring percentage errors and comparing blood glucose monitors

It is important to know the level of accuracy that apparatus can measure to. If we know how much error each measurement may have we can be more or less confident in our results. It is also important with clinical measuring devices such as glucose monitors that we know how much we can trust a reading.

Some measuring equipment such as balances will often give a measure of error such as 0.01 g. This means that the balance is accurate to ± 0.01 g of the reading given.

For example, a balance with a measuring error of ± 0.05 g was used to measure out 1 g of sodium carbonate.

The actual mass measured out will lie somewhere between 1.00 g ± 0.05 g (0.9–1.05 g).

If we carry out two measurements in a sequence, the errors will be added together. For example, in our previous example, if we were investigating the change in mass of our sodium carbonate after heating it:

Start mass = 1.00 g ± 0.05g.

Finish mass = 0.55 g ± 0.05 g.

The change in mass will be 1.00 g – 0.55 g = 0.45 g.

The measuring error could have occurred twice, so will be 0.05 g $\times 2 = 0.10$ g.

So, our final result for the change in mass will be 0.45 g ± 0.10 g (0.35–0.55 g).

When measuring volumes of liquids, unless otherwise stated on the equipment, we generally assume that the error is half of the smallest graduation on the scale.

For example, a 1 cm^3 graduated pipette has increments of 0.1 cm^3. This means that the pipette is accurate to $\pm(0.1 \div 2) = \pm 0.05$ cm^3.

1 Calculate the ranges that the true values will lie between for the following:

a 2.500 g of glucose measured using a balance accurate to 0.005 g

b 25 g of glucose measured in five batches of 5 g using a balance accurate to 0.005 g

c the change in mass of 5 g of starch after digestion by amylase left a mass of 2.4 g, using a balance accurate to 0.01 g

d a temperature of 33 °C on a thermometer with the smallest graduations on the scale of 1 °C

e the change in body temperature of a reptile over a one hour period. Start temperature = 17 °C, finish temperature = 21 °C. Smallest graduations on the thermometer scale are 0.1 °C

f the change in volume of oxygen produced by pond weed, using a gas syringe. Start volume = 0.1 cm³, finish volume = 11.2 cm³. Smallest graduations on the scale = 0.1 cm³.

It is also useful to express the amount of error in a measurement as a percentage error. To do this, you use the formula below:

$$\text{Percentage error (\%)} = (\text{error} \div \text{reading}) \times 100$$

In other words, for our first example where we measured out 1 g of sodium carbonate, the percentage error would be:

$$(0.05 \div 1.00) \times 100 = 5\%$$

Looking at percentage error of equipment should help you to choose the correct sized apparatus. For example, if we want to measure out 25 cm³ of 1% glucose solution and have three measuring cylinders:

- 250 cm³ cylinder   smallest graduations on scale: 5 cm³
- 50 cm³ cylinder   smallest graduations on scale: 2 cm³
- 10 cm³ cylinder   smallest graduations on scale: 1 cm³

the percentage errors when using each of the measuring cylinders would be:

- 250 cm³ cylinder: (2.5 cm³) ÷ 25 cm³ × 100 = 10%
- 50 cm³ cylinder: (1.0 cm³) ÷ 25 cm³ × 100 = 4%
- 10 cm³ cylinder: (1.5 cm³) ÷ 25 cm³ × 100 = 6%.

If we use the 10 cm³ cylinder, we would have to measure out two sets of 10 cm³ and one set of 5 cm³, which would give us a combined error of 0.5 × 3 = 1.5 cm³.

So for this experiment, we would opt to use the 50 cm³ measuring cylinder as it would give the lowest percentage error.

Generally (although not always), you should choose the smallest piece of measuring equipment that would measure your volume in one batch. The smaller the volume being measured, the higher the percentage error becomes in a particular piece of apparatus.

For example, the percentage error with 250 cm³ of liquid measured in a 250 cm³ measuring cylinder graduated into 5 cm³ is:

$$(2.5 \text{ cm}^3 \div 250 \text{ cm}^3) \times 100 = 1\%$$

The same measuring cylinder used to measure out 1 cm³ of glucose gives a percentage error of:

$$(2.5 \text{ cm}^3 \div 1 \text{ cm}^3) \times 100 = 250\%$$

which is obviously not acceptable!

2 Calculate the percentage errors of the following:

a 34 cm³ water measured in a 100 cm³ beaker with graduations of 2 cm³

b the change in distance moved by the fluid in a respirometer: start height 5 cm, finish height 2.5 cm, graduations of 1 mm on the scale

c 10 cm³ of 2% sucrose solution measured out using a 1 cm³ syringe, scale graduations of 0.1 cm³

   d the change in temperature of calorimeter using a thermometer, scale graduations of 0.5 °C. Start temperature 17 °C, finish temperature 64 °C

   e a 27.3 s time assuming that human reaction time error is 0.1 s.

3 Percentage error is often used in a different way when placed on clinical equipment. People with diabetes need to constantly monitor blood sugar levels. This can be done using several methods, such as:

- Using urine dip sticks (shown in Figure 14.3). These use two different enzymes to produce a brown colour that will change in intensity according to the concentration of glucose.

Urine glucose dip stick

Negative	Cyan	Light green	Dark green	Light brown	Dark brown
	1.0	2.5	5.0	10.0	20.0 mg cm^{-3}

Figure 14.3 Reference chart for urine glucose dip stick.

- Using a blood glucose concentration monitor. These use the same enzyme but also generate a measurable electric current.

   a Use your knowledge of the enzymes in dip sticks to draw out and complete the flow chart in Figure 14.4 to show how the colour changes in the dip sticks occur.

Figure 14.4 Flow chart showing how the enzymes in glucose urine dip sticks produce a brown colour.

   b Describe whether the dip stick test for the presence of glucose in urine is a quantitative, semi-quantitative or qualitative test. Explain why it could not be used to predict or detect hypoglycaemia.

Blood glucose monitors offer a more quantitative method of measuring blood glucose concentration. The glucose monitors detect the glucose concentration in the blood at a particular time and can identify low as well as high concentrations. There are many different brands available which have varying levels of accuracy (which depend on how the skill of the user and the sensitivity of the equipment). In 2013, the International Organization for Standardization (ISO) set the following guidelines for the accuracy of blood glucose monitors:

- accurate to within ±0.15 mg cm^{-3} at concentrations of under 1 mg cm^{-3}
- accurate to within ±20% at concentrations of 1 mg cm^{-3} or more.

   c Use the guidelines to calculate the maximum acceptable range and percentage error of blood glucose concentration from a reading of 0.55 mg cm^{-3}.

   d Use the guidelines to calculate the maximum acceptable range of readings for blood glucose concentrations from a reading of 1.25 mg cm^{-3}.

   e Suggest why it is important for people with type 1 insulin-dependent diabetes to consider the accuracy of the blood glucose monitors when injecting insulin.

   f Blood glucose concentrations are often screened to identify those who have diabetes and those who are at risk of developing diabetes. Those who show elevated blood glucose concentrations but are not full diabetics are classed as prediabetics or are said to be suffering from prediabetes. If untreated, prediabetes will often develop into type 2 diabetes. Two measures of blood glucose are carried out:

- The fasting test. Blood glucose concentrations after 24 hours of fasting are measured.
- Oral blood glucose tolerance test. The patient is given a measured dose of glucose and blood glucose concentrations are tested after two hours.

Figure 14.5 shows the recommended guidelines on blood glucose concentrations used to classify a person as having diabetes, prediabetes or neither.

	A1C / per cent	Fasting plasma glucose / mg cm^{-3}	Oral glucose tolerance test / mg cm^{-3}
Diabetes	6.5 or above	1.26 or above	2.00
Prediabetes	5.7 to 6.4	1.00 to 1.25	1.40 to 1.99
Normal	About 5	0.99 or below	1.39 or below

Figure 14.5 Blood glucose concentrations that enable classification of diabetic, prediabetic or normal patients. The higher the test result, the higher the risk of diabetes.

i Suggest why both tests are carried out.

ii Evaluate the ISO guidelines on blood glucose monitor accuracy when used to identify diabetic and prediabetic patients.

g A further test for diabetes is a test called the A1C test. This test is based on the attachment of glucose to haemoglobin. In the body, red blood cells are constantly forming and dying, but typically they live for about three months. The A1C test reflects the average of a person's blood glucose levels over the past three months. The A1C test result is reported as a percentage. The higher the percentage, the higher a person's blood glucose levels have been. A normal A1C level is below 5.7%. Figure 14.5 shows the typical A1C test results for normal, prediabetic and diabetic patients.

Figure 14.6 shows the fluctuations in blood glucose concentration of a diabetic patient over one week and the A1C value. Use the data to evaluate how effective the A1C test would be in identifying patients with prediabetes.

Figure 14.6 Fluctuations in blood glucose concentration of a prediabetic patient and A1C value of same patient.

Exercise 14.4 Stomatal opening in plants

Plants open and close their stomata in response to a variety of factors, including light intensity, humidity, water stress and high carbon dioxide. This exercise should help you to understand how plants open and close their stomata, understand the difference between the **mean**, **median** and **mode**, and appreciate the use of the **interquartile range**.

1 Plants often open and close their stomata in a rhythmic pattern that persists for a while if the light/dark pattern is stopped. An experiment was carried out into the natural rhythm of stomatal opening in *Tradescantia* sp. plants. The plants were illuminated daily from 06:00 hours until 18:00 hours and then placed in darkness from 18:00 hours until 06:00 hours the next day. This cycle was continued for two weeks. Each day at 13:00 hours, over 80% of stomata were found to be open on leaves, and at 00:00 hours fewer than 5% of stomata were found to be open. After continuing the cycle of light and dark for two weeks, the plants were placed into complete darkness and the percentage of stomata open determined at 12:00 hours 24 hours later and then again 48 hours later. The results for 50 different leaves are shown below.

Percentage of stomata open at 12:00 hours after 24 hours	Percentage of stomata open at 12:00 hours after 48 hours
54, 56, 58, 59, 58, 62, 62, 61, 63, 64, 65, 67, 68, 68, 67, 69, 67, 68, 68, 70, 73, 72, 71, 72, 71, 71, 73, 74, 73, 75, 74, 73, 74, 75, 78, 76, 78, 77, 78, 79, 78, 79, 78, 81, 84, 82, 83, 83, 87, 89	44, 44, 48, 48, 49, 49, 49, 49, 51, 51, 51, 52, 52, 52, 52, 52, 53, 54, 56, 56, 57, 57, 57, 58, 58, 58, 58, 59, 59, 59, 60, 61, 61, 61, 61, 62, 62, 63, 63, 64, 64, 66, 67, 68, 68, 69, 69, 69, 73, 74

We can plot frequency distributions to compare the two sets of data. First, select suitable intervals; for this, intervals of 5% are ideal. The table below is a frequency table for the data. It has been completed for percentage of stomata open after 24 hours.

a Copy out and complete the table by writing down the frequencies of the different percentages of stomata open after 48 hours.

Range	Number of leaves after 24 hours	Number of leaves after 48 hours
≤45	0	
46–50	0	
51–55	1	
56–60	4	
61–65	6	
66–70	9	
71–75	14	
76–80	9	
81–85	5	
≥86	2	

To represent these data, we can plot a histogram. A histogram can be plotted when both axes have continuous variables, as opposed to a bar chart which is plotted when one axis has categorical data.

165

TIP

Remember:

Histograms have bars that touch.

Bar charts have gaps between the bars.

To plot the histogram, write down the intervals on the *x*-axis, as shown in Figure 14.7, and label the *x*-axis 'Percentage of stomata that are open / %'. The *y*-axis is the frequency of each group – label this axis 'Frequency'.

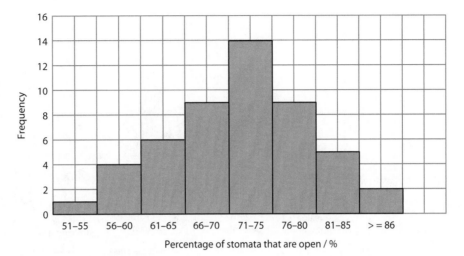

Figure 14.7 Histogram showing the frequency of leaves with different percentages of stomata open.

    b   Plot a histogram to show the frequency of stomata open after 48 hours.

    c   Calculate the mean number of stomata open after 24 hours and 48 hours.

Sometimes means do not tell the whole story and it is useful to determine the median (middle value) and modal class (most frequent group).

Follow the following steps to calculate the median value:

Step 1   Arrange the raw data in order of smallest to largest. For the percentage of stomata open after 24 hours, this is:

            54, 56, 58, 58, 59, 61, 62, 62, 63, 64, 65, 67, 67, 67, 68, 68, 68, 68, 69, 70, 71, 71, 71, 72, 72, 73, 73, 73, 73, 74, 74, 74, 75, 75, 76, 77, 78, 78, 78, 78, 78, 79, 79, 81, 82, 83, 83, 84, 87, 89

Step 2   If there are an odd number of values, the median is the middle value. If there are an even number of values, the median is the mean of the two middle values.

In the data for percentage of stomata open after 24 hours, there are 50 values. The median will be the mean of the 25th and 26th values:

$$(72\% + 73\%) \div 2 = 72.5\%$$

    d   Now calculate the median of the percentage of stomata open after 48 hours.

The mode is the most frequent number from the raw data, which for the percentage of stomata open after 24 hours is: 78%.

The true mode is not always as useful as the modal class, which is the range on the histogram that has the highest frequency. Figure 14.7 shows that for the percentage of stomata open after 24 hours, this is: 71–75%.

    e   Calculate the mode and modal class for the percentage of stomata that are open after 48 hours.

Sometimes it is helpful to look at the interquartile ranges. This is the range of your data into which the middle 50% of your data fall and so ignores the extreme values. This is shown in Figure 14.8.

Figure 14.8 Frequency distribution showing the interquartile range.

To calculate the interquartile ranges we need to calculate the first quartile, Q_1 and the third quartile, Q_3, as shown in Figure 14.8. Do this as follows:

- Determine the median value and n, the number of values there are.
- The first quartile point will be value $(n + 1) \div 4$, the second quartile will be value $(n + 1) \div 2$, the third quartile will be $3(n + 1) \div 4$ and the final 100% quartile will be at n. If the value for the first and third interquartiles are not whole numbers, we again take a mean of the higher and lower number.

For the percentage of stomata open after 24 hours:

$$\text{Median} = \text{mean of the 12th and 13th value; } 72.5\%$$

The first quartile value, $Q_1 = (n + 1) \div 4 = (50 + 1) \div 4 = 12.75$. This means that the first quartile, Q_1 will be the mean of value 12 and 13.

$$Q_1 = (67 + 67) \div 2 = 67\%$$

The third quartile value, $Q_3 = 3(n + 1) \div 3 = 3(50 + 1) \div 4 = 38.25$. This means that the third quartile, Q_3 will be the mean of values 38 and 39.

$$Q_3 = (78 + 78) \div 2 = 78\%$$

Our interquartile range is thus $78\% - 67\% = 11\%$. This means that 50% of our values for percentage of stomata open after 24 hours are between 67% and 78%.

- **f** Calculate the interquartile range for the number of stomata open after 48 hours.
- **g** Compare the percentage of stomata open at 12:00 hours after 24 hours with the percentage of stomata open after 48 hours. Use the means, medians, modal classes and interquartile ranges in order to suggest what conclusions can be made from these data.

Exam-style questions

1 **a** Explain what is meant by the term *homeostasis* and outline why it is important to living organisms, using specific examples. [5]

   b A student carried out an investigation into the effect of drinking iced water on the skin and core body temperature. They measured the skin and core body temperature, consumed 250 g of iced water and then monitored the temperature continuously using electronic temperature probes for 35 minutes. The results are shown in Figure 14.9.

Figure 14.9 Change in skin and core temperature after drinking iced water.

   i   Compare the effects of the iced water on the core and skin temperatures. [3]
   iii Using your knowledge of **thermoregulation**, explain the changes in core and skin temperatures. [6]

[Total marks: 14]

2 Figure 14.10 shows the effect of increasing intensity of exercise on the muscle, core body and skin temperature.

Figure 14.10 Graph showing effects of exercise on skin, core and muscle temperature.

a **i** Describe and explain the effect of increasing intensity on the temperature of the muscles and core blood temperature. [4]

ii Suggest and describe an explanation for the effect of increasing exercise on skin temperature. [4]

b After exercise, athletes often take a cold shower to cool down. An experiment was carried out into the effect of water temperature of a shower on core body temperature. Athletes exercised and then took a shower for 10 minutes. Three different athletes were exposed to different temperatures of water in the shower. The core body temperature was measured every two minutes during the shower and for 10 minutes after. The results are shown in the table below.

Temperature of shower water / °C	Core body temperature / °C										
	0 min	2 min	4 min	6 min	8 min	10 min	12 min	14 min	16 min	18 min	20 min
4	39.5	39.4	38.9	38.5	38.4	38.5	38.7	38.9	38.5	38.3	38.1
12	41.2	40.9	40.4	39.8	39.7	38.7	38.6	38.4	38.3	38.1	37.9
16	42.1	41.1	40.5	39.7	38.5	38.5	38.5	38.2	38.1	37.8	37.6

i State the independent variable. [1]

ii Suggest two variables that should have been controlled. [1]

iii Explain whether a reliable conclusion could be drawn from the experiment. [2]

iv Compare the effect of different shower temperatures on the cooling of the athletes' core body temperature. [3]

v Suggest and explain a reason for the effect of shower temperature of 4 °C on the core body temperature. [3]

[Total: 18 marks]

3 Figure 14.11 shows a diagram of the renal capsule.

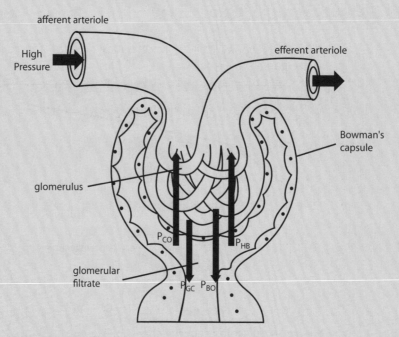

Figure 14.11 Diagram of the renal capsule showing the pressures that bring about ultrafiltration.

Ultrafiltration pressure is the net force that moves the filtrate from the glomerular **capillaries** into the **Bowman's capsule**. It is calculated using the following equation:

(P_F) Filtration pressure = (hydrostatic glomerular capillary pressure (P_{GC}) + Bowman's capsule oncotic pressure (P_{BO})) – (capillary oncotic pressure (P_{CO}) + hydrostatic Bowman's capsule pressure (P_{HB}))

a **i** The following pressures were determined for a normally functioning kidney:

$P_{GC} = 8.0$ kPa, $P_{BO} = 0.0$ kPa, $P_{CO} = 3.8$, $P_{HB} = 2.0$ kPa

Use these pressures to determine the filtration pressure, P_F. [1]

ii Oncotic pressure is the pressure exerted by proteins in the plasma or filtrate attracting water towards them. Use your knowledge of the structure of the renal capsule to explain why the Bowman's capsule oncotic pressure, P_{BO} is 0. [2]

Under normal conditions, 625 cm³ of blood plasma enters the afferent **arteriole** every minute and 500 cm³ of blood plasma exits the **glomerulus** via the efferent arteriole.

iii Calculate the amount of filtrate produced in one day. [2]

b If hydrostatic blood pressure falls, the kidneys release an enzyme called renin which converts a plasma protein called angiotensinogen into a protein called angiotensin I. Angiotensin I is then converted by another enzyme called ACE into angiotensin II. Angiotensin II stimulates contraction of the circular muscles in the efferent arterioles of the glomerulus. This is shown in Figure 14.12.

Figure 14.12 Flowchart showing cascade leading to circular muscle contraction in efferent arterioles in response to low hydrostatic blood pressure.

i Suggest why a cascade of enzyme activation is used to generate active angiotensin II. [1]

ii ACE inhibitors are drugs used in the treatment of hypertension. Explain how ACE inhibitors result in reduced filtration rates. [3]

[Total: 9 marks]

4 A medical student was presented with three urine samples and several simple laboratory tests. The urine samples came from:

- a diabetic patient
- a patient identified as having prediabetes; the blood glucose level does not rise as high as a patient with full diabetes
- a patient with high blood pressure causing high levels of protein to be present in the urine.

The samples were not labelled and the student had to identify each one by carrying out a range of tests.

The student was also asked to determine the concentration of glucose in the urine of the diabetics.

a Describe how you could identify each urine sample using biochemical tests. Include all practical details.

The table below shows the relative concentrations of some substances in the regions of the nephron labelled **A**, **B**, **C** and **D** on Figure 14.13. [6]

Area of nephron	Relative concentration of substance compared to concentrations at position A			
	Protein	Glucose	**Urea**	Salt
A	1	1	1	1
B	0	1	50	45
C	0	0	175	125
D	0	0	500	295

Figure 14.13 Diagram of a nephron.

b Explain the changes in relative concentration of the substances as they pass through the nephron:

   i protein [3]

   ii glucose [3]

   iii urea and salt. [4]

c Explain in detail why the concentration of urea at **D** will be higher after exercising without drinking. [5]

[Total: 21 marks]

5 a Describe how mammals break down excess amino acids. [4]

b The **loop of Henle** is described as a **counter-current multiplier**. Explain the term *counter-current multiplier* and describe how the loop of Henle maximises the reabsorption of water. [7]

c Explain why sodium and potassium ions are required for the reabsorption of glucose by the cells of the proximal convoluted tubule. [4]

[Total: 15 marks]

6 Figure 14.14 shows the fluctuations in blood plasma insulin, glucagon and glucose concentrations over a 24 hour period in a human. The times that meals were taken are shown on the graph.

Figure 14.14 The fluctuations in the concentrations of blood plasma insulin, glucose and glucagon over a 24 hour period.

a Explain the changes in concentrations of blood glucose plasma insulin and plasma glucagon over the 24 hour period. [7]

b Figure 14.15 shows the changes in blood glucose concentration over a 24 hour period for three patients, **A**, **B** and **C**. One patient is normal, one suffers from diabetes and the third from undiagnosed prediabetes. Prediabetes is diagnosed where a patient is less able to control their blood glucose concentration than normal. It will often develop into full type 2 diabetes if left untreated.

Figure 14.15 Changes in blood glucose concentrations over a 24 hour period in a diabetic, prediabetic and normal patient.

i State which of the patients is most likely to be suffering from diabetes. Explain your answer. [1]

ii The patients were told to eat three meals during the 24 hour period. One patient also had a snack as well as the three meals. State which patient had an additional snack and state the approximate time that the snack was taken. [1]

iii Glucose undergoes **selective reabsorption** in the kidney. Figure 14.16 shows the effect of increasing blood glucose concentrations on the reabsorption and excretion of glucose into the urine.

Figure 14.16 Effect of blood plasma glucose concentration on the reabsorption and excretion of glucose.

Describe and explain the effect of increasing blood glucose concentration on glucose reabsorption and excretion. [4]

iv The patient suffering from diabetes and the patient with undiagnosed prediabetes were given sets of glucose dip sticks that identify the presence of glucose in urine. The dipsticks confirmed the diagnosis of diabetes in one patient but did not indicate any blood glucose regulation problems in the prediabetic patient. Use Figures 14.15 and 14.16 to explain these results. [3]

[Total: 16 marks]

7 Cobalt chloride paper is coloured blue when dry and turns pink when wet. It can be placed on the lower surface of a leaf and secured between two microscope slides as shown in Figure 14.17.

a i Explain why the cobalt chloride paper will turn from blue to pink on the lower surface of the leaf. [1]

ii Predict and explain the effect of increasing light intensity on the time taken for the cobalt chloride paper to turn from blue to pink. [2]

iii Figure 14.18 shows some laboratory apparatus. Plan a controlled investigation using a plant, cobalt chloride paper as shown in Figure 14.17 and the apparatus shown in Figure 14.18 to investigate the effect of light intensity on stomatal opening. [7]

Figure 14.17 Diagram showing position of cobalt chloride paper on leaves.

Figure 14.18 Apparatus that can be used to investigate the effect of light intensity on time taken for cobalt chloride paper to turn pink.

b Stomatal conductance is the amount of gas that can pass through the stomata and is a measure of stomatal opening or closing. Low conductance is the result of few stomata opening or narrow stomatal apertures.

Abscisic acid (ABA) is produced by plants that undergo water stress due to dehydration. Scientists carried out an experiment to investigate whether there is a correlation between the mass of ABA found in leaves and stomatal conductance.

The results from the leaves from 10 plants are shown in the table below.

Leaf number	ABA mass/ μg g^{-1} dry leaf	Rank$_1$, r_1	Stomatal conductance / arbitrary units	Rank$_2$, r_2	Difference in rank, D	D^2
1	6		17	8		
2	6		26	6		
3	2		65	1		
4	9		24	7		
5	12	2.0	4	9		
6	14	1.0	2	10		
7	8		27	5		
8	8		43	4		
9	4		56	3		
10	5		58	2		

  i   Formulate a null hypothesis for the relationship between mass of ABA and stomatal conductance.   [1]

  ii   Copy out the table and use it to calculate the Spearman's rank correlation coefficient for the results.   [3]

  iii

n	5	6	7	8	9	10	11	12	14	16
Critical value of r_s	1.00	0.89	0.79	0.76	0.68	0.65	0.60	0.54	0.51	0.51

Use the table above to determine whether or not there is a significant correlation between mass of ABA in the leaves and stomatal conductance. Explain your answer using the terms *probability* and *chance*.   [3]

[Total: 17 marks]

Chapter 15
Coordination

Chapter outline

The questions in this chapter cover the following topics:

- the ways in which mammals coordinate responses to internal and external stimuli
- the structure and function of neurones, including their roles in simple reflexes
- the roles of sensory receptor cells
- the transmission of nerve impulses
- the structure, function and roles of synapses
- the ultrastructure of striated muscle and how muscles contract in response to impulses from motor neurones
- the roles of hormones in controlling the human menstrual cycle, and the biological basis of the contraceptive pills
- how responses in plants, including the rapid response of the Venus fly trap, are controlled

Exercise 15.1 The nerve impulse

You need to understand the nature of the nerve impulse in detail. This includes how the resting potential is maintained, and how depolarisation and repolarisation occur. This exercise should help you to understand the roles of the different membrane proteins and how drugs and toxins interfere with them.

Figure 15.1 shows the potential difference across the membrane of a **neurone**, showing the resting potential and an **action potential**. There are several different types of membrane protein that generate both the **resting potential** and action potential.

Figure 15.1 An action potential.

1 **a** Copy out and complete the table below to show which membrane channels and proteins are active during the resting potential, **depolarisation** and **repolarisation** phases, and explain the direction of ion movement for each.

Membrane protein	Phase					
	Resting		Depolarisation		Repolarisation	
	Open / closed / active	Direction of ion movement	Open / closed / active	Direction of ion movement	Open / closed / active	Direction of ion movement
sodium channel	open	sodium ions enter neurone	open	sodium ions enter neurone	open	sodium ions enter neurone
potassium channel						
voltage gated sodium channel						
voltage gated potassium channel						
sodium–potassium exchange pump						

b There are many different drugs and neurotoxins that affect resting potentials and action potential generation. Ouabain is an inhibitor of the **sodium–potassium (Na⁺–K⁺) exchange pump**. It is a naturally occurring toxin made by *Acokanthera schimperi* plants in East Africa and was used to make poison darts. The African crested rat deliberately chews the roots and bark of the tree and smears its saliva onto especially absorbent fur on its back as a defence against predators.

Figure 15.2 shows a resting potential across a neurone membrane. Copy out and complete the graph to predict the effect of the application of ouabain on the resting potential. Explain the graph that you have sketched.

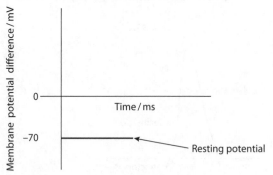

Figure 15.2 Resting potential in a neurone prior to the application of ouabain.

c Tetrodotoxin (TTX) is a neurotoxin that is produced by a wide variety of species including the pufferfish, *Takifugu* sp. It binds to **voltage gated sodium channels**, blocking their activity. The effects of poisoning due to consumption of the fish include loss of sensation in the mouth, difficulty in breathing and muscle paralysis.

Use your knowledge of action potentials to explain the effect of TTX.

Synapses are the junctions between neurones or between neurones and their target tissues such as skeletal muscle. You need to understand the **sequence** of events that occur at synapses.

2 a The table below shows the sequence of events beginning when an action potential reaches the **presynaptic terminal** of a **neuromuscular junction**. Place the events in the correct order.

A	Action potential arrives at presynaptic terminal.
B	**Acetylcholinesterase** enzyme digests acetylcholine in **synaptic cleft** and presynaptic membrane absorbs the products of the digestion.
C	Postsynaptic receptor / sodium channels open causing Na⁺ to diffuse into postsynaptic neurone.
D	Vesicles move towards the presynaptic membrane and fuse with it.
E	Ca²⁺ diffuses into the presynaptic terminal.
F	Acetylcholine (ACh) diffuses across the synaptic cleft and binds to postsynaptic receptors proteins in postsynaptic membrane.
G	**Acetylcholine** is released into the synaptic cleft.
H	If threshold voltage is reached, voltage gated sodium channels open resulting in action potential in **postsynaptic neurone.**
I	Voltage gated Ca²⁺ channels open.

Many questions in exams will give you examples of unfamiliar neurotoxins and drugs that act at synapses and ask you to work out the effects of them. You are not expected to learn the effects of every drug or toxin – you need to apply your knowledge of synapses to each situation.

b Curare is a toxin found in several South American plants including *Chondrodendron tomentosum*. It was used to make poison darts and arrow heads. α-Bungarotoxin is a toxin found in snake venom from the Taiwanese banded krait. Both toxins bind to and block the postsynaptic ACh receptors. This will prevent muscles from contracting, causing paralysis. Figure 15.3 shows the sites of action of several toxins, drugs and conditions on a neuromuscular junction.

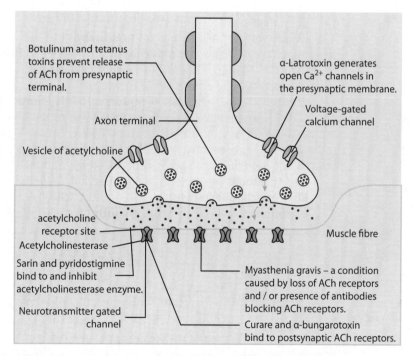

Figure 15.3 Sites of toxin action at neuromuscular junction.

Read the text below and predict explain the effects of these toxins:

i α-Latrotoxin is the venom found in the bite of the black widow spider. It generates a large number of open calcium channels in the presynaptic membrane. Predict and explain its effects.

ii Botulinum and tetanus toxins prevent fusion of vesicles with the presynaptic membrane. Predict and explain their effects.

   iii The nerve gas agent sarin and the drug pyridostigmine inhibit the action of the acetylcholinesterase enzyme in the synaptic cleft. Predict and explain their effects.

   iv Myasthenia gravis is a condition that causes muscle weakness. In some cases, there are fewer ACh receptors found on the postsynaptic membrane and in others, autoimmune antibodies bind to the ACh receptors. Explain why pyridostigmine is often used to help treat the condition.

   v Explain why pyridostigmine is often used to treat cases of curare and α–bungarotoxin poisoning but is not useful in cases of tetanus or botulinum poisoning.

Exercise 15.2 The use of technical language

It is very important to use language that is technically correct and is precise. You must be absolutely clear in your answers what you mean, give as much detail as possible and ensure that the standard is high enough. Do not expect the examiners to fill in things that you have missed – they can only give you credit for what you have written. This exercise looks at three different extended answers to show how important precision in writing is in order to gain maximum credit.

1 Mark the following essays using the attached mark scheme. The first is done for you as an example with comments.

   Question: Describe the events that occur at a neuromuscular junction after the stimulation of a motor neurone.

   [9]

Mark scheme

1 action potential / impulse / depolarisation arrives at presynaptic terminal / button / knob

2 (voltage gated) calcium / Ca^{2+} channels open

3 calcium / Ca^{2+} diffuses into the **presynaptic** neurone (only penalise once for Ca^+)

4 vesicles move towards **presynaptic** membrane and **fuse / bind**

5 acetylcholine is released into the **cleft / exocytosis**

6 (acetylcholine) diffuses across the cleft

7 (acetylcholine) binds with **receptors** on **postsynaptic membrane**; (must be membrane not just neurone) (only penalise once for wrong neurotransmitter / use of term neurotransmitter rather than acetylcholine)

8 sodium channels open in postsynaptic membrane / postsynaptic neurone

9 sodium diffuses into postsynaptic neurone / equivalent

10 if **threshold** / equivalent is reached, actions potential occurs / impulse is generated

11 **acetylcholinesterase** hydrolyses acetylcholine / ACh

12 **choline** is reabsorbed by **presynaptic** neurone / equivalent

---

Mp1

Not mp2 as Ca^+

Mp3

Mp6

Mp4

Mp5

Not mp7 as not receptors

Not mp12 as not in presynaptic neurone

Not mp10 as no ref to threshold

Not mp11 as no name of enzyme

An action potential arrives at the presynaptic terminal. The action potential opens voltage gated Ca^+ channels and Ca^+ diffuses through the membrane into the neurone. This causes vesicles to move towards the presynaptic membrane with which they fuse. When they fuse, acetylcholine is released into the cleft. It diffuses across the cleft and binds with the postsynaptic membrane causing sodium ions to diffuse into the neurone. This generates an action potential in the muscle cell. The acetylcholine is now broken down by enzymes and the products reabsorbed.

This extended answer would be awarded five marks. The candidate clearly knows the events that happen and would probably understand all the points on the mark scheme, but did not include sufficient detail and precision to gain all marks.

Now, have a go at marking these answers.

a

An impulse reaches the presynaptic terminal. This causes calcium channels to open and calcium ions move inside the presynaptic neurone. Calcium then enters the vesicles, which then move towards the end of the presynaptic neurone. The vesicles release the calcium into the cleft and it then diffuses into the postsynaptic membrane, generating an action potential.

b

An action potential reaches the end (terminal) of the presynaptic neurone. It opens voltage gated calcium channels so that calcium ions diffuse into the presynaptic neurone. Vesicles move towards the presynaptic membrane and release acetylcholine into the cleft. The acetylcholine then binds to ACh receptors on the postsynaptic neurone. Sodium channels in the postsynaptic membrane open and sodium ions floods in. If a threshold voltage is reached, voltage gated channels then open so that an action potential is generated in the postsynaptic neurone. Acetylcholine is then reabsorbed by the presynaptic membrane to stop it binding to the postsynaptic receptors.

c

An action potential arrives at the presynaptic terminal. This opens calcium channels, and calcium ions enter the presynaptic neurone. The calcium stimulates the vesicles to move towards the presynaptic membrane, fuse with it and release the neurotransmitter (acetylcholine or dopamine) into the cleft. The neurotransmitter binds with receptors in the postsynaptic membrane, which causes sodium channels to open leading to an inflow of sodium ions down their gradient. This inflow of sodium ions into the postsynaptic neurone generates an action potential. The enzyme acetylcholinesterase digests up the neurotransmitters and the choline is reabsorbed.

Exercise 15.3 The effect of auxin on root and shoot growth

Auxin hormones can have a range of effects on plant growth. In addition, different concentrations of auxins can have different growth effects on the same tissues. This exercise should help you to understand how auxins can inhibit and stimulate root and shoot growth at different concentrations and how we use logarithmic scales when there are variables that have very high ranges.

An experiment was carried out to investigate the concentration of auxin that generated the largest increase in root and shoot growth of tomato seedlings.

Tomato seedlings were grown in nutrient agar for five days. Different concentrations of auxin were added either to the nutrient agar, for root stimulation, or to the stem and leaves as spray. Growth of roots and shoots was measured after five days.

The results of the effects of the different concentrations of auxin on root and shoot growth are shown in the tables below.

Concentration of auxin applied / mg dm^{-3}	Log$_{10}$ concentration / mg dm^{-3}	Initial length of root / mm	Final length of root /mm	Ratio of final length / initial length
0.000001	−6	12	24	
0.000010		14	32	
0.000100		12	30	
0.001000		15	34	
0.010000		14	25	
0.100000		12	19	
1.000000		11	13	
10.000000		16	16	
100.000000		14	14	
1000.000000		12	12	

Concentration of auxin applied / mg dm^{-3}	Log$_{10}$ concentration / mg dm^{-3}	Initial length of shoot / mm	Final length of shoot / mm	Ratio of final length / initial length
0.000001	−6	17	17	
0.000010		16	16	
0.000100		17	17	
0.001000		14	15	
0.010000		18	27	
0.100000		21	82	
1.000000		23	90	
10.000000		17	87	
100.000000		18	32	
1000.000000		19	21	

The auxin concentrations used range from 0.000001 mg dm^{-3} to 1000 mg dm^{-3}. This is obviously a very large range, and if we wanted to plot a graph of this it would require a very long axis or some of the smallest increments would be cramped up together. The solution is to plot a graph using a logarithmic axis. This can be done by taking logarithms to base 10 of the concentrations.

Logarithms are calculated as follows: log$_{10}$ of a number is the power to which 10 is raised to obtain that number. For example:

The concentration 0.00001 is the same as 10^{-6}, so log$_{10}$ 0.00001 is −6.

You should be able to use your calculator to determine the log$_{10}$ values of numbers. How to do this will vary according to the make and model of calculator, but most will have a button labelled 'log'.

1 Use your calculator to determine the log$_{10}$ values of:

   a   0.00006

   b   12 000 000

   c   12

   d   0.0000325

   e   0.0025.

You should have found that the $\log_{10}$ values are numbers that are within a similar magnitude of each other and so could be plotted on a graph.

> **f** Now, copy out the tables and write down the $\log_{10}$ values for all the concentrations of auxin.

The mean growth of the roots and shoots is expressed as a ratio of the final length to initial length. A ratio of 1.0 would mean that the two values were the same, in other words the root or shoot had not grown at all.

For the root in auxin at a concentration of 0.000010 mg dm^{-3}, the ratio of final length to initial length is:

$$32 \text{ mm} \div 14 \text{ mm} = 2.3$$

> **g** Calculate the final length to initial length ratios for all the concentrations of auxin for the roots and shoots and enter them in your table.
>
> **h** Now we have got logarithms of the concentrations, we can now plot a graph to visualise the results. Follow the following steps to draw the graph:
>
> | | |
> |---|---|
> | **Step 1** | Label the x-axis: $\log_{10}$ concentration of auxin /mg dm^{-3}. Add a scale with even increments for each $\log_{10}$ value of concentration, starting at -6. |
> | **Step 2** | Label the y-axis ratio of final length / start length and add a continuous scale. |
> | **Step 3** | Plot your points for both root and shoot data, join the points for each and add a key. |
>
> **i** Compare the effect of increasing concentration of auxin on the roots and shoots.

To refer to concentrations of auxin used you will have to reconvert the $\log_{10}$ number back to a concentration. This is called the 'antilog' or 'inverse log' and should be easy to do on a calculator. For example, the antilog of -5 is 0.00001 (or 10^{-5}).

2 In a further experiment designed to identify the optimal concentration of auxin concentration for root and shoot elongation, different ranges of concentrations of auxins would be used. Explain what range of concentrations would be chosen for the root and shoot elongation experiments.

Exercise 15.4 The hormonal control of the human menstrual cycle

The human menstrual cycle is controlled by the interaction of four main hormones. The control is complex and you will need to have a strong understanding of it and apply it to different situations. This exercise will help you understand the events of the cycle, the functions of the hormones and the changes that contraceptive and fertility drugs bring about.

1 Figure 15.4 shows the stages leading up to and following ovulation in an ovary.

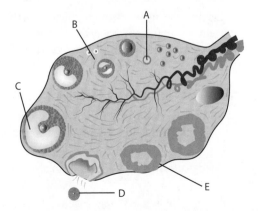

Figure 15.4 Diagram of ovary showing ovarian cycle.

Match up the labels below with the letters on the diagram:

- primary follicle
- gamete
- secondary follicle
- corpus luteum
- Graafian follicle.

2 You need to know the chemical nature of the hormones, the sites of production and effects of them. This is best summarised in a table.

The table below summarises the effects of **follicle stimulating hormone (FSH)**, **luteinising hormone (LH)**, **oestrogen** and **progesterone**.

Copy out the table and use the statements below to complete it.

Hormone	Chemical nature of hormone	Site of production	effects
FSH	protein	anterior pituitary	simulates follicle development. stimulates secretion of oestrogen from ovarian follicle
LH			
oestrogen			
progesterone			

- stimulates secretion of oestrogen from ovarian follicle
- steroid
- maintains uterine endometrium
- anterior pituitary
- stimulates follicle development
- corpus luteum
- stimulates ovulation
- ovarian follicle
- reduces production of FSH and LH by negative feedback
- stimulates secretion of progesterone and oestrogen from corpus luteum
- protein
- stimulates sudden rise in LH and LH prior to ovulation
- stimulates repair and development of uterine endometrium.

3 There are several drugs that can influence the production of the menstrual cycle hormones. These are often used either to enhance fertility or as a contraceptive. Looking at how these drugs work and at other factors that affect them can help you to understand the interactions between the hormones.

CLOMIPHENE CITRATE AND FERTILITY TREATMENT

a Some women produce low amounts of FSH. A drug called clomiphene citrate is used to boost FSH levels. It binds to and blocks oestrogen receptors, causing an increase in FSH and LH levels.

   i Use your knowledge of negative feedback to explain the rises in FSH and LH due to clomiphene citrate.

   ii Explain why the higher FSH and LH levels may increase the chance of pregnancy.

   iii Suggest why one of the side effects of clomiphene citrate is a thinner endometrial lining.

FSH, THE MENOPAUSE AND FERTILITY TREATMENT

b In vitro fertilisation (IVF) requires the production of a large number of eggs in order to improve the chances of a successful pregnancy. This is often achieved by injection of high daily doses of FSH. In early attempts at IVF, FSH and LH were purified from the urine of nuns who had passed through the menopause. Women who have passed through the menopause have constant high levels of FSH and LH, which are excreted in the urine.

    i Use your knowledge of negative feedback to explain why post-menopausal women are likely to have higher levels of FSH and LH.

    ii Explain why FSH must be injected rather than taken as an oral drug.

    iii Suggest why scientists collected the urine of nuns rather than other volunteers.

c Hormonal contraception uses synthetic steroid hormones to suppress the natural production of FSH and LH. Different forms of contraceptive pills and implants use different concentrations of oestrogen and progesterone.
Figure 15.5 shows the effect of the combined oestrogen and progesterone pill on FSH and LH levels.

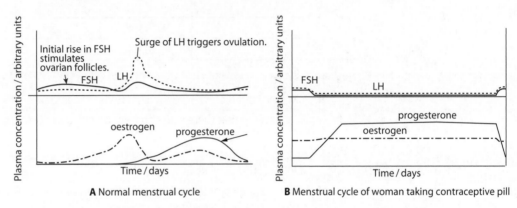

Figure 15.5 Plasma concentrations of FHS, LH, oestrogen and progesterone in **A** normal menstrual cycle and **B** woman taking contraceptive pill.

Use your knowledge of negative feedback to explain why the combined contraceptive pill reduces the chance of pregnancy.

183

Exam-style questions

1 The sea hare, *Aplysia*, has been used to investigate simple animal behaviours. It is a marine mollusc that has a protruding siphon and gill system for gas exchange, as shown in Figure 15.6. The siphon pumps water over the gills for gas exchange. Touching the siphon initiates a reflex arc that brings about the withdrawal of the gills.

Figure 15.6 Diagram of the sea hare, *Aplysia* showing the siphon withdrawal response.

An investigation was carried out into the effect of repeated touching of the siphon on the length of time the gills were withdrawn for. The siphon was touched with a paint brush and the time taken for the gills to fully open recorded. When the gills were fully open, the siphon was touched again. This was repeated for a total of 10 times. The results are shown in the table below.

Touch number	Rank, r_1	Time gill withdrawn / s	Rank, r_2	D	D^2
1	10	25	1		
2	9	15	2		
3	8	10			
4	7	8			
5	6	6			
6	5	4			
7	4	3			
8	3	2			
9	2	1			
10	1	3			

a **i** State the dependent variable. [1]

    ii Give two variables that would need to be standardised. [2]

b It was suggested that there was a correlation between the number of touches and the length of time that the siphon was withdrawn for.

    i State a null hypothesis for the association between number of touches of the siphon and gill withdrawal time. [1]

    ii Copy out and complete the table. Use the equation below to calculate the Spearman's rank correlation coefficient, r_s: [3]

$$r_s = 1 - \frac{6\Sigma D^2}{n^3 - n}$$

    where r_s is Spearman's rank correlation coefficient

    ΣD^2 is the sum of the differences between the ranks of the pairs

    n is the number of pairs of items in the sample.

    iii Use your calculated value for r_s and the critical values for r_s given below to evaluate your null hypothesis. Use the terms *probability* and *chance* in your answer. [3]

n	5	6	7	8	9	10	11	12	14	16
Critical value of r_s	1.00	0.89	0.79	0.76	0.68	0.65	0.60	0.54	0.51	0.51

c Plot a graph to show the effect of the number of trials on the withdrawal time of the gills. [3]

d *Aplysia* lives in areas of kelp forest that are inhabited by predators. Suggest reasons for the effect of repeatedly touching the siphon on gill withdrawal time. [2]

[Total: 15 marks]

2 Figure 15.7 shows the change in potential difference across the membrane of a neurone.

    a Explain how the membrane maintains the resting potential, labelled **A** in Figure 15.7. [3]

    b Explain how the membrane depolarises and repolarises over section **B** in Figure 15.7. [4]

Figure 15.7 Changes in the potential difference across a membrane during an action potential.

c Suggest and explain the effect of the application of a respiratory inhibitor on the resting potential. [2]

[Total: 9 marks]

3 Serotonin is a neurotransmitter that has several functions in the body. One of its functions is thought to be as a mood enhancer. Figure 15.8 shows a synapse in the CNS that uses serotonin. Prolonged stimulation of the postsynaptic neurone sends impulses to 'pleasure centres' in the brain.

Figure 15.8 Diagram showing action of serotonin at synapses.

a Describe how an impulse would be transferred from the presynaptic neurone to the postsynaptic neurone in Figure 15.8. [5]

b Some antidepressant drugs have a similar shape to serotonin but do not directly stimulate an action potential in the postsynaptic neurone. Use Figure 15.8 to suggest how they may work to improve mood. [3]

[Total: 8 marks]

4 a Figure 15.9 shows an electron micrograph of a muscle **sarcomere**.

i Calculate the length of the sarcomere labelled **A** in Figure 15.9. [2]

ii Use your answer to part **a i** to calculate the number of sarcomeres present if the muscle it was removed from had a length of 20 cm. [1]

Figure 15.9 Electron micrograph of skeletal muscle. Magnification: ×13 500.

iii Figure 15.10 shows a sarcomere from a relaxed muscle. Draw the sarcomere as it would appear in a fully contracted muscle, clearly labelling the **actin** and **myosin** filaments. [2]

Figure 15.10 Diagram of relaxed sarcomere.

b Figure 15.11 shows the maximum forces that a muscle is able to generate when contractions are initiated with sarcomeres of different starting lengths.

Figure 15.11 Effect of sarcomere length on force generated by a muscle.

i Describe the effect of changing length of sarcomere on the force generated by the muscle. [2]

ii Explain the effect of changing the initial length of the sarcomere on the maximum force generated by the muscle. [3]

[Total: 10 marks]

5 There are several distinct types of muscle fibre found within skeletal muscle, including type I, type IIa and type IIx fibres. The characteristics of each of these fibre types are shown in the table below.

A scientist made a hypothesis that type IIx fibres are mainly used for sprinting at high speed. Scientists investigated this by examining the percentage of skeletal muscles in different animals that were type IIx fibres and comparing it with the maximum sprint speed the animal is capable of. The results are shown in Figure 15.12.

Figure 15.12 Percentage of skeletal muscle fibres that are type IIx fibres in different animals.

a Explain whether the results in Figure 15.12 support the scientist's hypothesis. [3]

b This table shows some of the properties of the different muscle fibre types.

	Muscle fibre type	
	type I fibres	type IIx fibres
contraction time	slow	fast
resistance to fatigue	high	low
power produced	low	high
myoglobin presence	yes	no
capillary density	high	low
mitochondria density	high	low
major storage fuel	triglycerides	ATP, creatine phosphate

Use the information to explain why animals adapted for endurance running have a different muscle composition than animals adapted for sprinting. [5]

[Total: 8 marks]

6 A scientist carried out an experiment to investigate the roles of the different parts of a barley seed in germination. The scientist made three sterile starch agar plates and cut out two wells from each of them. The embryos were separated from the remainder of the seeds and both parts were sterilised. The following plates were set up:

- Plate A: embryo and remainder of seed
- Plate B: remainder of seed alone
- Plate C: embryo alone.

The plates were incubated at 37 °C for 24 hours, after which they were flooded with iodine solution. A clear, unstained area was seen around the remainder of the seed in plate A.

187

The results are shown in Figure 15.13.

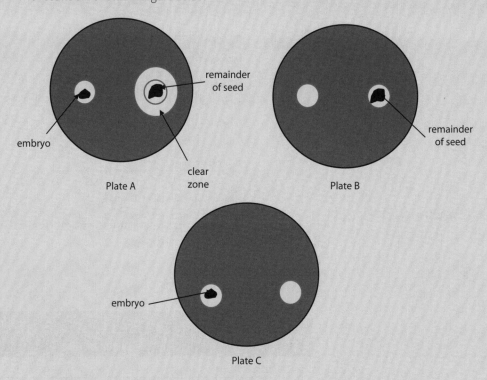

Figure 15.13 Effect of different parts of barley seeds on starch agar plate.

a **i** Explain why the starch agar plates and seeds were sterilised. [2]

ii Explain why the plates were flooded with iodine. [1]

b Use your knowledge of seed germination to explain the results shown in Figure 15.13. [5]

[Total: 8 marks]

7 Figure 15.14 shows the changes in reproductive hormones during a menstrual cycle that led to a pregnancy.

Figure 15.14 Graph showing levels of FSH, LH, oestrogen and progesterone before and immediately after pregnancy.

a **i** State the day at which ovulation occurred. [1]

ii Explain how the levels of progesterone and oestrogen from day 23 and onwards prevent another pregnancy. [3]

b Spermatogenesis and testosterone production in men is stimulated by FSH and LH. Use your knowledge of the regulation of hormones in the female menstrual cycle and the information in Figure 15.15 to explain why injection of extra testosterone can result in lower sperm production. [4]

Figure 15.15 Role of FSH and LH in production of sperm and testosterone in males.

[Total: 8 marks]

Extended answer questions

8 a Explain how the design of **myofibril** structure enables muscle contraction. [9]

b Describe the events that occur between the arrival of an impulse along a motor neurone and the initiation of muscle contraction. [6]

[Total: 15 marks]

9 a Describe how auxins bring about changes in plant growth. [9]

b Describe how a Venus fly trap is able to trap and digest insects. [6]

[Total: 15 marks]

Chapter outline

The questions in this chapter cover the following topics:

- the process of meiosis, and its importance in life cycles and in generating genetic variation
- solving genetics problems
- the chi-squared test
- mutations
- how gene expression is controlled

Exercise 16.1 Describing meiosis

This exercise tests your knowledge and understanding of the sequence of events in meiosis, and also how it compares with mitosis. You will need to think very carefully about some of the statements in part 4.

1 The second column in the chart below lists the different stages in meiosis. The statements in the third column describe some of the events that take place at different stages during meiosis.

Copy the columns. Write the numbers 1 to 8 in the first column, to show the sequence in which the stages take place.

Sequence	Name of stage	Events during this stage
	anaphase 1	Centromeres split and chromatids are pulled to the poles by the spindle fibres.
	metaphase 2	Chromatids arrive at the poles and nuclear membranes form around them.
	prophase 1	Pairs of homologous chromosomes line up on the equator of the spindle.
	telophase 1	Individual chromosomes, each made of a pair of chromatids joined at a centromere, line up on the equator of the spindle.
	prophase 2	Homologous chromosomes separate and are pulled to the poles by the spindle fibres.
	telophase 2	Homologous chromosomes form groups at either end of the cell; a nuclear membrane may form.
	metaphase 1	Chromosomes condense and become visible; the homologous chromosomes associate to form bivalents.
	anaphase 2	The nuclear membrane breaks down, and individual chromosomes are visible.

2 Draw a line from the name of each stage to the description of the events that take place during it.

3 In the 'Name of stage' column, add an asterisk, *, to any stages where crossing over can occur.

4 Copy the table below. For each statement, use a tick if the statement is true for a type of cell division, and a cross if it is not true.

Statement	Mitosis	Meiosis
can produce haploid cells from haploid cells		
can produce haploid cells from diploid cells		
can produce diploid cells from diploid cells		
can only take place in a cell with an even number of chromosomes		
produces genetically identical daughter cells		
involves independent assortment of chromosomes		
involves crossing over between chromatids of homologous chromosomes		
takes place in the formation of gametes		
takes place in gametes		
takes place in a zygote		

Exercise 16.2 Terms in genetics

Genetics has a very large number of specialist terms. You need to know and be able to use these correctly – and it helps if you can spell them correctly, too.

Each sentence below requires one or more genetic terms to complete it. Choose the terms from the list below, and then write out the complete sentence, highlighting the term or terms you have chosen. You may need to use some of the terms more than once. In some cases, you will need to use the plural form of the term.

allele   autosomal linkage   codominant   dominant   F1   F2
gene   genotype   heterozygous   homozygous   locus   multiple alleles
phenotype   recessive   sex linkage   test cross   X   Y

1 A chromosome is a length of DNA, containing a large number of .... , each of which codes for a particular protein. The position of each one on the chromosome is known as its ....

2 Homologous chromosomes have the same genes at the same .... However, the .... of the genes may not be the same.

3 Some genes are found on the part of the .... chromosome that does not have a matching length on the .... chromosome. Recessive alleles of these genes are more likely to show in the phenotype of male organisms than females, because there is only one copy of the allele present, and this is known as ....

4 In a diploid cell, there are two copies of each ...., whereas a haploid cell has only one copy.

5 The term .... is used to describe the characteristics of an organism, which are partly determined by its ....

6 A .... allele is one that only affects the phenotype if a .... allele of the same gene is not present.

7 When two parents are both .... but for different alleles, their resulting offspring are known as the .... generation. They all have a .... genotype. When these offspring are crossed, they produce the .... generation.

8 The term .... is used to describe two .... that both have an effect on the phenotype when they are present in a .... organism.

9 Some genes have three or more different forms, which are known as ....

10 When two genes are found close together on the same chromosome, other than a sex chromosome, they tend to be inherited together. This is known as ....

11 It is not possible to tell the genotype of an organism that has the phenotype produced by a dominant .... You can use a .... to determine its genotype.

Exercise 16.3 Answering questions involving a dihybrid cross

If you can feel confident about answering genetics problems, this is an excellent way to get a lot of marks fairly quickly on an exam question. But it is very important to have a reliable strategy for tackling a problem, and also to be meticulous in the way that you set out your answer.

Here's a straightforward genetics problem, involving a dihybrid cross.

The type of hair on a guinea pig is determined by two different genes, which are found on two different chromosomes. One gene, A/a, determines the length of hair, with the dominant allele A giving short hair and allele a giving long hair. The second gene, B/b, determines whether the hair is smooth or produces rough 'rosettes'. The dominant allele B produces rough hair, whereas b produces smooth hair.

1 Copy and complete this table:

genotype	phenotype
AABB	short hair, rough
AaBB	
aaBB	
AABb	
AaBb	
aaBb	
AAbb	
Aabb	
aabb	

Here are some tips to help you when you are working through genetics problems.

- If you are given particular symbols to use to represent alleles in a genetics question, you must use those symbols and not invent ones of your own.
- If you do need to invent your own symbols, you should choose one letter for each gene, and then use an upper case (capital) letter for the dominant allele and a lower case (small) letter for the recessive allele. Here, it would not be sensible to use S/s for the hair length gene, because it will be very difficult to tell the upper case and lower case letters apart when you are writing them.
- It's almost always a good idea to construct a table showing all the possible genotypes and phenotypes. Do this before you start answering the question itself – you can do it on a piece of rough paper, or in an empty space on the exam paper. You'll find it really helpful to have this to refer to as you work through the rest of the question.
- When you write down a dihybrid genotype, write the two alleles of one gene, followed by the two alleles of the second gene.

2. Construct a genetic diagram to predict the genotypes and phenotypes of the offspring produced by a cross between a short haired, smooth coated guinea pig that is heterozygous for the hair length gene, and a short haired, rough coated guinea pig that is heterozygous at both gene loci.

Try doing this yourself, then check your answer against the example below in Figure 16.1.

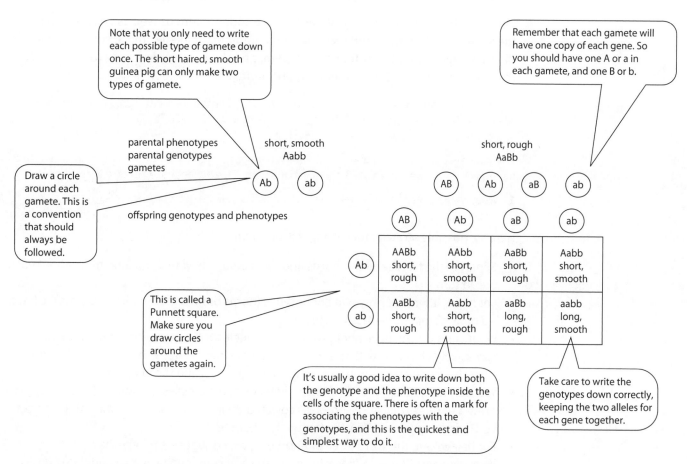

Figure 16.1 How to set out a genetic diagram.

3   What are the expected ratios of the different phenotypes in the offspring of this cross?

4   Eleven baby guinea pigs were produced from this cross. How many would you expect to have long hair and a smooth coat?

5   Imagine that you have a guinea pig with short, rough hair. You want to find out its genotype, which you can do by crossing it with another guinea pig and looking at the phenotypes of their offspring. This is called a **test cross**.

   a   What type of guinea pig would you cross your short haired, rough haired guinea pig with? Explain your choice.

   b   Explain how you would use the offspring phenotypes to work out the genotype of the short, rough haired parent. You might want to use a genetic diagram to help your explanation.

Exercise 16.4 Another dihybrid cross question

This cross involves one pair of alleles that are codominant, as well as another where the alleles are dominant and recessive. For codominant alleles, make sure that you use the same upper case letter for both of them, and then use superscripts to represent the different alleles. This problem requires quite a bit of detective work.

A bull without horns and with red hair was bred on several occasions with a cow with horns and white hair. Six calves were born. All the calves were roan (with a mixture of red hairs and white hairs). Two of the offspring had horns, and four did not.

The same bull was also bred many times with a different cow that did not have horns and had white hair. Seven calves were born. All of them had roan hair. Five did not have horns, and two had horns.

1   What were the genotypes of the bull and the two cows? Use genetic diagrams to explain your answers.

Here's a possible strategy for solving this problem:

• Separate the two features – horns and hair colour – in your mind, and think about each one in turn.
• For horns, there are only two phenotypes (horns or no horns), which suggests we have a simple dominant/recessive situation.
• What clues do you have about whether the allele for having horns is dominant or recessive? (The cross with the second cow is the most helpful for working this out.) Now choose suitable symbols for the allele for horns and the allele for no horns.
• You may find it helpful to draw little sketches of the crosses. So, for the first cross, draw a hornless bull and a hornless cow and their six calves. Sometimes, that can get you started on seeing how the feature is inherited.
• For hair colour, there are three phenotypes, which suggests that we have codominance. Choose a 'base' letter for the hair colour gene (e.g. C) and then choose two different letters to use as superscripts. For example, you could use C^R for the allele for red hair, and C^W for the allele for white hair.

- At the start of your answer, write down clearly what each of your symbols represents, e.g.:

C^R is the allele for red hair

- Now construct a table, like the one in Exercise 16.3.1, listing the nine possible genotypes and their phenotypes.
- Now go back to what you were told about the bull, the cows and their offspring. Can you work out any of their genotypes? Start with coat colour – it's always easy to work out genotypes where there is codominance. And where there is a dominant allele and a recessive allele, remember that you always know the genotype of an organism that shows the recessive characteristic.
- Sketch out genetic diagrams to see if your ideas work out. Lastly, draw fully complete genetic diagrams to answer the question.

Exercise 16.5 Autosomal linkage

When two genes are found on the same chromosome, they do not show independent assortment. Instead, the two genes are inherited together and are said to be linked. This is called autosomal linkage, to distinguish it from sex linkage (when a gene is found on a part of the X chromosome that does not have a homologous region on the Y chromosome).

1 A plant with red flowers and serrated leaves, which was heterozygous at both loci, was crossed with a plant with yellow flowers and smooth leaves.

   a By means of a genetic diagram, predict the ratios of phenotypes in the offspring from these two plants, assuming that the two genes are on different chromosomes. Use the symbols R/r for the flower colour gene, and T/t for the leaf shape gene.

   b Now, using the same symbols, construct a genetic diagram predicting the ratios of phenotypes if the two genes are close together on the same chromosome.

TIP

Remember:

- Always start by constructing a table showing all the possible genotypes and phenotypes.
- Then construct a complete genetic diagram, remembering to draw circles around the gametes.
- Finally, write a sentence summarising the expected ratios of the different phenotypes.

TIP

Remember:

- If two genes are on the same chromosome, they are linked. They are inherited together.
- We can tell which alleles are linked together by looking at the organism with the double recessive genotype. This one has the genotype rrtt, so we know that r and t are found together.
- The heterozygous parent has the genotype RrTt. The alleles r and t are linked together on one chromosome, and R and T are linked together on the other. Instead of the four kinds of gamete you should have shown in a, if the genes are linked like this they can make only the genotypes RT and rt.

Exercise 16.6 Linkage and crossing over

It's very rare for two genes to be completely linked. Almost always, crossing over between chromatids of the two homologous chromosomes happens during meiosis, so that some gametes are made with different combinations of alleles. This can give us unusual ratios of phenotypes.

1   In a species of insect, the allele for green body is dominant to the allele for brown body. The allele for long wings is dominant to the allele for short wings.

An insect with green body and long wings was crossed with an insect with brown body and short wings.

The offspring obtained were:

green body, long wings	132
green body, short wings	31
brown body, long wings	29
brown body, short wings	135

Construct a genetic diagram to explain the results of this cross.

> **TIP**
> - As we have offspring showing the features resulting from the recessive alleles, the green, long parent must be heterozygous at both loci.
> - You should recognise that this looks roughly like a 1 : 1 ratio of the two parental phenotypes (green and long, and brown and short), with a small number of 'different' phenotypes. The 'different' ones are called 'recombinants', because their combinations of features differ from those of their parents.
> - When you construct the genetic diagram, you should show all four possible gametes from the heterozygous parent, but indicate that two of them will be relatively rare (because they will only occur if crossing over takes place between the two gene loci).

Exercise 16.7 The chi-squared test

Genetics is all about chance, so we almost never get exactly the ratio of phenotypes that we predict. The chi-squared test allows us to determine whether the results we have obtained are a good fit for our ideas about the type of inheritance we are dealing with, or whether the results are so different that we need to come up with a different explanation for them.

1   Let's imagine we cross two plants, both with green stems and curly petals. The offspring we obtain are:

green stems, curly petals	121
green stems, straight petals	22
red stems, curly petals	23
red stems, straight petals	26

a Using the symbols G/g for stem colour, and P/p for petal shape, construct a genetic diagram to show that you would expect a 9 : 3 : 3 : 1 ratio of phenotypes in the offspring if these two genes are not linked.

b i Calculate the total number of offspring.

   ii Assuming a 9 : 3 : 3 : 1 phenotypic ratio, calculate the numbers of these offspring you would expect to show each phenotype.

We can see that the numbers of offspring with each phenotype don't quite match the results we would expect if the ratio is 9 : 3 : 3 : 1. But are they different enough to suggest that the genes are linked?

Let's assume that the genes are not linked. We can write our null hypothesis:

The genes for stem colour and petal shape are not linked.

The chi-squared test will tell us how likely it is that the difference between our observed results and the results we would expect if our hypothesis is correct is just due to chance – or whether the difference is so great that it is unlikely to be due to chance, and our hypothesis is wrong.

The formula for finding chi-squared is:

$$\chi^2 = \sum \frac{(O-E)^2}{E}$$

c Copy out this table:

Phenotypes	green, curly	green, straight	red, curly	red, straight
observed number (O)	121			
expected ratio	9 :	3 :	3 :	1
expected number (E)	108			
$O - E$	13			
$(O - E)^2$	169			
$\dfrac{(O - E)^2}{E}$	1.40			

   i   The cells for the green curly phenotype have already been completed. Complete the cells for the other three phenotypes.

   ii Use your answer to **i** to show that the value for chi-squared is 25.20.

Now we have to use this value to work out the **probability** that the difference between our observed results and the expected results is due to chance. This requires us to look at a table of chi-squared values, like this one:

Degrees of freedom	Probability that the differences between observed and expected results are due to chance			
	0.1	0.05	0.01	0.001
1	2.71	3.84	6.64	10.83
2	4.60	5.99	9.21	13.82
3	6.25	7.82	11.34	16.27
4	7.78	9.49	13.28	18.46

First of all, decide on the number of degrees of freedom in your data. You can calculate this using the formula:

$$v = c - 1$$

where v is the number of degrees of freedom
  c is the number of classes.

   iii Here the classes are the different phenotypes. Calculate the number of degrees of freedom.

   iv Looking along the row for this number of degrees of freedom, find the chi-squared value that most closely matches your calculated value.

You should find that there is no number anywhere near as large as yours. Our value of chi-squared is way off to the right of the table somewhere. This shows that the probability that the differences between the observed and expected values differ just by chance is much lower than 0.001.

In biology, we normally take a probability of 0.05 to be our cut-off point. If the probability is greater than 0.05, then we must accept that the differences between our observed and expected results could be due to chance. In other words, our hypothesis could be correct.

If the probability is less than 0.05, then it is extremely unlikely that the differences are due only to chance.

   v On this basis, what can you say about the null hypothesis that we used to calculate the expected results? Justify your answer.

2 Now work out this chi-squared problem for yourself.

A homozygous fish with a black stripe and a forked tail was crossed with a homozygous fish with a blue stripe and a smooth tail. All the offspring (the F1 generation) had black stripes and forked tails.

a Construct a genetic diagram to predict the results of crossing two of these offspring (the F2 generation). Remember to explain the symbols that you are using.

b The phenotypes in the F2 generation were as follows:

black stripe, forked tail   189
black stripe, smooth tail   52
blue stripe, forked tail   53
blue stripe, smooth tail   63

Suggest an explanation for these results.

c Construct a null hypothesis, and then use the chi-squared test to determine whether the results differ significantly from those you would expect from your hypothesis. Show all of your working.

TIP

For part c, it may seem odd to construct a null hypothesis that states that your suspected explanation is actually wrong! If you were right with your explanation, then the chi-squared test will indicate that your null hypothesis is wrong.

198

Exercise 16.8 Interacting genes

Quite frequently, one gene affects another. For example, one gene might encode an enzyme that is needed in order for a protein encoded by a second gene to be converted to a product. Without both of these genes being present, no product can be produced.

1 In horses, a gene E/e controls the production of the black pigment, eumelanin. Allele E causes the pigment to be produced, while allele e does not produce eumelanin.

A second gene, A/a, determines the distribution of black pigment in the coat. Allele A restricts the black colour to the mane, tail, ears and lower legs, with the rest of the body being brown. Allele a causes black pigment to be produced all over the body.

A horse that is brown with black mane, tail, ears and lower legs is said to be bay (see Figure 16.2). A horse that it brown all over is chestnut.

a Copy and complete this table.

genotype	phenotype
EEAA	bay
EEAa	
EEaa	
EeAA	
EeAa	
Eeaa	
eeAA	
eeAa	chestnut
eeaa	

Figure 16.2 A bay horse.

TIP

In part b, start off by writing down what you can work out about the genotype of the chestnut foal. Then think about how he got these alleles. Then work out the genotype of the black stallion.

b A bay mare was crossed with a black stallion. The foal was chestnut.

i What is the genotype of the black stallion? Explain your answer.

ii What are the two possible genotypes of the bay mare and the two possible genotypes of the chestnut foal? Explain your answer.

Exercise 16.9 Control of gene expression

The *lac* operon in *Escherichia coli* is one of the best-studied examples of how the expression of a gene is controlled. In this exercise, you will practise using the correct names for the various components of the operon and neighbouring DNA, and also describe how the process works.

1 The boxes below represent the various components that control the translation of the genes for β-galactosidase in the bacterium *Escherichia coli*.

a Copy the boxes, but arrange them as they are organised in the bacterial chromosome.

promoter for regulatory gene	β-galactosidase gene	operator

promoter for structural gene	regulatory gene

b Identify the component of the *lac* operon and neighbouring DNA with each of the following roles. Some components may fit more than one description:

i codes for mRNA that is used in the production of β-galactosidase

ii codes for mRNA that is used in the production of the *lac* repressor protein

iii is a binding site for the *lac* repressor protein

iv is a binding site for mRNA polymerase, which can then begin to transcribe the structural gene

v is a structural gene

vi is a binding site for mRNA polymerase, which can then begin to transcribe the regulatory gene.

c Explain what happens to cause the production of the enzyme β-galactosidase when the bacterium takes up lactose.

Exam-style questions

This question tests your knowledge and understanding of meiosis and gametogenesis in a flowering plant.

1 a The micrograph in Figure 16.3 shows a pollen mother cell in anaphase 1 of meiosis.

Figure 16.3 Pollen mother cell in anaphase 1.

   i   Name the type of microscope that was used to make this image. Explain your answer. [2]
   ii Identify the parts of the cell labelled **A** and **B**. [2]
   iii The structure labelled **C** is a chromosome. Describe what is happening to the chromosomes at this stage of meiosis. [2]

   b Figure 16.4 is a flow diagram showing the formation of pollen grains in an anther.

A pollen mother cell   **B**   **C** young pollen grains   **D** mature pollen grains

X   Y   Z

Figure 16.4 Pollen formation.

   i   For each of the cells, **A**, **B**, **C** and **D**, state whether the nuclei are 2*n* (diploid) or *n* (haploid). [2]
   ii For each of the arrows, **X**, **Y** and **Z**, state whether it represents mitosis, meiosis or neither. [2]

[Total: 10 marks]

2 Figure 16.5 shows the sex chromosomes of a male cat and a female cat. The alleles of a gene at a locus on the X chromosome are also shown.

Figure 16.5 Sex chromosomes of two cats.

This gene affects fur colour. Allele G produces ginger (reddish orange) fur, while allele g produces black fur.

In female cats, only one of the X chromosomes is functional in each cell. This is determined randomly in the early embryo, so if the cat is heterozygous at this gene locus, one of the X chromosomes is expressed in some groups of cells and the other X chromosome in others. This results in a cat with black and orange patches, a colour known as tortoiseshell.

a **i** State the phenotypes of the cats whose cells are shown in Figure 16.5. [1]

    ii Use a genetic diagram to show the expected ratio of colours in the offspring of a cross between the male cat and the female cat. [5]

b Another gene, found on one of the autosomes, also affects fur colour. The dominant allele W reduces the formation of cells that produce the pigments that give the fur its colour, so the cat is white.

A male cat with genotype X^gYWW is crossed with a female cat with genotype X^GX^gww.

State the colour or colours of their offspring. Explain your answer. [2]

c A third gene, with alleles T/t, codes for the production of tyrosinase.

Explain why a cat with the genotype tt is albino, no matter what genotype it has for other genes that affect coat colour. [4]

[Total: 12 marks]

3 Male pattern baldness is a condition in which hair is lost from the top of the head. This condition is at least partly caused by elevated levels of an enzyme called 5α-reductase, which converts testosterone to dihydrotestosterone (DHT).

DHT is a steroid that is transported in the blood to all cells of the body. Its receptor, the androgen receptor, is found in the cytoplasm of cells at the base of hair follicles. The androgen receptor is normally bound with proteins called heat shock proteins. When DHT is present, it binds with the androgen receptor, freeing this receptor from the heat shock proteins. The androgen receptor then moves to the nucleus and binds with specific DNA sequences that regulate gene expression. This in turn affects the production of proteins that are involved in the loss of hair, although the exact mechanism by which this happens is not yet understood.

a Name the substance described in the passage above that acts as a transcription factor. Explain your answer. [2]

b DHT is a steroid. Suggest why the androgen receptor is found in the cytoplasm and not in the cell surface membrane. [2]

c Finasteride is a drug whose molecules have a shape that is similar to the normal substrate of 5α-reductase.

This question begins with an example of sex linkage, involving just one gene locus – a monohybrid cross. Part **b** then moves on to consider how this gene interacts with another. You should be able to see a very quick and simple way to answer this part. The final part asks you to remember what you have learnt about the enzyme tyrosinase.

Despite all that has been learnt in recent years about the human genome, there is still a huge amount to be discovered about how our genes affect our phenotypes. Many bald men would love to be able to regrow their hair, and research is taking place to find drugs that might be able to achieve this. This question ranges across several different areas of the syllabus, including some topics that you learnt about in the AS year.

201

i Explain how finasteride could inhibit the production of DHT. [3]

ii Explain how this drug could prevent male pattern baldness. [3]

d Different forms of the gene that controls the production of the androgen receptor appear to be associated with the likelihood of developing male pattern baldness. A study was carried out in which the presence of an allele *Stu*I was determined in a sample of 552 men. Each of the men was also assessed for baldness. The results are shown in the 'observed' row in the table below.

The researchers used the chi-squared test to determine whether or not there was an association between baldness and the *Stu*I allele.

	Bald, *Stu*I present	Bald, *Stu*I absent	Not bald, *Stu*I present	Not bald, *Stu*I absent
observed	415	31	82	25
expected	138	138	138	138

i State the null hypothesis that was used to calculate the expected values. [1]

ii State the number of degrees of freedom in these data. [1]

iii The calculated value of chi-squared was 755.01.

Use the table below to explain how this value can be used to interpret the results obtained by the researchers.

Degrees of freedom	Probability that the differences between observed and expected results are due to chance			
	0.1	0.05	0.01	0.001
1	2.71	3.84	6.64	10.83
2	4.60	5.99	9.21	13.82
3	6.25	7.82	11.34	16.27
4	7.78	9.49	13.28	18.46

[4]

[Total: 16 marks]

4 Figure 16.6 shows a length of DNA in a bacterium that controls the production of the amino acid tryptophan. The structural genes code for enzymes that catalyse the synthesis of tryptophan.

You will have learnt about how the synthesis of enzymes that catalyse the metabolism of lactose is controlled in bacteria. In this question, you will need to apply what you have learnt in an unfamiliar context.

Figure 16.6 Bacterial DNA controlling tryptophan production.

When tryptophan is present, it binds to a repressor protein. This protein then allows the repressor protein to bind with the operator.

a Give the correct biological term for the length of DNA shown in Figure 16.6. [1]

b State the function of the regulatory gene in Figure 16.6. [1]

c With reference to Figure 16.6, explain how the presence of a large quantity of tryptophan in a cell will affect the production of more tryptophan. [3]

d Suggest the advantage of this control mechanism to the bacterium. [2]

e State whether the enzymes for the production of tryptophan are repressible or inducible enzymes. Explain your answer. [2]

[Total: 9 marks]

This question tests your understanding of the different types of mutation. You will also construct a genetic diagram for a dihybrid cross involving multiple alleles at one of the gene loci.

5 a New alleles arise by mutation. The mutation of a gene can involve insertion, deletion or substitution of a base pair in DNA.

Suggest explanations for each of the following facts:

i Gene mutation is most likely to take place during interphase of the cell cycle. [1]

ii Organisms that have inherited mutations from their parents are most likely to survive if the mutation involves either substitution or the insertion of three base pairs or multiple sets of three base pairs. [5]

b In humans, blood group is controlled by multiple alleles, for which the symbols I^A, I^B and I^O are used. Albinism is controlled by a recessive allele of a gene that determines the production of melanin.

i Suggest suitable symbols for the alleles of the gene that controls the production of melanin. [1]

ii A woman with blood group A and normal skin pigmentation, and a man with blood group B and normal skin pigmentation, had a child with blood group O and albinism.

Construct a genetic diagram to explain how this could happen. [5]

iii What is the chance that the couple's next child will also have blood group O and albinism? [1]

[Total: 13 marks]

Chapter outline

The questions in this chapter cover the following topics:

- the causes of variation, and why variation is important in selection
- using the *t*-test
- natural selection and selective breeding
- using the Hardy–Weinberg equations
- evolution and speciation

TIP

Remember: your answer should be to the same number of significant figures as, or one more than, the smallest number of significant figures in the raw data.

TIP

In the exam, you would not be asked to work through all of the calculations for a *t*-test. However, you could be asked to work through one or more steps in the calculation, so it is a good idea to know how to do each one. Another helpful point is that you will always be given the formula – you do not need to remember it.

Exercise 17.1 Using the *t*-test to analyse variation

In Chapter 5, Exercise 5.3, we looked at using tally counts to draw a bar chart. You will use that skill again here, to analyse two sets of measurements from two populations of plants. You will then go on to use a statistical test to determine whether there is a significant difference between the measurements for the two populations.

1 The leaf lengths of 30 plants belonging to the same species, growing in two different areas, were measured. These were the results. The lengths are in mm.

Area A

19, 12, 13, 13, 16, 18, 17, 16, 19, 17, 16, 18, 15, 17, 19, 18, 18, 18, 15, 17, 16, 14, 16, 18, 13, 17, 15, 21, 14, 14

Area B

29, 27, 24, 26, 30, 27, 23, 19, 26, 28, 25, 26, 30, 29, 29, 24, 25, 29, 12, 31, 26, 28, 22, 29, 17, 28, 23, 29, 30, 31

First, you are going to construct histograms to get a visual representation of the variation within each of these two populations.

    a Begin by looking at the complete range of lengths in each population – the spread between the smallest and largest lengths. Use this to decide how to group the lengths into around 10 different classes.

Next, make two tally charts to show the numbers of plants in each area with leaf lengths in each of your classes. Look back to Chapter 5, Exercise 5.3, if you are not sure how to do this.

    b Use your tally charts to construct a pair of histograms to display these results.

2 Use the raw results to calculate the mean leaf length for each population.

It looks as though these populations really are different from one another. However, when we look at the two histograms, we can see that there is overlap between the range of leaf lengths, which might make us question whether the difference between them really is significant. We can use the *t*-test to decide whether the difference between the means is significant or not. As for the chi-squared test, we need to construct a null hypothesis. This can be:

There is no significant difference between the mean leaf lengths of these two populations.

TIP

Look at Exercise 12.1 in Chapter 12 to remind yourself how to calculate standard deviation. If you have set up a spreadsheet, you could use that. If not, you could use a website to do the calculation quickly for you, or use a function on your calculator.

3 a Step 1   Calculate the standard deviation for the data sets for each area.

   Step 2   Substitute into the *t*-test formula:

$$t = \frac{|\bar{x}_1 - \bar{x}_2|}{\sqrt{\left(\dfrac{s_1^2}{n_1} + \dfrac{s_2^2}{n_2}\right)}}$$

where

t is the value of *t* that you will calculate

$\bar{x}_1$ is the mean for area A

$\bar{x}_2$ is the mean for area B

s_1 is the standard deviation for area A

s_2 is the standard deviation for area B

n_1 is the number of individual measurements in area A

n_2 is the number of individual measurements in area B.

   Step 3   Next, decide on the number of degrees of freedom in your data, using the formula:

$$v = n_1 + n_2 - 2$$

where *v* is the number of degrees of freedom.

   Step 4   Now, look at the table of probabilities (below) for different values of *t*. The numbers in the table cells are values of *t*.

You may remember, from the chi-squared test, that:

- The table gives you the probability that the difference between the results is due to chance rather than being a significant difference.
- We take a probability of 0.05 as our cut-off value.

When a value of *t* gives us a probability of greater than 0.05, we can say that the difference between the means is just due to chance. This leads us to the conclusion that the differences are not significant. In other words, our results support the null hypothesis.

However, if the value of *t* shows a probability of less than 0.05 that the difference between the means is due to chance, then we can say that there is a significant difference, and our two populations really are significantly different from one another. In other words, our results do not support the null hypothesis.

Degrees of freedom	Probability that the difference between the means is due to chance			
	0.10	0.05	0.01	0.001
15	1.75	2.13	2.95	4.07
20	1.73	2.09	2.85	3.85
30	1.70	2.04	2.75	3.65
>30	1.64	1.96	2.58	3.29

TIP

Remember to choose the row that is for the correct number of degrees of freedom.

   b Look up your calculated value of *t* in the probability values table.

   What can you say about the significance of the difference between the means for the populations in area A and area B?

205

Exercise 17.2 Answering questions about selection

Great care is needed when answering questions about how natural selection takes place. Examiners will be looking out for any language in an answer that suggests that you think the organisms might have changed 'on purpose' or in response to the selection pressure. It's very important to make absolutely clear that mutations happen by chance, and that selection acts on variation that is already in place, rather than causing new variants to emerge. You also need to take care over using the terms *gene* and *allele* – remember that an allele is a particular form of a gene.

1   Here are three answers to an examination question. Start by reading the question carefully – you might also like to try to answer it yourself. Then read each of the three answers, and comment on what has been done well and what is not so good about each one.

Question: Explain the role of natural selection in the evolution of antibiotic resistance in bacteria. [5]

Answer A

If a bacterium is exposed to an antibiotic, susceptible ones will die while those that can resist will survive. Mutation may arise, therefore the frequency of alleles may change. Some will become resistant due to mutation and some will not. This is due to selective advantages.

Answer B

Natural selection acts by exerting selection pressures on bacteria, which includes antibiotics. Increased selection pressures increase the chance that one or more bacteria might have genes that confer resistance to the antibiotics. These bacteria can reproduce with members of the same species. Therefore more antibiotic resistant strains are created.

Answer C

In a bacterial population, some individual bacteria will, by chance, have alleles that give them resistance against an antibiotic. These alleles will have arisen by mutation. Normally, these individuals have no better chance of survival than all the others, but when they are exposed to an antibiotic, the ones with the alleles for resistance have a better chance of survival. They are more likely to reproduce, while the ones without these alleles will die. So the next generation of bacteria will inherit the allele for resistance and, after a while, all the bacteria in the population will have this resistance allele.

Exercise 17.3 Using the Hardy–Weinberg equations

The Hardy–Weinberg equations enable us to work out the frequency of an allele in a population. Students most often have problems with this if they are not clear in their minds what the symbols used in the equations, p and q, stand for. And, of course, you also need to be able to substitute numbers in the two equations correctly, and manipulate the equations to help you to find out what you need to know.

The Hardy–Weinberg equations are two equations that we can use when a trait in a population is controlled by a gene with two alleles, where one allele is dominant and the other is recessive.

Imagine there is a population of animals where the length of ears is controlled by a gene with two alleles, **E** and **e**. Allele **E** is the dominant allele and gives long ears. Allele **e** gives short ears.

We can use the symbol p to represent the frequency of the dominant allele, in this case **E**. The 'frequency of E' means the proportion of all the alleles of the gene that are allele **E**.

Similarly, we can use the symbol q to represent the frequency of the recessive allele, in this case **e**.

> p is the frequency of the dominant allele.
> q is the frequency of the recessive allele.

The frequencies are expressed as decimal values:

- If every allele in the population is **E**, then p is 1.
- If no alleles in the population are **E**, then p is 0.
- If 50% of the alleles in the population are **E**, then p is 0.5.

Because there are only the two alleles, the frequencies of the two alleles together always add up to 1. So:

- If 50% of the alleles in the population are **E**, then the other 50% of the alleles must be **e**. So p is 0.5 and q is 0.5
- If 70% of the alleles in the population are **E**, then the other 30% must be **e**. So p is 0.7 and q is 0.3.

This is shown by the first of the two Hardy–Weinberg equations:

$$p + q = 1$$

Now let's think about the genotypes of the organisms in the population. There are three possible genotypes, **EE**, **Ee** or **ee**.

There are four possible ways in which an organism can inherit these alleles:

- The chance of an animal inheriting allele **E** from each parent is $p \times p$ or p^2.
- The chance of an animal inheriting allele **e** from each parent is $q \times q$ or q^2.
- The chance of an animal inheriting allele **E** from its father and allele **e** from its mother is $p \times q$, or pq.
- The chance of an animal inheriting allele **E** from its mother and allele **e** from its father is $p \times q$, or pq.

Overall, the frequency of all of these chances must add up to 1.

So we can write the second Hardy–Weinberg equation:

$$p^2 + 2pq + q^2 = 1$$

where
p^2 is the frequency of homozygous dominant genotypes
$2pq$ is the frequency of heterozygous genotypes
q^2 is the frequency of homozygous recessive genotypes.

Now let's look at how these two equations can be used. Here's a question to be answered:

In a population of animals, 18 animals out of every 100 have short ears. The other 82 have long ears. What is the frequency of heterozygous organisms in the population?

Because the allele for long ears is dominant, heterozygous organisms with the genotype **Ee**, and those with the genotype **EE,** all have long ears – we can't tell which is which. But we do know that the genotype of each of the short-eared animals is **ee**.

The frequency of the homozygous recessive genotypes is represented by q^2. So we can say that q^2 is 0.18.

From this, we can now work out the frequency of the recessive allele, **e**, which is represented by q:

$$q = \sqrt{0.18}$$
$$= 0.42$$

To answer the question, we need to know the frequency of the dominant allele, **E**. This is represented by p, and we know that $p + q = 1$.

$$p = 1 - q$$
$$= 1 - 0.42$$
$$= 0.58$$

We want to know the frequency of the heterozygous organisms in the population. This is represented by $2pq$:

$$2pq = 2 \times 0.42 \times 0.58 = 0.49$$

In other words, about 49% of the organisms in the population are heterozygous, with the genotype **Ee**.

Here's a question for you to try:

1 In a population of 350 woodlice, 22 animals are red-brown, while the rest are grey.

   Assuming that the allele for the production of grey pigment is dominant, and the allele for red-brown pigment is recessive, calculate:

   a the frequency of the allele for red-brown pigment in the population

   b the frequency of animals that are homozygous for the allele for grey pigment in the population.

Exercise 17.4 Assumptions when using the Hardy–Weinberg equations

The Hardy–Weinberg equations assume that the chances of inheriting the two different alleles are affected **only** by their relative frequencies in the population. In this exercise, we will use this principle to determine whether selection is acting against a particular genotype or allele.

The Hardy–Weinberg equations assume that the frequencies of alleles do not change from generation to generation. This will only happen if:

- there is no significant migration into the population, or emigration from it
- every organism in the population is equally likely to breed
- mating is random – that is, organisms do not 'choose' a mate by their phenotype, so organisms of either phenotype are equally likely to mate with each other
- new mutations do not occur
- the population is large.

Drongos are small, black birds that live in many tropical regions of the world. In a population of 1270 drongos, 15 albino birds were counted. It is known that the allele for albino colouration is recessive.

1 Use the Hardy–Weinberg equations to calculate the frequencies of the two alleles for colouration in this population.

2 a Two years later, a second survey of the same drongo population found that, out of 2654 individuals, 17 albino birds were counted.

Use your answers from **1** to calculate the number of albino birds that you would expect in this population.

b Name a statistical test that you could use to determine whether the observed number of albino birds in the population differs significantly from the expected number.

3 What do your answers to **1** and **2 a** suggest about selection pressures on the two phenotypes in the drongo population?

Exam-style questions

We generally think of selective breeding in relation to crops that are grown in fields, and farm animals, but selective breeding can also be used for trees to be harvested for timber. It is a very slow process for trees, as breeders may have to wait many years for the young trees to grow large enough to reproduce. In this question, you will think about how the discovery of the involvement of a gene for a desired characteristic could speed up the process of selective breeding.

1 Spruce trees, *Picea* sp., are grown for timber in North America. They are frequently damaged by a pest called the spruce budworm, which is a caterpillar that feeds on the needles (leaves) of the trees and can kill even mature trees. However, some spruce trees have varying degrees of natural resistance to the budworm.

a Outline how a selective breeding programme could be carried out to produce populations of spruce trees that are resistant to the spruce budworm. [5]

b Researchers have discovered a gene in white spruce, *Picea glauca*, whose expression is related to the degree of resistance to the budworm. The gene is present in all white spruce trees, but is expressed to different degrees. The degree of resistance to the budworm is passed on from parents to offspring.

Suggest why the gene is expressed to a greater extent in some individual spruce trees than others. [3]

c The gene codes for the enzyme β-glucosidase, which catalyses the cleavage of molecules of acetophenone sugars to produce compounds called piceol and pungenol, which are active against spruce budworm.

Figure 17.1 shows the results of tests to determine the concentration of these compounds in resistant and non-resistant spruce trees in June and August in 2010.

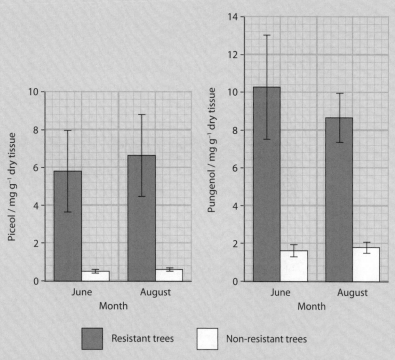

Figure 17.1 Piceol and pungenol concentrations in resistant and non-resistant spruce trees.

i   Compare the results for piceol and pungenol. [4]

ii Error bars are shown on the bar charts. Explain how the lengths of the error bars are determined, and what they indicate. [3]

iii Suggest how the discovery of this gene could enable faster development of strains of spruce tree that are resistant to spruce budworm. [2]

[Total: 17 marks]

> The reproductive barriers that keep similar species separated in the wild may be made up of many different components. This question asks you to describe and explain data about the possible isolating mechanisms that keep two closely related species of flowering plant separate from one another.

2   *Mimulus cardinalis* and *Mimulus lewisii* are two species of monkeyflower that grow in moist, streamside habitats in North America. *M. cardinalis* grows at altitudes between 0 and about 2000 m above sea level, and has red flowers that are pollinated by hummingbirds. *M. lewisii* grows at altitudes of about 1600 m to 3000 m, and has pink flowers that are pollinated by bumblebees.

Figure 17.2 shows these two species of monkeyflowers.

Figure 17.2 A *Mimulus cardinalis.* **B** *Mimulus lewisii.*

DNA analysis suggests that these two species are very closely related. They can be crossed artificially to produce fertile hybrids, but hybrids are only very rarely found in the wild.

a   Use the information above to suggest why hybrids of these two monkeyflowers are only rarely found in the wild. [3]

b   The fruits of these monkeyflowers contain large numbers of tiny seeds. Researchers grew both species in controlled conditions, and then pollinated the flowers either with pollen from their own species, or with pollen from the other species. The results are shown in the table.

Experiment number	Species from which pollen was taken	Species onto whose stigma the pollen was placed	Mean number of seeds contained in resulting fruits
1	*M. cardinalis*	*M. cardinalis*	2700
2	*M. lewisii*	*M. cardinalis*	1200
3	*M. cardinalis*	*M. lewisii*	800
4	*M. lewisii*	*M. lewisii*	1400

i   Use a suitable calculation to compare the number of seeds produced by *M. cardinalis* when pollinated with pollen from its own species and with pollen from *M. lewisii*. [2]

ii With reference to the data, suggest explanations for the difference between the number of seeds produced in experiments 2 and 3. [3]

c The researchers grew plants from the seeds obtained from experiments 1, 2, 3 and 4. They allowed the plants to grow to adulthood and flower. They then collected pollen from each of the plants and tested its fertility by determining whether it could germinate and produce pollen tubes.

The results are shown in Figure 17.3.

Figure 17.3 Bar chart showing pollen fertility.

Suggest explanations for the results shown in Figure 17.3. [3]

d With reference to all of the information provided in this question, list **three** isolating mechanisms between *M. cardinalis* and *M. lewisii*, and classify each one as pre-zygotic or post-zygotic. [3]

[Total: 14 marks]

3 Cone snails are predatory marine molluscs. Cone snails produce venom that paralyses their prey, making it easier for the snail to feed on them. In most species of cone snails, these venoms contain various neurotoxins. One of these neurotoxins is a protein that inhibits voltage dependent sodium ion channels.

a Suggest how this neurotoxin could paralyse the cone snail's prey. [4]

b In some species of cone snail, the venom also contains insulin.

All molluscs, including cone snails, produce insulin that has a different structure from vertebrate insulin. The molluscan-type insulin produced by cone snails is called con-ins G2.

Cone snails also produce a different type of insulin called con-ins G1.

Below are the amino acid sequences from the polypeptide chain A in con-ins G2, con-ins G1 and insulin from a zebra fish. Each letter stands for a different amino acid.

con-ins G2   T G Y K G I A C E C C Q H Y C T D Q E F I N Y C P P V T E S S S S S S A

con-ins G1   G V V E H C C H R P C S N A E F K K Y C

zebra fish   G I V E Q C C H K P C S I F E L Q N Y C N

i Compare the amino acid sequence for con-ins G1 with those for con-ins G2 and zebra fish insulin. [3]

ii The letter C stands for the amino acid cysteine. Disulfide bonds form between cysteine molecules.

Explain what the information in the table implies about the tertiary and quaternary structure of con-ins G1 and insulin from zebra fish. [3]

iii Discuss what the information in the amino acid sequences suggests about the closeness of the evolutionary relationship between molluscs and fish. [3]

This question requires you to use knowledge and understanding of facts and concepts from several different areas of the syllabus, including protein structure, the transmission of nerve impulses, the action of insulin and evolution by natural selection.

211

c In 2015, researchers discovered that the cone snail *Conus geographicus* releases con-ins G1 into the water when it is hunting fish. This causes hypoglycaemia in fish, so that they stop swimming and can more easily be captured by the cone snail. In contrast, other species of cone snails, which hunt worms and do not hunt fish, only produce con-ins G2, and do not produce con-ins G1.

Suggest how *C. geographicus* may have evolved from worm-hunting cone snails. [6]

[Total: 19 marks]

Extended answer questions

4 a Barriers to interbreeding between species can involve both pre-zygotic and post-zygotic isolating mechanisms.
Classify each of these barriers to interbreeding between two species of animals, **A** and **B**, as pre-zygotic or post-zygotic.
  i Species **A** and species **B** have different courtship displays.
  ii The sperm of species **A** have different glycoproteins in the cell surface membrane than species **B**.
  iii The chromosome numbers of species **A** and species **B** are different. [3]

b Outline how geographical isolation can result in the formation of a new species. [7]

c Explain, with reference to specific examples, the difference between stabilising and directional forces of natural selection. [5]

[Total: 15 marks]

5 Rice is a cereal crop that is grown for food in many countries. In the 1970s, the discovery of a mutant rice plant with short stems, broad dark green leaves and short, round grains led to the development of a dwarf variety called Daikoku. It was found that Daikoku was dwarf because it was completely insensitive to gibberellin. Gibberellin normally causes the expression of genes that are involved with stem elongation.

a Outline the advantages of growing dwarf varieties of cereals such as rice. [2]

b In the early 21st century, it was discovered that Daikoku contains a recessive allele of a gene, *gid1*, that codes for a protein that normally functions as a gibberellin receptor. This receptor, known as GID1, interacts with the rice DELLA protein. The protein coded for by *gid1* has one amino acid different from the protein coded for by the normal, dominant allele *GID1*.

Explain why a plant with two copies of *gid1* remains dwarf, even if treated with gibberellin. [7]

c Rice blast is a serious fungal disease that greatly reduces yields of rice. Some varieties of rice have some degree of natural resistance to rice blast. Suggest how a breeding programme could be carried out to produce a variety of rice that has the dwarf phenotype of Daikoku, and is also resistant to rice blast. [6]

[Total: 15 marks]

Chapter outline

TIP

All of the different species living in an area at the same time are known as a community.

Exercise 18.1 Collecting and analysing data on species richness and species diversity

Various techniques can be used to assess the number of different species in an area, and their relative abundance. This exercise will help you to decide on appropriate techniques to use in different contexts, and to analyse the data that are obtained.

One aspect of biodiversity is the number of species in an area and their relative **abundance**.

1   The table summarises some of the techniques that can be used to collect data on the number of species and their abundance in a defined area.

Technique	How it is used	Type of data collected	Notes
frame **quadrat**	Quadrats are placed randomly within a defined area. The species within the quadrat are identified and their relative abundance is assessed.	for animals and large plants including trees (which can be counted as individuals): numbers of each species in the quadrats for small plants (which often cannot be counted individually): percentage cover or abundance measured on an abundance scale (e.g. the Braun–Blanquet scale)	Appropriate sizes of quadrats need to be used, e.g. a quadrat with 10 m sides might be appropriate to assess trees in a forest, while a quadrat with 0.5 m sides would be appropriate on a rocky shore or in a grassy field.
line **transect**	A tape is placed on the ground to make a 'line', and the species touching the tape are recorded.	species present at different distances along the line	This is useful when you want to know how the species change as environmental factors change, e.g. from sunlight into shade.
belt transect	A tape is placed along the ground as for a line transect. Frame quadrats are then placed along the line, either continuously or at intervals (interrupted belt transect), and abundance assessed as for frame quadrats.	abundance of each species at different distances along the line	As for line transect, but more data are collected and assessment of relative abundance along the line is more reliable.

Decide which technique or techniques you could use in each of the following situations, and outline what you would do:

a You want to know whether the species of seaweed that grow on a rocky shore change as you go up the shore from mean sea level.

b You want to compare the species that grow around the edge of a rice field with those that grow around the edge of a wheat field.

2 We can use **Simpson's Index of Diversity** to calculate the species diversity of an area.

> **TIP**
> **Species richness** is simply the number of different species living in an area.
> **Species diversity** also takes into account the evenness of these species.
> Imagine two communities both containing 10 different species. In one community, nearly all the organisms are of just two of these species, while the other eight are rare. In the other community, numbers of all the different species are quite similar. This second community has a higher species diversity than the first.

Here are some data that a student collected from two different areas of grassland. The two areas were the same size, and the student used the same sized quadrats, and the same number of quadrats in each area. The quadrats were placed randomly.

Species	Number in area P, n	Number in area Q, n
A	282	310
B	141	103
C	376	292
D	0	49
E	132	2
F	21	0
G	210	14
H	63	1

> **TIP**
> Note that you do not actually need to identify the species by name to be able to calculate species diversity.

You are going to calculate Simpson's Index of Diversity for area P, and then for area Q.

The formula for calculating Simpson's Index is:

$$D = 1 - \left(\Sigma \left(\frac{n}{N} \right)^2 \right)$$

where
D = Simpson's Index of Diversity
n = the number of each species in the sample
N = the total number of organisms, of all species:

a Calculate the total number of organisms, N, found in area P.

b Calculate $\frac{n}{N}$ for each of the species in area P.

c Square each of your values of $\frac{n}{N}$.

d Add up all these squared values.

e Subtract your answer from 1.

f Repeat the calculation for area Q.

g Which area has the greater species diversity?

214

> **TIP**
>
> You may find it helpful to do steps **a** to **d** in this calculation in a chart or spreadsheet like this:
>
> | Species | n | $n \div N$ | $(n \div N)^2$ |
> |---------|-----|------------|----------------|
> | A | | | |
> | B, etc. | | | |
> | | | | |
> | Total | $N =$ | $\Sigma \left(\dfrac{n}{N}\right)^2 =$ | |

3 We can use the **mark–release–recapture** technique to estimate the population of a mobile animal.

To estimate the size of a woodlouse population, you could:

- Capture a fairly large number of woodlice, say 50.
- Mark each one with a small spot of non-toxic paint. Record the number of woodlice you have marked.
- Then release the woodlice where you found them, and leave them for long enough to mix back into the rest of the population – perhaps two or three days.
- Catch a second sample, and count the number of marked animals and the total number of animals caught.
- Calculate an estimate of the size of the whole population using the formula:

> **TIP**
>
> This is known as the Petersen or Lincoln index. An easy way to remember the formula is that you multiply the two largest numbers together and divide by the smallest one.

$$\text{Estimated size of population} = \frac{\substack{\text{number caught and marked} \\ \text{in first sample}} \times \substack{\text{total number in second} \\ \text{in second sample}}}{\text{number of marked animals in second sample}}$$

a A student caught and marked 62 woodlice. She released them, then caught a second sample two days later. There were 73 woodlice in the second sample, of which 9 were marked. Calculate the estimated number in the population.

b Suggest why this method gives us only an estimated number, not a true value for the population size.

Exercise 18.2 Using Pearson's linear correlation

In ecology, we often want to know if the distribution and abundance of a particular species correlates with that of another species, or with a particular biological factor such as light intensity. Pearson's linear correlation tells us if there is a linear correlation between the two variables.

> **TIP**
>
> Note that scatter graphs tend to be used when there is no independent variable. You do not have control over, or choose, values for either of the variables. You simply measure their values. It therefore does not matter which variable you put on which axis.

In Chapter 13, you practised using Spearman's rank correlation to determine whether there was a correlation between two continuous variables. This is also very useful in ecology. However, there is also another correlation test that we can use, if we think that there could be a linear correlation between the two variables.

When you are wondering about a possible correlation between two variables, it is a good idea to begin by drawing a scatter graph. The pattern of results on the graph can give you a good idea of whether or not the two variables may have a relationship with one another. Here are three examples:

In graph **A**, it doesn't look as though there is any relationship between the two variables. It is not worth doing any statistical test to look for a correlation.

In graph **B**, it looks as though the numbers of species P might be lower in high light intensities. There seems to be a **negative correlation**. If we drew a best fit line through the points, however, it probably would not be a straight line, but would be a curve. The relationship is not linear. We could use Spearman's rank correlation to test this relationship.

In graph **C**, it looks as though the numbers of species R and the numbers of species Q are related. If large numbers of species R are found, there are also large numbers of species Q. We could possibly draw a straight best fit line through these points. The relationship looks as though it might be a positive **linear correlation**. We could use Pearson's linear correlation test to decide whether this relationship exists.

Figure 18.1 Scatter graphs of pairs of variables.

Figure 18.2 Galls on a leaf of *Tilia* sp. Each gall is caused by an insect that lays an egg in the leaf. Substances in the egg affect cell division and differentiation in the leaf, causing it to produce these growths in which the insect egg develops.

1 A student wanted to know if the number of galls on a leaf was correlated with the surface area of the leaf. She collected 20 leaves from a lime tree. She measured the surface area of one side of each leaf, and counted the number of galls on the leaf.

    a Suggest the variables that the student should control when collecting the leaves for her study.

    b Suggest how the student could calculate the area of each leaf.

c   The table shows the student's results.

Leaf	Surface area / cm²	Number of galls
1	101	180
2	143	139
3	53	119
4	61	98
5	111	120
6	92	131
7	149	151
8	123	105
9	47	88
10	63	107
11	120	149
12	62	134
13	141	156
14	83	101
15	76	137
16	142	123
17	21	101
18	104	142
19	65	98
20	137	114

i   Plot a scatter graph to display these results.

ii Describe the relationship that there appears to be between these two variables.

The formula for Pearson's linear correlation is:

$$r = \frac{\sum xy - n\bar{x}\,\bar{y}}{n s_x s_y}$$

where

r = Pearson's correlation coefficient

x is the value of one variable (in this case, the surface area of the leaf)

y is the value of the other variable (in this case, the number of galls)

n is the number of readings (in this case, 20)

$\bar{x}$ is the mean value of x

$\bar{y}$ is the mean value of y

s_x is the standard deviation for the surface area of the leaf

s_y is the standard deviation for the number of galls.

TIP

You will not be expected to remember this formula, nor will you be asked to work through an entire calculation on an exam paper.

2   a   Construct a table like this, and complete it by filling in the values of x and y, and calculating xy for each pair of values. The first row has been done for you.

Leaf	Surface area / cm² x	Number of galls y	xy
1	101	180	18 180
2			
3			
4			
5			

i   Calculate Σxy by adding up all the values in the last column.

ii Calculate $\bar{x}$ and $\bar{y}$.

iii Calculate $n\overline{x}\,\overline{y}$.

iv Calculate s_x and s_y. (Use a calculator that can do this quickly for you, or input the numbers to a website or spreadsheet that will do the calculation.)

v Substitute your values into the formula, and calculate *r*.

vi Does your value of *r* suggest that there is a positive linear correlation between the surface area of the leaf and the number of galls?

Exercise 18.3 Answering structured questions about conservation

It's important to ensure that you write answers that will get you the very best marks possible, using the knowledge that you have. This exercise asks you to identify strong and weak points in three students' answers and then write an answer yourself that would get full marks.

Conservation can be an awkward subject on which to get full marks. The problem is often that students answer using general knowledge, rather than using specific knowledge that they have gained through the A level course. The trick is to show the examiner that you have studied this topic to A level, by using terminology, phrases and explanations that a non-biologist would not be able to use correctly.

1 Here is part of an examination question, worth four marks, about conserving gorillas. Read the question, and then each of the answers. Rank the answers according to which one you think is best and which is least good, and justify your ranking. Finally, try writing an answer yourself.

Question: The western lowland gorilla, *Gorilla gorilla*, lives in west central Africa. It is largely herbivorous, feeding on foliage and fruit that is rarely in short supply. This species is currently listed as endangered.

Explain how captive breeding programmes in zoos could help to protect the western lowland gorilla.

[4]

Student A

Breeding programmes in zoos help an endangered species by maintaining the animal alive so they can reproduce and produce offspring. They then take care of the offspring until they reproduce. Keeping them captive means they will not be harmed by outside enemies. They can be kept safe in a healthy environment, so that they can breed.

Student B

Captive breeding ensures the gorillas can continue to reproduce even when threatened in the wild. Zoos can ensure that the animals are healthy, which improves the chances of successful breeding. They could coordinate with one another to ensure that only unrelated gorillas are bred together to maximise genetic diversity. They could use reproductive techniques such as IVF, or use frozen embryo transfer, to increase the number of young gorillas produced. Eventually, the zoos would hope to be able to transfer some gorillas back to the wild to increase their numbers there, if their habitat can be made safe.

Student C

They can help as the gorillas are protected from any harm and competition with other animals. Competition for food will be non-existent as they can be given plenty of food and kept healthy. Reproduction can take place without danger for the young.

Exam-style questions

It is not easy to do controlled experiments in the field to investigate the effects of biodiversity. This question describes one such experiment that was carried out in the year 2000. You may need to read the information at the start of the question more than once in order to get a clear picture of exactly what the researchers did. Try making some sketches to help you to understand their method.

1 An investigation was carried out to investigate the hypothesis that a higher level of diversity in a community results in greater plant biomass.

The study was done in a grassy field that had been mowed regularly but never ploughed. Three plant species dominated the community:

- Kentucky blue grass, *Poa pratensis*
- wild strawberry, *Fragaria virginiana*
- dandelion, *Taraxacum officinale*.

The researchers cleared all the vegetation from 45 plots of 40 cm × 40 cm. They then planted a total of 14 plants from these three species in each of these plots, to achieve three levels of evenness in the species in the plot. Fifteen plots were planted, with the ratios of the different species as follows:

1.5 : 1 : 1   5 : 1 : 1   12 : 1 : 1

a The researchers used a diversity index to calculate the species evenness in each of the three types of plot. The diversity indices were 0.45, 0.61 and 0.96. Match these three diversity indices to the three different treatments. [1]

b Within each of the evenness treatments, five plots were planted with *Poa* as the dominant species, five with *Fragaria* as the dominant species and five with *Taraxacum* as the dominant species.

   i How many plants of the dominant species would be planted in a plot in which the ratio was 5 : 1 : 1? [1]

   ii Suggest **two** variables that the researchers should have tried to keep the same in all of the plots. [2]

c The above- and below-ground plant material was harvested from all 45 plots at the end of the growing season, and its biomass determined. The table below shows the results.

Diversity index (species evenness)	Total biomass / g per plot					
	Poa dominant		*Fragaria* dominant		*Taraxacum* dominant	
	Mean	SE	Mean	SE	Mean	SE
0.45	319.9	54.4	301.2	27.3	246.5	57.5
0.61	336.9	26.1	410.5	30.3	205.5	33.8
0.96	348.7	41.0	381.5	35.3	358.3	27.5

   i On graph paper, plot the results for the *Fragaria* dominant plots as a bar chart. [3]

   ii Use the values for standard error to show error bars on your bar chart. [2]

   iii Discuss the extent to which these results support or disprove the hypothesis that was being tested. [3]

[Total: 12 marks]

The design of captive breeding programmes for mammals requires good knowledge of the genetic diversity and physiology of the animals concerned. This question asks you to think about these issues in the context of an endangered small cat species.

2 The fishing cat, *Prionailurus viverrinus*, is a small cat that lives in wetland habitats in South and South-East Asia. Fishing cats are largely nocturnal and feed mainly on fish, which they catch by wading or swimming into water. They are classified by the IUCN, the International Union for Conservation of Nature, as an endangered species.

Figure 18.3 shows a fishing cat.

a **i** Suggest **two** reasons why fishing cats are endangered.   [2]

  ii Fishing cats are listed in Appendix 1 of CITES, the Convention on International Trade in Endangered Species.

    Explain how this can help in their conservation.   [2]

b Several zoos in North America keep fishing cats, and a captive breeding programme has begun. In 2006, there were a total of 71 fishing cats in these zoos, all bred from 8 founder animals imported from Asia. The genetic diversity of these 71 animals was 0.85, meaning that 85% of gene loci had more than one allele present in the population.

A computer model was used to predict how the genetic diversity of this population would change in the next 50 years, if breeding was restricted to these 71 animals and their offspring, or if new animals were imported from Asia. The model assumed that the maximum number of fishing cats that could be kept in zoos in North America would be 100. Figure 18.4 shows some of these predictions.

Figure 18.3 A fishing cat, *Prionailurus viverrinus.*

220

Figure 18.4 Results of modelling genetic diversity in captive fishing cats.

i With reference to the data in Figure 18.4, explain why it is important to continue to import fishing cats from elsewhere to add to the population in North American zoos. [5]

ii Suggest **one** reason why the importation of new animals to North American zoos might **not** be desirable. [1]

iii There is concern that genetic drift might lead to loss of genetic diversity in the remaining wild populations of fishing cats. Explain how this could occur. [3]

c Many species of small cats, including fishing cats, breed only once a year, and often have only small numbers of young. Assisted reproduction techniques such as embryo transfer could potentially increase the number of young cats that are born, and also help to maintain or increase genetic diversity.

i Outline how embryo transfer could potentially be used in a captive breeding programme for fishing cats. [5]

ii At present, scientists do not have detailed knowledge of the hormonal control of reproductive cycles in most small cat species. Suggest how this limits the use of assisted reproduction techniques for these animals. [3]

[Total: 21 marks]

> In Chapter 17, you practised using the *t*-test to compare the variation in two different populations, by testing for the significance of difference between their mean values. In this example, you will use the *t*-test again, but this time in an ecological context.

3 A student investigated whether the abundance of a plant species growing in a shady habitat was significantly different from that in a sunny habitat.

The student measured the area covered by the plant species, in cm², in each of 10 areas of 1 m² in the shady habitat, and another 10 areas of 1 m² in the sunny habitat.

a i What was the independent variable in this investigation? [1]

ii What was the dependent variable? [1]

b State a suitable null hypothesis for the student's investigation. [1]

c The student used random sampling in his survey. Explain what is meant by *random sampling*, and why it was important to use this method. [2]

d The results were as follows:

Area of ground (in cm²) covered by the plant in a 1 m² area:

shady habitat: 43, 52, 31, 61, 56, 47, 22, 42, 33, 40

sunny habitat: 54, 56, 32, 65, 23, 43, 59, 41, 45, 31

Calculate the mean area covered per m² in each habitat. [2]

e The student calculated the standard deviation, *s*, for the two samples:

s for the shady area = 11.945

s for the sunny area = 13.609

He used a *t*-test to determine whether the difference between the means of the two samples was significantly different.

i Explain why the *t*-test is a suitable statistical test to use for these data. [3]

ii The formula for the *t*-test is:

$$t = \frac{\left| \bar{x}_1 - \bar{x}_2 \right|}{\sqrt{\left(\dfrac{s_1^2}{n_1} + \dfrac{s_2^2}{n_2} \right)}}$$

where

t is the value of *t* that you will calculate

$\bar{x}_1$ is the mean for one sample

$\bar{x}_2$ is the mean for the other sample

221

s_1 is the standard deviation for one sample

s_2 is the standard deviation for the other sample

n_1 is the number of individual measurements in one sample

n_2 is the number of individual measurements in the other sample.

Calculate the value of t. Show your working. [3]

iii The table below shows the probability that chance could have produced a particular value of t for a range of degrees of freedom.

$$\text{degrees of freedom, } v = (n_1 - 1) + (n_2 - 1)$$

Use your value of t, and the table below, to decide whether the null hypothesis that you gave as your answer to **b** is supported or not. Explain your answer. [4]

Degrees of freedom	Probability that the difference between the means is due to chance			
	0.10	0.05	0.01	0.001
15	1.75	2.13	2.95	4.07
18	1.73	2.10	2.88	3.92
20	1.73	2.09	2.85	3.85
22	1.72	2.07	2.82	3.79
30	1.70	2.04	2.75	3.65
>30	1.64	1.96	2.58	3.29

[Total: 17 marks]

Extended answer questions

This is a relatively straightforward question about classification. Try to answer the question without looking up any facts.

4 **a** Explain what is meant by a taxonomic hierarchy, with reference to the classification system used for living organisms. [5]

b Outline the characteristic features of the domain Archaea. [5]

c Describe how viruses are classified, and explain why they are not included in any of the three domains. [5]

[Total: 15 marks]

5

The first part of this question requires some precise definitions of technical terms. By all means make use of what you have learnt by doing a similar investigation yourself, but take great care that you adapt your experience to fit the particular situation outlined in the question.

In the second part, you should aim to give a clear, simple but full account that someone else could follow to do the investigation. Don't forget to include a description of how you will record and analyse your results, and any calculations that you will carry out on them.

a Explain the meaning of the terms *ecosystem*, *niche* and *biodiversity*. [5]

b Describe how you could carry out an investigation to test the hypothesis that the abundance of limpets on a rocky shore shows a negative correlation with the abundance of seaweeds. [10]

[Total: 15 marks]

Notice that this question has three different command words, and make sure that you tailor your answers to match them. In particular, remember that 'discuss' means that you should include points from both sides of an argument. or from opposing viewpoints.

6 a Describe why it is important to attempt to maintain biodiversity. [5]

b Explain the roles of seed banks in protecting endangered species. [5]

c Discuss the use of culling in the conservation of protected species. [5]

[Total: 15 marks]

Chapter outline

The questions in this chapter cover the following topics:

- the principles of genetic technology
- bioinformatics
- screening for and treating genetic diseases
- GM crops
- social and ethical issues in genetic technology

Exercise 19.1 Choosing the right tools to analyse data

During your A level course, you have come across a number of different statistical tests and calculations that you can use to help you to make sense of data that have been collected. This exercise will help you to think about when you should use some of these calculations and tests.

When you plan an experiment, it is important to consider how you will analyse your results. You can then plan what data to collect, and how you will collect them, in order to allow you to use your chosen statistical test to interpret what the data mean.

In the examination, however, you may be given information about an investigation, and asked to suggest how you would analyse the results.

The table summarises some of the data analysis calculations that you have been using in your A level course.

Calculation	Criteria for using it	How to interpret the value you calculate	Notes
Lincoln / Petersen index (mark–release–recapture)	You want to estimate the size of a population of mobile animals. You can mark an animal without affecting its chances of survival. Marked animals mix randomly and fully into the rest of the population after release.	The value gives you an estimate of the size of a population.	The value is only an estimate; the only way to find the absolute number of organisms in a population is to count every one of them.
Simpson's Index of Diversity, D	You have collected quantitative data about the numbers of individuals belonging to the different species in an area.	The greater the value, the greater the species diversity (that is, the higher the number of species and the greater the evenness of their population sizes).	There are several different versions of the formula for Simpson's Index of Diversity; make sure you are familiar with the one in Chapter 18.

Calculation	Criteria for using it	How to interpret the value you calculate	Notes
Hardy–Weinberg equations	In a population, a gene has two alleles. There is random mating between organisms with different phenotypes. There is no significant immigration or emigration from the population. Each phenotype has an equal chance of survival (i.e. there is no selection against any of the phenotypes).	If you use the equations to calculate the frequency of a recessive allele in a population, you can then predict the proportion of people in the population who are likely to be carriers of that allele.	
Standard deviation, s	You have data that show a normal distribution. You want to know how much these data are spread on either side of the mean value.	The greater the standard deviation, the more widely the data are spread on either side of the mean.	
Standard error, S_M	You have data that show a normal distribution. You want to know how close the mean value is likely to be to the true mean – in other words, how likely it is that if you collected another set of data, the mean would be the same.	The greater the standard error, the less chance that a second set of data would give you exactly the same mean value. You can be 95% certain that the true mean lies with $2 \times$ the standard error either above or below your calculated mean. If this shows overlap between the possible true mean values of two sets of data, you cannot be sure that the true means are different.	Standard error can be used to draw error bars on graphs. These are usually drawn as vertical lines extending to $2 \times S_M$ above and below the data plot.
t-test	You have two sets of continuous, quantitative data. You have more than 10 but fewer than 30 readings in each set. Both sets of data come from populations with normal distributions. The standard deviations for the two data sets are similar.	Construct a null hypothesis, predicting that there is no significant difference between the two data sets. Determine the number of degrees of freedom in your data. Look up your calculated value of t in a table of probabilities. If the probability table tells you that the probability of your null hypothesis being correct (that is, the difference between the two populations being due to chance) is 0.05 or greater, then the null hypothesis is supported.	In general, the greater the value of t, the smaller the probability that the null hypothesis is correct. The value of 0.05 means that there is a 5% chance that the differences between the two data sets are due to chance. This is the critical value that is generally used in biology. If the value is less than 0.05, then we can reasonably assume that the differences are real, and not just due to chance.

Calculation	Criteria for using it	How to interpret the value you calculate	Notes
chi-squared test, χ^2	You have two or more sets of quantitative data, which belong to two or more discontinuous categories.	Construct a null hypothesis predicting that there is no significant difference between the observed and expected values. Determine the number of degrees of freedom in your data. Look up your calculated value of χ^2 in a table of probabilities. If the probability table tells you that the probability of your null hypothesis being correct (that is, the difference between the two populations being due to chance) is 0.05 or greater, then the null hypothesis is supported.	See notes on the *t*-test.
Spearman's rank correlation, r_s	You have collected data for two variables, both of which can be ranked. The samples for both sets of data have been collected randomly. You have at least 5 pairs of data, but preferably between 10 and 30. You have plotted a scatter graph, and it looks as though there may be a relationship between the two variables.	Values of r_s can lie anywhere between −1 and +1. A value of −1 indicates a perfect negative correlation, and +1 a perfect positive correlation. A value of 0 indicates no correlation. Use a correlation coefficient table to look up your value of r_s. If your value of r_s is greater than the value with a probability of 0.05, then you can say there is a significant correlation between the two variables.	Remember that correlation does not prove causation.
Pearson's linear correlation, r	You have two sets of interval data. You have at least 5 pairs of data, but preferably 10 or more. Both sets of data have an approximately normal distribution. You have plotted a scatter graph, and it looks as though there might be a linear correlation between the two variables.	Values of r can lie anywhere between −1 and +1. A value of −1 indicates a perfect negative correlation, and +1 a perfect positive correlation. A value of 0 indicates no correlation.	Remember that correlation does not prove causation.

TIP

Note that the table does not provide information about how to do the calculations. You can find guidance on this in earlier chapters in this book.

1 For each of these situations, decide which of the calculations in the table you might use. In some cases, you could use more than one.

a You want to know if the yield per plant from a variety of rape genetically modified for herbicide resistance is significantly different from the yield of a non-GM variety.

b You have counted the numbers of animals of every visible species in 10 quadrats placed randomly on a rocky shore.

c You know the percentage of children born each year with a genetic disease caused by a recessive allele. You want to know the frequency of that allele in the population.

d You want to know if the numbers of offspring obtained in a genetic cross are significantly different from the values you would expect from your predictions.

e You are using the mark–release–recapture technique for estimating the number of water boatmen in a pond.

f You have measured the test scores of all the members of the biology group who also study physics and also the test scores of all the members of the biology group who do not study physics. You are interested in finding out whether the true mean values for the scores of the physicists and non-physicists are likely to be different.

Exercise 19.2 Gene technology terminology

There are many technical terms associated with this topic. This exercise will help you to use each term appropriately.

1 Choose the term from the list that matches each description. If you find that you are not absolutely sure about any of them (even if you can guess the answer), this signals that you need to do a little more work on that topic.

bioinformatics	biopsy	DNA ligase	DNA microarray
gel electrophoresis	gene therapy	liposome	polymerase chain reaction (PCR)
primer	promoter	recombinant	restriction endonuclease
reverse transcriptase	*Taq* polymerase	vector	

a An enzyme used to cut DNA at a specific base sequence.

b An enzyme derived from bacteria that are adapted to live in hot water springs; the enzyme has a very high optimum temperature, and is used to synthesise new strands of DNA during PCR.

c An enzyme that catalyses the formation of bonds between phosphate groups and deoxyribose during the synthesis of DNA.

d An enzyme that produces complementary DNA strands using an RNA template.

e A length of DNA that controls the expression of a gene.

f A short length of DNA with a base sequence complementary to the part of a DNA strand that is to be copied during the PCR.

g Taking a small sample of tissue from a living organism, which can later be tested, e.g. to determine whether the organism is homozygous for a recessive allele of a gene.

h An adjective used to describe DNA, or an organism, in which the DNA has been modified so that it contains base sequences from more than one organism.

i A 'go-between' used to insert genes into a cell. Examples include liposomes, viruses and plasmids.

j The collection, processing and analysing of biological information using computerised databases.

k   A small piece of glass or plastic on which thousands of tiny pieces of single-stranded DNA are attached in a regular arrangement; the DNA pieces act as probes and allow rapid analysis of DNA of unknown composition.

l   A method of separating lengths of DNA or proteins according to their relative mass or charge.

m   A small sphere of lipid and protein; it can be used in genetic technology to transport DNA into a cell.

n   Inserting DNA into the cells of an organism to correct a harmful genetic condition.

o   A (usually fully automated) method of rapidly producing many copies of a small DNA sample.

Exam-style questions

Exam questions about genetic technology will often introduce unfamiliar contexts and data, asking you to apply your knowledge and understanding. They may also cross over into other topics. Here, the question begins by asking about a topic relating to enzymes, and finishes by asking you to consider the use of a novel technique for producing hybrid herbicide-resistant plants.

1   a   Plants contain an enzyme called glutamine synthase, which catalyses the reaction of glutamate and ammonia to produce glutamine.

Some types of herbicide contain glufosinate. This compound can bind to the glutamate binding site of glutamine synthase. This results in a build-up of ammonia in the plant, and kills it.

Explain how glufosinate results in a build-up of ammonia.   [3]

b   Several varieties of rape, *Brassica napus*, have been genetically modified for resistance to herbicides containing glufosinate.

Herbicide-resistant rape varieties contain the *bar* gene, which codes for an enzyme called phosphinothricin acetyl transferase (PAT). PAT changes glufosinate into an inactive compound.

Explain how growing rape plants containing the *bar* gene can result in higher yields of rape seed.   [3]

c   A company that produces and sells GM herbicide-resistant rape seed has developed an F1 hybrid variety, produced by crossing two herbicide-resistant pure-breeding varieties called MS8 and RF3.

i   Explain what is meant by the term *F1 hybrid*.

ii   Suggest **one** advantage to a farmer of growing a hybrid variety of oil-seed rape, rather than a pure-breeding variety.   [1]

iii   MS8 (male-sterile) contains a gene called *barnase*, which encodes for a ribonuclease that is expressed only in the anthers of the flowers. This affects RNA synthesis and stops anther development.

RF3 (restoration of fertility) contains a gene called *barstar*, which codes for a ribonuclease inhibitor that is only expressed in the anthers. This can inactivate the ribonuclease encoded by *barnase*.

Explain how the company can use these two varieties for large-scale production of seed that is 100% hybrid.   [3]

iv   Predict whether plants grown from the hybrid seed would be fertile. Explain your answer.   [2]

[Total: 12 marks]

The first part of this question involves genetics, but then moves on to topics relating to evaluating data and discussing ethical issues. Ethical issues and social issues overlap; in general, ethical issues are ones that relate to values of right and wrong, and social issues relate to effects on situations and conflicts in society. Remember that the command word 'discuss' means that you should address two different viewpoints of an issue.

factor VIII gene (haemophilia A)
colourblindness gene

Figure 19.1 The positions of two genes on the human X chromosome.

2 **a** Figure 19.1 shows the positions on the human X chromosome of two genes that are associated with hereditary conditions.

  i State the term used to describe the position of a gene on a chromosome. [1]

  ii These two genes are sex-linked. Explain what is meant by this term. [2]

b The gene that is associated with haemophilia A codes for a protein called factor VIII. A man with haemophilia A has one of several different recessive alleles of this gene, which do not produce functioning factor VIII. Haemophilia A can be treated by injecting the person with factor VIII, and a man with haemophilia who has such treatment whenever required will have a life expectancy similar to that of a man without the condition.

  i It is now possible to screen embryos for the presence of a haemophilia A allele. Outline the advantages of this screening. [3]

  ii Suggest the ethical considerations that should be taken into account when screening embryos for the presence of a haemophilia allele. [2]

c Haemophilia A is treated with factor VIII extracted from donated human blood plasma, or with recombinant factor VIII made by genetically engineered mammalian cells grown in tissue culture.

Doctors and patients may be able to choose which of these types of factor VIII are used. Both are equally good at controlling the condition. However, other issues to be considered are cost (recombinant factor VIII is more expensive) and the likelihood of development of immune reactions to the products. Some patients produce antibodies to the injected factor VIII, preventing it from working, and it is possible that the source of the factor VIII could affect the likelihood of antibodies being produced.

  i Many studies have been carried out to try to determine which type of factor VIII is more likely to cause patients to develop antibodies. The table below shows the results from 12 of these studies.

Study	Type of factor VIII used	Number of people in the study	Percentage developing antibodies
1	plasma derived	48	6.25
2	plasma derived	16	0.00
3	plasma derived	37	2.70
4	plasma derived	89	28.09
5	plasma derived	19	5.26
6	plasma derived	135	21.48
7	recombinant	59	23.73
8	recombinant	50	18.00
9	recombinant	181	29.28
10	recombinant	35	5.71
11	recombinant	47	36.17
12	recombinant	101	31.68

Suggest reasons for the wide variation in the results shown in the table. [4]

  ii A further independent trial is planned. In this trial:

  • The parents of boys who have just been diagnosed with haemophilia will be asked to participate in a randomised trial.

  • The parents will be given full information about the known safety and effectiveness of both types of treatment.

  • If the parents agree, the boys will be randomly allocated to a group being given plasma-derived factor VIII, or a group being given recombinant factor VIII.

229

- The boys will be tested at frequent intervals for the production of antibodies, and measures will be taken to deal with this if it occurs.

Suggest why only boys who have just been diagnosed with haemophilia will be included in the study. [2]

iii Discuss the ethical and social issues that are raised by the implementation of this study. [4]

[Total: 18 marks]

3 Maize is a cereal crop grown in many parts of the world. In many countries, more than 90% of the maize plants that are grown are F1 hybrids. Hybrid maize has significantly higher yields of grain than pure-breeding maize.

> This question links material relating to Chapter 17 (inbreeding and hybridisation in maize) and Chapter 19 (genetic technology, including the use of microarrays and bioinformatics). Some of the questions are quite straightforward, but the question ends with a very difficult three-mark section. Even if you are very unsure about this, it is worth having a try – just think about what you know about the control of gene expression and make a suggestion or two.

a Explain what is meant by:

i an F1 hybrid [1]

ii pure-breeding. [1]

b The greater vigour and yield of hybrids compared with pure-breeding parents is termed *hybrid vigour*. Biologists still do not fully understand what causes hybrid vigour. One theory is that harmful recessive alleles that are present in the parents are masked by dominant alleles in the hybrid. Another is that the level of expression of a particular allele might be greater or lower in the hybrid than in either of the parents.

An investigation was undertaken to determine the level of expression of 13 999 genes in two pure-breeding maize varieties, B73 and Mo17, and a hybrid between them.

- Large numbers of seedlings of B73, Mo17 and the hybrid Mo17 × B23 genotypes were grown in controlled conditions.
- Ten replicates of each genotype were grown.
- After 14 days, above-ground tissue was harvested from all three genotypes.
- RNA was extracted from the seedlings.
- The RNA was used to make single-stranded cDNA with a complementary base sequence.
- The cDNA was labelled with fluorescent dyes.
- A microarray with 13 999 spots containing single-stranded DNA with specific sequences (each known to be part of the maize genome) was used to determine the quantity of the different types of cDNA produced from each of the three maize genotypes.

i Suggest **two** conditions that would be controlled when growing the seedlings. [2]

ii Explain why the researchers extracted RNA from the seedlings and not DNA. [2]

iii Name the enzyme that would be used to make single-stranded DNA from the extracted RNA. [1]

iv Outline how the microarray would be used, and how it would enable the researchers to determine the level of expression of the genes in the maize seedlings. [5]

c The researchers found that, of the 13 999 genes tested, 1367 were expressed to different levels in the hybrid than in either of the parents.

Of these 1367 genes:

- 1062 were expressed to a degree half-way between that of the two parents.
- 34 were expressed to a higher degree in the hybrid than in either of the parents.
- 10 were expressed to a lower degree in the hybrid than in either of the parents.

Suggests reasons why a gene in the hybrid could be expressed to different levels than in either of the parents. [3]

[Total: 15 marks]

In 2015, details of the largest-ever set of human genomes and the results of various analyses of these data were published. The population of Iceland was chosen for this study because the Icelandic population was founded only 1100 years ago from a relatively small number of people, and full genealogies of a very high proportion of the people are known. This question asks you to apply knowledge to an unfamiliar situation, to make some calculations, and to think about ethical issues relating to genome sequencing.

4 Genotyping of 104 000 individuals in Iceland has been carried out, and the complete sequences of the genomes of 2636 people have been determined. Bioinformatics based on these data is providing new insights into genetic variation in humans and its consequences.

a Explain the meaning of the term *bioinformatics*. [2]

b It has been found that 93% of differences in base sequences between the 2636 people were caused by a change in a single base, and the remaining 7% were insertions or deletions.

One group of researchers was interested in loss-of-function mutations, which prevent the gene coding for a useful protein.

In the 2636 genomes analysed, 6795 loss-of-function mutations in 4924 genes were found. Of these, 3979 mutations were changes in a single base, and 2816 were insertions or deletions.

i Calculate the percentage of loss-of-function mutations that were insertions or deletions. [1]

ii Explain the reasons for the difference between the value you have calculated in i, and the value of 7% given in the introduction to part b. [3]

iii Many of the loss-of-function mutations were very rare, with an allele frequency of 0.002. Calculate how many individuals in a population of 250 000 you would expect to be homozygous for such a mutation. Show your working. [2]

c The Icelandic population from which these data have been collected gave their permission for the information about their genomes to be used for research. The analysis of the genomes has identified many people who carry mutations that may increase the risk of the development of harmful conditions such as breast cancer or Alzheimer's disease.

Discuss the ethical issues involved in making a decision about whether or not these people should be contacted through their doctors and given information about the results of their genome analysis. [5]

[Total: 13 marks]

Extended answer questions

5 a Describe the use of plasmids in genetic technology. [5]

b With reference to named examples, explain the significance of genetic engineering in improving the quality and yield of crop plants. [10]

[Total: 15 marks]

6 a Describe the principles of the polymerase chain reaction (PCR). [8]

b Describe how PCR and DNA analysis can be used in criminal investigations. [7]

[Total: 15 marks]

Glossary

abundance the quantity of organisms in a particular habitat

accessory pigment a pigment that is not essential to photosynthesis but which absorbs light of different wavelengths and passes the energy to chlorophyll *a*

acetylcholine (ACh) a transmitter substance found, for example, in the presynaptic neurone at neuromuscular junctions

acetylcholinesterase an enzyme that rapidly breaks down acetylcholine at synapses

actin the protein that makes up the thin filaments in striated muscle

action potential a brief change in the potential difference across cell surface membranes of neurones and muscle cells caused by the inward movement of sodium ions followed by the outward movement of potassium ions; it rapidly travels along the length of the neurone or muscle cell

alveolus (plural alveoli) one of the tiny air sacs of the lungs which allow for rapid gaseous exchange

amylopectin a polymer of α-glucose monomers linked by both 1,4 linkages and 1,6 linkages, forming a branched chain; amylopectin is a constituent of starch

amylose a polymer of α-glucose monomers linked by 1,4 linkages, forming a curving chain; amylose is a constituent of starch

anomalous a result or value that lies well outside the range of other results or values

antibiotic a substance produced by a living organism that is capable of killing or inhibiting the growth of a microorganism

antibody a glycoprotein (immunoglobulin) made by plasma cells derived from B-lymphocytes, secreted in response to an antigen; the variable region of the antibody molecule is complementary in shape to it specific antigen

arteriole small blood vessel that carries blood from arteries to capillaries; arterioles determine how much blood flows through capillaries

artery a blood vessel that carries blood away from the heart; it has a relatively thick cell wall and contains large amounts of elastic fibres

auxin a plant growth regulator (plant hormone) that stimulates cell elongation

bar chart a graph in which the variable on the *x*-axis is discontinuous; the bars are drawn so that they do not touch

Benedict's test a test for the presence of reducing sugars; the unknown substance is heated with Benedict's reagent, and a change from a clear blue solution to the production of yellow, red or brown precipitate indicates the presence of reducing sugars such as glucose

biuret test a test for the presence of amine groups and thus for the presence of proteins; biuret reagent is added to the unknown substance, and a change from pale blue to purple indicates the presence of protein

Bowman's capsule the cup-shaped part of a nephron that surrounds a glomerulus and collects filtrate from the blood

C3 plant a plant in which the first product of photosynthesis is a three-carbon compound

C4 plant a plant in which the first product of photosynthesis is a four-carbon compound; most tropical grasses (but not rice) are C4 plants

calorimeter the apparatus in which the energy value of a compound can be measured by burning it in oxygen

Calvin cycle a cycle of reactions in photosynthesis in which carbon dioxide is fixed into carbohydrate

capillary the smallest type of blood vessel, whose function is to facilitate exchange of substances between the blood and the tissues; capillary walls area made up of a single layer of squamous epithelium, and their internal diameter is only a little larger than that of a red blood cell

cardiac cycle the sequence of events taking place during one heart beat

carotenoid a yellow, orange or red plant pigment used as an accessory pigment in photosynthesis

causal link (relationship) where one factor directly brings about an effect in another

cell surface membrane very thin membrane (about 7 nm diameter) surrounding all cells; it is partially permeable and controls the exchange of materials between the cell and its environment

cellulose a carbohydrate that is a polymer composed of β-glucose units; it is the main component of the cell walls of most plants

channel protein a membrane protein of fixed shape which has a water filled pore through which selected hydrophilic ions or molecules can pass

chemiosmosis the synthesis of ATP using energy stored as a difference in hydrogen ion concentration across a membrane in a chloroplast or mitochondrion

chlorophyll a green pigment responsible for light capture in photosynthesis in algae and plants

chloroplast the photosynthetic organelle in eukaryotes

chronic obstructive pulmonary disease (COPD) a disease of the lungs characterised by bronchitis and emphysema

collecting duct the last section of the nephron, from which water can be absorbed back into the bloodstream before urine flows into the ureter

collenchyma a modified form of parenchyma in which the corners of the cells have extra cellulose thickening, providing support, as in the midrib of leaves and at the corners of square stems; in three dimensions the tissue occurs in strands (as in celery petioles)

companion cell a cell with an unthickened cellulose wall and dense cytoplasm that is found in close association with a phloem sieve element to which it is directly linked via many plasmodesmata; the companion cell and the sieve element form a functional unit

condensation reaction a chemical reaction involving the joining together of two molecules by removal of a water molecule

95% confidence limits a measure of how accurate a mean value is. There is a 95% probability that the true mean lies between ±2 standard errors of the mean

control experiment an experiment in which the factor whose effect is being investigated (the independent variable) is absent; it is used as a standard of comparison

control group the group in an experiment or study that does not receive treatment by the researchers and is then used as a benchmark to measure how the other tested subjects do; often referred to as the **placebo group**

controlled variables see standardised variables

corpus luteum the 'yellow body' that develops from an ovarian follicle after ovulation

correlation a relationship or connection between two things based on co-occurrence or pattern of change may be a **positive correlation** or a **negative correlation** indicates the extent to which one variable increases as the other decreases

dependent variable in an experiment, the variable that changes as a result of changing the independent variable

depolarisation the reversal of the resting potential across the cell surface membrane of a neurone or muscle cell, so that the inside becomes positively charged compared with the outside

diabetes an illness in which the pancreas does not make sufficient insulin, or where cells do not respond appropriately to insulin

diploid possessing two complete sets of chromosomes

disaccharide a sugar molecule consisting of two monosaccharides joined together by a glycosidic bond

efferent leading away from

electron transport chain chain of adjacently arranged carrier molecules in the inner mitochondrial membrane, along which electrons pass by redox reactions

emphysema a disease in which alveoli are destroyed, giving large air spaces and decreased surface area for gaseous exchange; it is often associated with chronic bronchitis

endoplasmic reticulum a network of flattened sacs running through the cytoplasm or eukaryotic cells; molecules, particularly proteins, can be transported through the cell inside the sacs separate from the rest of the cytoplasm; ER is continuous with the outer membrane of the nuclear envelope

error (in measurement) the possible difference between a measured value and the true value; this is usually calculated as plus or minus half the value of the smallest division on the scale of the measuring instrument

error (general) any factor that could cause the measured results of an experiment to differ from 'true' results; this could be caused by factors such as measurement error (see above) or inability to control variables

error bars there is a 95% certainty that the true mean lies within the range of an error bar that extends two standard errors above the mean and two standard errors below the mean

follicle stimulating hormone (FSH) glycoprotein hormone secreted by the anterior pituitary gland to stimulate the development of follicles in the ovary

glomerulus a group of capillaries within the 'cup' of a Bowman's capsule in the cortex of the kidney

glucagon a small peptide hormone secreted by the a <alpha symbol> -cells in the islets of Langerhans in the pancreas that brings about an increase in the blood glucose level

glycogen a polysaccharide made of many glucose molecules linked together, that acts as a glucose store in liver and muscle cells

glycolysis the splitting (lysis) of glucose

glycosidic bond a C–O–C link between two monosaccharide molecules formed by a condensation reaction

guard cell a sausage-shaped epidermal cell found with another, in a pair bounding a stoma and controlling its opening or closure

haemoglobin the red pigment found in red blood cells, whose molecules contain four iron atoms within a globular protein made up of four polypeptides, and that combines reversibly with oxygen

histogram sometimes known as a frequency diagram; a type of graph used when the x-axis parameter is a series of continuous categories, and the y-axis shows the frequency of occurrence of each category; the bars touch

homoeothermic maintaining a constant body temperature

hormone a substance secreted by an endocrine gland, that is carried in blood plasma to another part of the body where it has an effect (plant hormone – see **plant growth regulator**)

hydrogen bond a relatively weak bond formed by the attraction between a group with a small positive charge on a hydrogen atom and another group carrying a small negative charge, e.g. between two $-O^{\delta+}H^{\delta+}$ groups

hydrolysis reaction a reaction in which a complex molecule is broken down to simpler ones, involving the addition of water

incidence (of a disease) the number of people diagnosed with a disease over a certain period of time

independent variables the variable (factor) that is deliberately changed in an experiment

infectious disease a disease caused by an organism such as a bacterium or virus

insulin a small peptide hormone secreted by the β-cells in the islets of Langerhans in the pancreas that reduces blood glucose levels

interquartile range the range which the middle 50% of data falls between

isotopes forms of an element that have the same proton number but different numbers of neutrons in their atoms

K_m see Michaelis–Menten constant

Krebs cycle a cycle of reactions in aerobic respiration in the matrix of a mitochondrion in which hydrogens pass to hydrogen carriers for subsequent ATP synthesis and some ATP is synthesised directly

light dependent reactions reactions in photosynthesis for which light energy is needed

light independent reactions reactions in photosynthesis for which light energy is not needed

lignin a complex organic compound that binds to cellulose fibres and hardens and strengthens the cell walls of plants (lignification); chief noncarbohydrate constituent of wood

linear correlation a relationship between two variables such that a straight best-fit line can be drawn when one is plotted against the other

line graph a type of graph used when both the *x*-axis parameter and the *y*-axis parameter are continuous variables; points are plotted as small crosses or circled dots, and the line drawn as ruled lines between points or as a best-fit line

loop of Henle the part of the nephron between the proximal and distal convoluted tubules; in humans, some of the loops of Henle are long and reach down into the medulla of the kidney

luteinising hormone (LH) a glycoprotein hormone that is secreted by the anterior pituitary gland to stimulate ovulation and the development of the corpus luteum

lymphocyte a type of white blood cell that is involved in the immune response; unlike phagocytes they become active only in the presence of a particular antigen that 'matches' their specific receptors or antibodies

magnification the number of times greater that an image is than the actual object; magnification = image size ÷ actual (real) size of the object

mark–release–recapture a method of estimating the numbers of individuals in a population of mobile animals

mean often referred to as the 'average'; calculated by adding up the values and dividing by the number of values

median the middle value of all the values in a set of data showing a normal distribution

menstrual cycle the changes that occur in the ovary and the uterus approximately every 28 days involving ovulation and the breakdown and loss of the lining of the uterus (menstruation)

mesophyll the internal tissue of a leaf blade with chloroplasts for photosynthesis and consisting of an upper layer of palisade mesophyll (the main photosynthetic tissue) and a lower layer of spongy mesophyll with large air spaces for gas exchange

Michaelis–Menten constant (K_m) the substrate concentration at which an enzyme works at half its maximum rate, used as a measure of the efficiency of an enzyme; the lower the value of K_m, the more efficient the enzyme

mitochondrion (plural: mitochondria) the organelle in eukaryotes in which aerobic respiration takes place

mode (modal class) the value that appears most frequently in a set of data

mole the amount of an element or substance that has a mass in grams numerically equal to the atomic or molecular weight of the substance

monomer a relatively simple molecule which is used as a basic building block for the synthesis of a polymer; many monomers are joined together to make the polymer, usually by condensation reactions; common examples of molecules used as monomers are monosaccharides, amino acids and nucleotides

monosaccharides a molecule consisting of a single sugar unit with the general formula $(CH_2O)_n$

myofibril one of the many cylindrical bundles of thick and thin filaments in striated muscle

myosin the contractile protein that makes up the thick filaments in striated muscle

negative correlation a relationship between two variables such as when one increases, the other decreases

neuromuscular junction a synapse between the axon of a motor neurone and a muscle

neurone a nerve cell; cell which is specialised for the conduction of action potentials

nicotine a chemical found in tobacco smoke that can bind with acetylcholine receptors on the postsynaptic membrane of cholinergic synapses

normal distribution a pattern shown by a set of data that are distributed symmetrically on both sides of the mean value

null hypothesis a hypothesis that assumes there is no relationship between two variables, or that there is no significant difference between two samples

oestrogen steroid hormone secreted by follicles in the ovary; used in some contraceptive pills

oral rehydration therapy (ORT) treatment for diarrhoea-related dehydration in which an electrolyte solution containing fluids and vital ions is administered

osmoreceptors a receptor cell that is sensitive to the water potential of the blood

osmoregulation the control of the water content of the fluids in the body

oxidation the name of the reaction that occurs if a substance gains oxygen, loses hydrogen or loses electrons anomalous a result or value that lies well outside the range of other results or values

oxidative phosphorylation the synthesis of ATP from ADP and P_i using energy from oxidation reactions in aerobic respiration (compare photophosphorylation)

palisade mesophyll see mesophyll

pancreas an organ lying close to the stomach that functions both as an exocrine gland (secreting pancreatic juice) and an endocrine gland (secreting insulin and glucagon)

parenchyma a basic plant tissue typically used as packing tissue between more specialised structures; it is metabolically active and may have a variety of functions such as food storage, support and transport via symplast and apoplast pathways

pathogen an organism that causes infectious disease

PEP phosphoenolpyruvate, the initial carbon dioxide acceptor in a C4 plant

peptide bond a C–N link between two amino acid molecule, formed by a condensation reaction

percentage error the actual error in a measurement calculated as a percentage of the measured value

phloem tissue containing sieve tubes and other types of cell, responsible for the translocation of assimilates such as sucrose through a plant

photolysis the splitting of water using light energy; $H_2O \rightarrow 2H^+ + 2e^- + \frac{1}{2}O_2$

photophosphorylation the synthesis of ATP from ADP and P_i using light energy in photosynthesis (compare oxidative phosphorylation)

photorespiration a wasteful reaction in which RuBP combines with oxygen rather than carbon dioxide; it is favoured by high temperatures and high light intensities

photosystem a cluster of light-harvesting accessory pigments surrounding a primary pigment or reaction centre

placebo group the group of participants in a study of the effectiveness of a drug who receive an inactive substance designed to resemble the drug; see **control group**

plant growth regulator (plant hormone) any chemical produced in plants that influences their growth and development, e.g. auxins, gibberellins, cytokinins and abscisic acid

plasmodesma (pleural: plasmodesmata) a pore-like structure found in plant cell walls; plasmodesmata of neighbouring plant cells line up to form tube-like pores through the cell walls, allowing the controlled passage of materials from one cell to the other; the pores contain ER and are lined with the cell surface membrane

polymer a giant molecule made from many similar repeating subunits joined together in a chain; the subunits are much smaller and simpler molecules known as monomers; polymers may also be referred to as macromolecules; examples of biological polymers are polysaccharides, proteins and nucleic acids; see monomer

polypeptide a long chain of amino acids formed by condensation reactions between the individual amino acids; proteins are made of one or more polypeptide chains; see peptide bond

polysaccharide a polymer whose subunits are monosaccharides joined together by glycosidic bonds

positive correlation a relationship between two variables such as when one increases, so does the other

postsynaptic neurone the neurone on the opposite side of a synapse to the neurone in which the action potential arrives

potometer a piece of apparatus used to measure the rate of uptake of water by a plant

presynaptic terminal (neurone) a neurone ending at a synapse from which a neurotransmitter is secreted when an action potential arrives

prevalence the number of people who have disease at any one time

primary pigments see reaction centre

probability mathematically, the probability (p) that an event will occur is expressed as a number between 0 and 1; if $p = 0$, the event will almost definitely not occur, if p is close to 0, there is only a small chance that the event will occur, if $p = 0.5$, there is a 50/50 chance that the event will occur, if p is close to 1, there is a strong chance that the event will occur, if $p = 1$, the event will almost definitely occur.

progesterone a steroid hormone secreted by the corpus luteum in the ovary after ovulation; used in contraceptive pills

purine a nitrogenous base containing two carbon–nitrogen rings; adenine and guanine are purines

pyrimidine a nitrogenous base containing one carbon–nitrogen ring; thymine, cytosine and uracil are pyrimidines

quadrat a square frame which is used to mark out an area for sampling of organisms

random errors uncertainties in experimental results that are caused by variations in variables that should be standardised, or by difficulties in measuring the independent or dependent variables; they can act in different directions for different parts of the experiment

range the minimum value to maximum value in a set of data

reaction centre a molecule of chlorophyll *a* that receives energy from the light absorbed by the surrounding accessory pigments in a photosystem

repolarisation returning the potential difference across the cell surface membrane of a neurone or muscle cell to normal following the depolarisation of an action potential

respiration enzymatic release of energy from organic compounds in living cells

respiratory quotient (RQ) the ratio of the volume of carbon dioxide given out in respiration to that of oxygen used

respirometer the apparatus for the measuring the rate of oxygen consumption in respiration or for finding the respiratory quotient

resting potential the difference in electrical potential that is maintained across a neurone when it is not transmitting an action potential; it is normally about -70mV inside and is maintained by the sodium–potassium pump

sarcomere the part of a myofibril between two z discs

sclerenchyma a supportive plant tissue that consists of thick-walled, usually lignified cells; sclerenchyma cells are either fibres or sclereids

selective reabsorption movement of certain substances from the filtrate back into the blood in the kidney nephron

sieve element or **sieve tube element** a cell found in phloem tissue, with non-thickened cellulose walls, very little cytoplasm, no nucleus and end walls perforated to form sieve plates, through which sap containing sucrose is transported

sieve tube tubes formed by sieve elements lined up end to end

Simpson's Index of Diversity a method to assess the biodiversity of an ecosystem

sodium–potassium ($Na^+ - K^+$) pump (sodium–potassium exchange pump) a membrane protein (or proteins) that move sodium ions out of a cell and potassium ions into it, using ATP

Spearman's rank correlation a statistical test to determine whether two variables are correlated

species diversity a measure of the number and evenness of species living in an area

species richness the number of different species living in an area

spongy mesophyll see mesophyll

standard deviation a measure of how widely a set of data is spread out on either side of the mean

standard error a measure of how likely it is that a mean calculated from a sample represents the true mean for the whole population

standardised variables variables (factors) that are kept constant in an experiment; only the independent variable should be changed

stoma (plural stomata) a pore in the epidermis of a leaf, bounded by two guard cells and needed for efficient gas exchange

stroma the matrix of a chloroplast in which the light independent redactions of photosynthesis occur

synapse a point at which two neurones meet but do not touch; the synapse is made up of the end of the presynaptic neurone, the synapse is made up of the end of the presynaptic neurone, the synaptic cleft and the end of the postsynaptic neurone

synaptic cleft a very small gap between two neurones at a synapse

systematic errors uncertainties in experimental results that are caused by lack of precision or accuracy in a measuring instrument; they always act in the same direction

tangent a straight line drawn to touch a curve at a single point

telomere a repetitive sequence of DNA at the end of a chromosome that protects genes from the chromosome shortening that happens at each cell division

test cross a genetic cross in which an organism showing a characteristic caused by a dominant allele is crossed with an organism that is homozygous recessive; the phenotypes of the offspring can be a guide to whether the first organism is homozygous or heterozygous

thermoregulation the control of core body temperature

thylakoid a flattened, membrane-bound, fluid-filled sac, which is the site of the light dependent reactions of photosynthesis in a chloroplast

transect a line along which samples are taken, either by noting the species at equal distances (line transect) or placing quadrats at regular intervals (belt transect)

translocation the transport of assimilates such as sucrose through a plant, in phloem tissue; translocation requires the input of metabolic energy; the term is sometimes used more generally to include transport in the xylem

transpiration the loss of water vapour from a plant to its environment by diffusion down a water potential gradient; most transpiration takes place through the stomata in the leaves

triglyceride a lipid whose molecules are made up of a glycerol molecule and three fatty acids

ultrafiltration filtration on a molecular scale e.g. the filtration that occurs as blood flows through capillaries, especially those in glomeruli in the kidney

uncertainty (in measurement) the possible difference between a measured value and the true value; this is usually calculated as plus or minus half the value of the smallest division on the scale of the measuring instrument

urea a nitrogenous excretory product produced in the liver from the deamination of amino acids

V_{max} the theoretical maximum rate of an enzyme-controlled reaction, obtained when all the active sites are occupied

vein a blood vessel that carries blood back towards the heart; it has relatively thin walls and contains valves

virus very small (20-300 nm) infectious particle which can replicate only inside living cells and consists essentially of a simple basic structure of a genetic code of DNA or RNA surrounded by a protein coat

voltage gated channels a channel protein through a cell membrane that opens or closes in response to changes in electrical potential across the membrane

xerophyte a plant adapted to survive in conditions where water is in short supply

xylem tissue containing xylem vessel elements and other types of cells, responsible for support and the transmission of water through a plant

xylem vessel a dead, empty tube with lignified walls, through which water is transported in plants; it is formed by xylem vessel elements lined up end to end

xylem vessel element a dead, lignified cell found in xylem specialised for transporting water and support; the ends of the cells break down and join with neighbouring elements to form long tubes called xylem vessels

CUP AS/A level Biology Workbook — Skills grid

AS level

AO2 Handling information and solving problems

Legend: ☐ Exercises ▨ Exam-style questions

Skill	Type	1	2	3	4	5	6	7	8	9	10	11
locate, select, organise and present information from a variety of sources	Exercises		1,4,5,7	1,2	4	1		3	1,2	3,4	1,4	
	Exam-style		6		2,3	3	3		3,5,6	3,4	1,2,3,4,5	4
translate information from one form to another	Exercises	6	1,3,4	2	4	4		4	1,3	3	2,4	
	Exam-style		5,	1,2	1, 2, 3	3		6	1,2,3,6	2,3	1	4
manipulate numerical and other data	Exercises		2,3,4	1,3,5		3		4	1,2,3	1,2,3,4	2,4	3
	Exam-style				2			3	2,3,	3,	5	4
use information to identify patterns, report trends and draw conclusions	Exercises	6	4	2,3	3,4	1	1,3	4	1,2,3	1,2,3,4	2,4	3
	Exam-style	3	2,3,5,	2	1,2	2,3	1,2	2,3,4,5,6	1,2,3,6	2,3	1,2,3,4,5	4
give reasoned explanations for phenomena, patterns and relationships	Exercises	6	4	1,2	3	4	3	4	1,2,3	2,3	2,4	3, 4
	Exam-style	4	2,3,4,5	1	1,3	3	1,2	3,3,4	1,2,3,6	1,2,3	1,2,3,4,5	1, 3
make predictions and hypotheses	Exercises			4							2,	
	Exam-style									1		
apply knowledge, including principles, to new situations	Exercises	6		1,3	3,4	1,4	1,3	4	1,2	1,3	2,3,4	3,4
	Exam-style	2,3,	1,2,3,6	1,2,3	1,2,3,4	2,3	1,3	2,3,4	1,2,3,5,6	1,2,3,4	1,2,3,4,5	1,3
demonstrate an awareness of the limitations of biological theories and models	Exercises								2		4	
	Exam-style							6		4		
solve problems	Exercises		4	2				4	2,3	3,4	2,3,4	
	Exam-style		3,5		2				1,2,3,6	2,3		

AO3 Experimental skills and investigations

Skill	1	2	3	4	5	6	7	8	9	10	11
Experimental design											
identify independent and dependent variables		6,	4	2	3		4	4			
choose range, number of values and interval for independent variable, and number of replicates		6,	4	2, 3	3		4	4			
describe an appropriate control experiment						3		4		3,4	
use simple or serial dilution		2,3	4	2						3,4	
identify important control variables and how to standardise them		3,6,	3, 4 / 3	2	3		4	4		3	
identify methods of measuring dependent variable, including when and how often		6	4 / 1	2 / 1			4	4		4	
assess risk and make decisions about safety			4					2		3,4	
suggest how to modify or extend an investigation to answer a new question			1	3							
Collecting , recording and processing data											
be able to measure an area using a grid								2			
measure using counting, e.g. using tally charts					3			2			
clearly describe qualitative results											
decide how to deal with anomalous results				3				2		4	
measure and record all results to an appropriate number of significant figures											

Skill	Chapter										
	1	2	3	4	5	6	7	8	9	10	11
describe how to identify biological molecules, and use a standardised test to estimate quantity		3, 3,5		2							
design, construct and complete results charts			4	1, 2, 3	3			1			
show calculations clearly; record calculated values to correct number of significant figures	2, 5,	2,	1	1, 3			4	1,2	1,2,3,4		3
draw graphs; determine the best type of graph or chart to display results		3,	3	1, 2, 3	3		4	1,3	2,		2, 3, 4
calculate percentage change; calculate rate as 1/time and as gradient of line graph			1								
find an unknown value using a graph, including extrapolation		3,	1,3	3				3 / 2,3			
describe patterns and trends shown in tables and graphs			1,2 / 2,3	1,3 / 2,3	4 / 3		4 / 6	1,3 / 1,2,3.6	1,2,3,4 / 2,3,4	2,4 / 1,2,3,4,5	4

Evaluating results

Skill	Chapter										
	1	2	3	4	5	6	7	8	9	10	11
identify significant sources of error, and classify them as systematic or random; calculate percentage error			4	1				2		4	
suggest improvements to reduce error, e.g. by improving standardisation of variables, methods of measurement, quantity of data							4	2		4	
evaluate uncertainty in quantitative results			4					2	4	4	
determine the confidence with which conclusions can be made					4		4	1,2	1,2	2,4	4
make conclusions from data			2, 3	1 / 3	4		4 / 3,4	2	1,2 / 3,4,	2,4 / 1,2,3,4,5	4

240

Skill	Chapter										
	1	2	3	4	5	6	7	8	9	10	11
Microscopy and observation of specimens											
use a microscope to identify and draw tissues from prepared slides	3						1,2	1			
calibrate an eyepiece graticule using a stage micrometer, and use it to measure cells and tissues	5						1,4				
draw and label plan diagrams							1,2 4,	1,			
draw and label details of cells using high power	3						1	4			
use scale bars and magnifications	2, 3				1		1	1,			
	4			3			4,6	4			
compare observable features of specimens							1,2,3	4			
							1,2,4	4	1		

241

CUP AS/A level Biology Workbook Skills grid

A level

AO2 Handling information and solving problems

Legend: ☐ Exercises ▨ Exam-style questions

Skill	Type	12	13	14	15	16	17	18	19
locate, select, organise and present information from a variety of sources	Exercises	1,2,4	1,4	1	1,2	3,4,5,6,7,8	1,2,3	1,2	
	Exam-style questions	1,2,3,4	1,2,3,4	1,2,5	1,2,3,7,8,9	2,3	1,2,3		1,4
translate information from one form to another	Exercises	1,3,4	1,2,3,4	1,2,4	1,4	1,9	1,3,4	1,2,3	
	Exam-style questions	2		4,6,7	1	4	1,2,3	1,2	4
manipulate numerical and other data	Exercises	1,2,4	1,2,3	1,3,4	3	3		1,3	1,2
	Exam-style questions		1	3,7	1		1,2,3		4
use information to identify patterns, report trends and draw conclusions	Exercises	1,2,3,4	1,2,3	1,2,3	1	3,4,5,6,7,8	1,3,4	1,2,3	1,3,4
	Exam-style questions	1,2,4,5	1,3,4,5	1,2,3,4,6	1,4,5,6	1,3,4	1,2,3,4,5	1,2	
give reasoned explanations for phenomena, patterns and relationships	Exercises	2,3,4	1,2,3	1,2,3	4	3,4,5,6,7,8		2	
	Exam-style questions	2,3,4,6	1,3,4,5	1,2,3,4,6	1,2,3,4,5,6,7	2,3,4,5	1,2,3		2,4
make predictions and hypotheses	Exercises		1,3			3,7		2,3	
	Exam-style questions		1		1		3		2
apply knowledge, including principles, to new situations	Exercises	2,3,4	1,2,3	1,2,3	1,4	3,4,5,6,7,8	3,4	1,2	1,2
	Exam-style questions	1,2,3,4,5	1,3,4,5	1,2,4,6	1,2,3,4,5,6	1,2,3,4,5	1,2,3,4,5	1,2,3	1,2,3,4
demonstrate an awareness of the limitations of biological theories and models	Exercises						4		
	Exam-style questions		2						
solve problems	Exercises	1,2,3,4	1,2,3	1		3,4,5,6,7,8	3,4		
	Exam-style questions	1,2,3,4,5	1,3,4,5	1,2,6	1,4,5,6	2,3	1,2,3,5	2,3	1,4

AO3 Experimental skills and investigations

Skill	12	13	14	15	16	17	18	19
Planning an investigation and describing method								
construct a testable hypothesis		1,3						
identify independent and dependent variables	1	1	7	1			4	
		1,3	1				3	
choose range, number of values and interval for independent variable, and number of replicates, and describe how to vary the independent variable		1	2,7	1			4	
	3	3		3				
describe any appropriate control experiments	1	1,3	1				4	
		1	7					
make up solutions in %(w/v) or mol dm_3 and use serial or proportional dilution			2,3	3				
		1						
identify key control variables and describe how to standardise them	1,4	1,3	1				2	
	1	1	2,7	1			1, 4	
identify methods of measuring dependent variable, including when and how often	1,4	1,3	1				4	
		1	7					
describe steps involved in the procedure in a logical sequence		3					4	
		1	7		.			
assess risk and describe precautions that would be taken to minimise risk		2					4	
Processing and evaluating data								
decide which calculations are necessary in order to draw conclusions	1,4	1	1,3		7		2	
		7	7		2		4	
use tables and graphs to identify key points in quantitative data, including variability	1,4	1,3	1,4			1	2	
	4	1,4,5	2,3		2			
draw graphs, including confidence limit error bars	4	1	1			1	2	
		1	1			1	1	

Skill	Chapter							
	12	13	14	15	16	17	18	19
choose and carry out appropriate calculations to simplify or compare data	1,4	1,3	4			1	2	
		1	3,7		2, 3		44	
use standard deviation or standard error to determine statistical significance of differences between means	1	1	1			1		
		1					1, 3	
choose appropriate statistical tests		1,3			7	1	2	1
					3		4	
apply statistical methods, including stating a null hypothesis, including t-test, chi-squared test, Pearson's linear correlation and Spearman's rank correlation		3	4		7	1	2	
			7	1	3		3	
recognise the different types of variable and different types of data presented	1	1	4					
				1				
identify anomalous results, suggest possible causes and suggest how to deal with them			1					
assess whether replicates were sufficient, and whether range and interval were appropriate		2						
assess whether the method of measuring was appropriate for the dependent variable	4,	1						
assess the extent to which variables have been effectively controlled	4,	1,3						
assess the spread of results by inspection and by using standard deviation and standard error or 95% confidence interval	1	1						
		1						
make conclusions from data	2,4,5	1,3	3,4					
	2,3,4		7	6			1,3	
discuss how much confidence can be put in any conclusions, including commenting on the validity of the investigation and how much trust can be placed in the data	1,2,4	1,2	3				1	
			7	6			1,3	

Acknowledgements

The authors and publishers acknowledge the following sources of copyright material and are grateful for the permissions granted. While every effort has been made, it has not always been possible to identify the sources of all the material used, or to trace all copyright holders. If any omissions are brought to our notice, we will be happy to include the appropriate acknowledgements on reprinting.

Cover isak55/Shutterstock; Chapter 1 Ryan McVay/Thinkstock; 1.1, 1.13 Martyn F Chillmaid/SPL; 1.2 Tek Images/SPL; 1.7 SPL; 1.8 Geoscience features; 1.9 Andrew Lambert/SPL; 1.10 Ben Johnson/SPL; 1.12, 1.15a-d Cambridge University Press; 1.14 GP Bowater/Alamy; 1.16 MedicImage/Alamy; Chapter 2 Jose Antonio Nicoli Andonie/Thinkstock; 2.1 IBM Research/SPL; 2.2 NASA/JAXA; 2.4 Prof Peter Fowler/SPL; 2.6 University of Cambridge Cavendish Laboratory; Chapter 3 Kheng Guan Toh/Shutterstock; 3.1 Charles D Winters/SPL; 3.3 Sheila Terry/SPL; Chapter 4 Sunagatov Dmitry/Thinkstock; 4.1 Tony Camacho/SPL; 4.3, 4.7, 4.28 Charles D Winters/SPL; 4.28 Tom McHugh/SPL; 4.28, 4.46 Andrew Lambert/SPL; 4.30 Alfred Paseika/SPL; 4.31 Natural Visions/Alamy; 4.38 sciencephoto/Alamy; 4.45 Steve Allen/SPL; Chapter 5 eugenesergeev/Thinkstock; 5.1 foodfolio/Alamy; 5.1 D. Hurst/Alamy; 5.7 bigjo5/Thinkstock; 5.9 Wikipedia; 5.14 Roberto de Gugliemo/SPL; 5.18b ogwen/Shutterstock; 5.19 Burke/Triolo Productions/Getty Images; Chapter 6 Design Pics/Thinkstock; 6.1 Peter Menzel/SPL; 6.2 David R Frazier Photolibrary. Inc/Alamy; Chapter 7 DanielPrudek/Thinkstock; 7.1 NASA; 7.2 Mar Photographics/Alamy; 7.3x2 Charles D Winters/SPL; Chapter 8 Blazej Lyjak/Shutterstock; 8.1 Camera lucinda lifestyle/Alamy; 8.2 Cambridge University Press; 8.7 Images of Africa Photobank/Alamy; 8.13 Linda Kennedy/Alamy; 8.13 Andrew Lambert/SPL; 8.14 mediablitzimages/Alamy; Chapter 9 Iculig/Shutterstock; 9.1 Cephas Picture Library/Alamy; 9.1 Sheila Terry/SPL; 9.11a GIPhotostock/SPL; 9.11b sciencephotos/alamy; Chapter 10 isak55/Shutterstock; 10.1a Wikipedia; 10.1b Gordon Woods, 3 Peterboro' Ave, LE15 6EB; 10.8, 10.9, 10.14 Andrew Lambert/SPL; 10.10 Phil Degginger/Alamy; 10.11 David R Frazier Photolibrary, Inc./Alamy; Chapter 11 E.R. Degginger/Alamy; 11.1 Avpics/Alamy; 11.5, 11.6, 11.7 Andrew Lambert/SPL; 11.8 Dirk Wiersma/SPL; Chapter 12 Roberto Anguita Escribano/Thinkstock; 12.1 africa924/Shutterstock; 12.2, 12.3, 12.4 Andrew Lambert/SPL; 12.6 Ron Bull/Alamy; Chapter 13 Nathalie Speliers Ufermann/Shutterstock; 13.1a Tor Eigeland/Alamy; 13.1b National Georgaphic Images Collection/Alamy;

13.3 Keith Kent/SPL; 13.6 Nigel Cattlin/SPL; 13.7 geophotos/Alamy; 13.8 CORDELIA MOLLOY/SPL; Chapter 14 Wildnerdpix/Thinkstock; 14.1 istock/Thinkstock; Chapter 15 think4photop/Shutterstock; 15.1 Stephane Compoint/eyevine; 15.5 Andrew Lambert/SPL; 15.6 dbimages/Alamy; 15.7 Tina Manley/Alamy; 15.8 National Geographic Image Collection/Alamy; 15.9 Document General Motors/Reuter R/Corbis Sygma; 15.11a Paul Rapson/SPL; 15.13 Realimage/Alamy; 15.19 Ashley Cooper/Alamy; Chapter 16 Ammit Jack/Shutterstock; 16.1 Caro/Alamy; 16.8 NASA/SPL; Chapter 17 PathomP/Thinkstock; 17.1 Bjorn Svensson/SPL; 17.3 AFP/Getty Images; 17.4, 17.5, 17.8 Andrew Lambert/SPL; 17.6 Goran Bogicevic/Shutterstock; Chapter 18 Jupiterimages/Thinkstock; 18.1a funkyfood London - Paul Williams/Alamy; 18.1b Art Directors & TRIP/Alamy; 18.3, 18.4, 18.5, 18.6 Andrew Lambert/SPL; Practice Test 1 luchschen/Thinkstock; P1.1 Decha Thapanya/Shutterstock; Chapter 19 FotoStocker/Shutterstock; 19.1 Scott Camazine/Alamy; Chapter 20 David Hanlon/Shutterstock; 20.1all, 20.6, 20.19, 20.21, 20.22 Andrew Lambert/SPL; 20.25 David J Green/SPL; 20.26 Michael Klinec/Alamy; Chapter 21 pixinoo/Shutterstock; 21.1 Bjorn Svensson/SPL; 21.2 Martin Shields/SPL; 21.3 Wikipedia; 21.4 Andrew Lambert/SPL; 21.12 CNRI/SPL; 21.13 Barry Slaven/Visuals Unlimited; 21.15 Douglas Faulkner/SPL; Chapter 22 Jupiterimages/Thinkstock; 22.1 Jack Finch/SPL; 22.2 Martyn F Chillmaid/SPL; 22.3 Andrew Lambert/SPL; 22.16 Roger Norris; 22.20 Elenac/BASF; Chapter 23 Martyn Vickery / Alamy; 23.1 Martyn F Chillmaid/SPL; 23.4 Korpithas/Sutterstock; 23.7 INTERFOTO/Alamy; Chapter 24 Ramon Espelt Photography/Shutterstock; 24.1 stock connection blue/Alamy; 24.1 Claire Dunn/Alamy; 24.1 moodboard/Alamy; 24.2, 24.3, 24.11, 24.12 Andrew Lambert/SPL; Chapter 25 zorandimzr/Thinkstock; 25.1 blickwimkel/Alamy; 25.5 Michael Brooke/SPL; 25.6 Andrew Lambert/SPL; Chapter 26 Khlongwangchao/Thinkstock; 26.1 Michael Rosenfeld/Getty Images; Chapter 27 Neale Cousland/Shutterstock; 27.1 Jake Lyell/Alamy; 27.6, 27.7 Andrew Lambert/SPL; 27.11 R.A Longuehaye/SPL; Chapter 28 Jozef Jankola/Shutterstock; 28.1 Charles D Winters/SPL; 28.3 Maxim Tupikov/Shutterstock; 28.24 Yganko/Shutterstock; 28.27 Roger Ressmeyer/Corbis; Chapter 29 Dmitry Kalinovsky/Shutterstock; 29.1 caro/Alamy; 29.12 speedpix/Alamy; 29.16 Colin Cuthbert/SPL; Chapter 30 MJTH / Shutterstock; 31.1 Bill Varie/Alamy; Practice Test 2 Jaroslav74/Thinkstock; P2.1 Radharc Images/Alamy; P2.2 Sealstep/Shutterstock; P2.3 Science Photo Library/Alamynds and undergoes catalytic reaction.

This is a legal agreement between 'You' (which for individual purchasers means the individual customer and, for network purchasers, means the Educational Institution and its authorised users) and Cambridge University Press ('the Licensor') for Cambridge International AS and A Level Biology Workbook with CD-ROM. By placing this CD in the CD-ROM drive of your computer You agree to the terms of this licence.

1. Limited licence

(a) You are purchasing only the right to use the CD-ROM and are acquiring no rights, express or implied to it or to the software ('Software' being the CD-ROM software, as installed on your computer terminals or server), other than those rights granted in this limited licence for not-for-profit educational use only.

(b) Cambridge University Press grants the customer the licence to use one copy of this CD-ROM either (i) on a single computer for use by one or more people at different times, or (ii) by a single person on one or more computers (provided the CD-ROM is only used on one computer at any one time and is only used by the customer), but not both.

(c) You shall not: (i) copy or authorise copying of the CD-ROM, (ii) translate the CD-ROM, (iii) reverse-engineer, alter, adapt, disassemble or decompile the CD-ROM, (iv) transfer, sell, lease, lend, profit from, assign or otherwise convey all or any portion of the CD-ROM or (v) operate the CD-ROM from a mainframe system, except as provided in these terms and conditions.

2. Copyright

(a) All original content is provided as part of the CD-ROM (including text, images and ancillary material) and is the copyright of, or licensed by a third party to, the Licensor, protected by copyright and all other applicable intellectual property laws and international treaties.

(b) You may not copy the CD-ROM except for making one copy of the CD-ROM solely for backup or archival purposes. You may not alter, remove or destroy any copyright notice or other material placed on or with this CD-ROM.

(c) The CD-ROM contains Adobe® Flash® Player.

Adobe® Flash® Player Copyright © 1996–2010 Adobe Systems Incorporated. All Rights Reserved. Protected by U.S. Patent 6,879,327; Patents Pending in the United States and other countries. Adobe and Flash are either trademarks or registered trademarks in the United States and/or other countries.

3. Liability and Indemnification

(a) The CD-ROM is supplied 'as-is' with no express guarantee as to its suitability. To the extent permitted by applicable law, the Licensor is not liable for costs of procurement of substitute products, damages or losses of any kind whatsoever resulting from the use of this product, or errors or faults in the CD-ROM, and in every case the Licensor's liability shall be limited to the suggested list price or the amount actually paid by You for the product, whichever is lower.

(b) You accept that the Licensor is not responsible for the persistency, accuracy or availability of any urls of external or third party internet websites referred to on the CD-ROM and does not guarantee that any content on such websites is, or will remain, accurate, appropriate or available. The Licensor shall not be liable for any content made available from any websites and urls outside the Software.

(c) Where, through use of the CD-ROM and content you infringe the copyright of the Licensor you undertake to indemnify and keep indemnified the Licensor from and against any loss, cost, damage or expense (including without limitation damages paid to a third party and any reasonable legal costs) incurred by the Licensor as a result of such infringement.

4. Termination

Without prejudice to any other rights, the Licensor may terminate this licence if You fail to comply with the terms and conditions of the licence. In such event, You must destroy all copies of the CD-ROM.

5. Governing law

This agreement is governed by the laws of England, without regard to its conflict of laws provision, and each party irrevocably submits to the exclusive jurisdiction of the English courts.